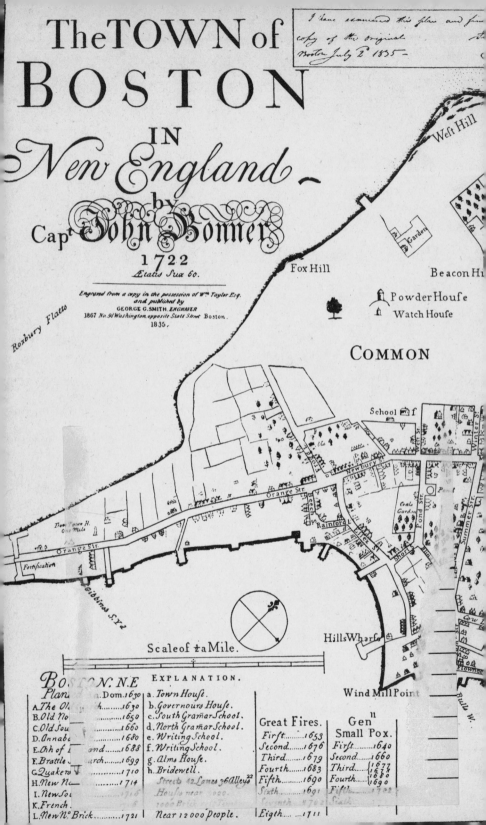

Charles River

Bartons Point

Copper Works

Rope Walk

Rope Walk

Lee's Ship Yard

E.b.N. Mill Damm

N. Water Mill

Ferry to Charles Town

Gees Ship Yd

Hudsons Point

Hunt & Whites Ship Yd

Mill Pond

Boling Green

Ferry Way

Hill

Burying Place

Bakery

Greenoughs Ship Y.

Salem Street

Hunts Wharfe

Sudbury

Hannover

Old Way

Back Street

Middle Street

North Street

Lyn Street

Thorntons Yard

ount St.

Union

Fifth Street

Ship Street

N. Battery

Burroughs W.

ornhill

King St

Lees Ship Y.

Wentworths Wharfe

Clark W.

Galloud W.

Clarks Ship Yd

Scarletts Wharfe.

Hutchinsons W.

Grant & Greenwood Ship Yd & Wharfe

Clarks Wharfe

Old Wharfe.

Melvills W.

Fools Dock

Long Wharfe

Old Wharfe.

Greenleafs Y.

Long Wharf

Wings sha Y.

Olivers Wharfe

Gibbs shy.

Old Wharfe.

Fort Hill

S. Battery.

Hubbards W.

HARBOUR

Boston

BOOKS BY JOHN JENNINGS

Boston: Cradle of Liberty, 1630–1776

The Salem Frigate

The Shadow and the Glory

Gentleman Ranker

Call the New World

Next to Valour
Non-Fiction

Our American Tropics

Boston

CRADLE OF LIBERTY

1630-1776

By

JOHN JENNINGS

Doubleday & Company, Inc.

GARDEN CITY 1947 NEW YORK

TO THE SEAMEN OF BOSTON WHO,
MORE THAN THE SHIPS THEY SAILED,
MORE THAN THE OWNERS WHO SENT THEM,
MADE THIS THE FOREMOST
PORT OF ALL.

Foreword

BOSTONIANS have been suckled on sea water for three
centuries, and more. They have salt in their veins. A cold
December fog, rolling in from off the bay, seasoned, if possible,
with a dash of spattering wet snow, is their notion of healthful
weather. But there is no fog in their brains, and the fellow who
thinks there is, if he deals with them, is likely to find himself
hard aground with the tide setting out before he is finished.

As anyone can see, this is a book about Boston and the sea. It
is the story of the first century and a half of her existence; when
she was growing up and coming of age and setting the pace for
the rest of the colonies to follow in becoming a nation.

Why tell it? Well, because, for one thing, we have just finished and helped to win the greatest war in history; a war in
which Boston ships and Boston men carried their share of the
sea-borne burden. It seems a good time now to look at how it
all began; how there came to be a port of Boston to carry on that
task. But this is not the only reason. Boston has always been the
pioneer of American trade. But she has been more than that.
She was the pioneer of American liberty as well.

It was Daniel Webster who, as far as I can discover, first used
the phrase, "cradle of American liberty." He was referring to

Faneuil Hall when he said it, and since he was speaking of the famous old meetinghouse it was only natural that he should hang it there. But he might, with equal justice, have used it with reference to a half a dozen other buildings as well—the Old North Meeting House, for a single instance. To my way of thinking, however, Black Daniel should have applied the phrase to no building or set of buildings at all, but rather to Boston as a whole. Indeed, to be more specific, he should have applied it to Boston Port.

From the very beginning Boston took the place of leadership in American trade. No other city, no other seaport—not Salem, not Newport nor Providence, not New York nor even Philadelphia—can claim roots that go as deep or as far back, or that flourished as rapidly, or that bore such fruit. It was colonial trade in general which first brought friction between the colonies and the mother country. But it was Boston's trade in particular which caused the rub, for Boston had the lion's share of it. It was Boston's success upon the sea, threatening their profits, which first roused British commercial interests to protest the activities of her upstart merchants and shipbuilders. It was this fear of Boston's competition which made those interests demand government intervention and point out the loss of revenue. It was these demands and this exposition which prompted the first repressive Acts of Trade and Navigation—which were aimed primarily at Boston and its livelihood. It was Boston, first, which sought to nullify those acts by smuggling and whatever other means came to hand, and it was this resistance on the part of Boston and the Bostonians which brought even harsher and more coercive measures. In the end, when it came to a showdown, it was Boston which fought first for its right to trade how and where and with whom it pleased. And when this was denied, it was Boston which became the martyr to the American cause and the rallying point of American arms. It was on Boston's hills that the flames of that revolution which was to bring liberty to us all burst forth.

This does not pretend to be the definitive history of Boston, even for the period which it covers. Such an undertaking would require more years of research than I can give it, and would fill many volumes. It would have to examine a great many more facets of Boston's past than are considered here, and it would be dry reading, for much of history is like that.

But this is not even the ultimate word on the Port. Here you will find no tables of statistics, no tabulated lists of imports and exports, no registers of vessels, no columns of customs receipts. Rather, what I have tried to do here is to tell the story of Boston Port in human terms. I have left out or tried to condense the drier details and have endeavored, as far as possible, to cling to the movement and the high action which when lumped together made the city what it was.

This is a story of people; of men and women and the sea; of their struggles and triumphs; their pains and their pleasures; their nobility and their greed. There is adventure here aplenty. There is disaster on the high seas. There are courage and devotion to duty and idealism, as well as piracy and murder and brutality and bigotry and lust for gain and personal aggrandizement. Stupidity and foresight, initiative and sloth, sacrifice and self-seeking are all a part of the tale, and the tale is a part of the story of us all.

In the writing of this story I have been often reminded of Doctor Johnson's remark that "a man will turn over half a library to make one book." I think I have turned over half of several libraries in the making of this one, and if I have brought to light no new facts, I think I have at least turned up much that is unfamiliar; much that will be new to most readers.

In doing so I have, of course, not been without aid. Much of the help I received was unwitting—found in the diaries, letters,

Foreword

and journals of men on the spot, who saw the events described take place; in the histories and studies that other men have written. To these authors, diarists, reporters I express my gratitude en masse. Other valuable assistance was rendered by persons whose names I do not even know, whose faces I sometimes never even saw—library personnel, bookshop employees, and others, who fetched and carried for me, and who dropped many invaluable little suggestions that gave clues to new and worth-while veins of information. Some of these will remember the man who was looking helplessly for Bostoniana. Others will have forgotten him entirely. To them all, however, I wish to express my sincere thanks.

But certain individuals must be mentioned personally for their particular assistance: Mr. Robert H. Haynes, of the Harvard College Library, gave invaluable practical aid in granting the author access to materials there. He was a treasure house of sound suggestions, and went out of his way to find other sources. Captain John Barleon, U.S.N., of Cambridge, offered valuable hints as to charts and the general cartography of the harbor and adjacent coast. Mr. Richard Parkhurst, chairman of the Port of Boston Authority, likewise made a number of valuable suggestions.

To all of these I wish to express my deepest appreciation. Without their combined help this book could never have been written.

THE AUTHOR

Washington, D.C.
December 1945.

Contents

	Foreword	vii
I	The Beginning	1
II	The Farmer Takes to the Sea	17
III	Business in Great Waters	34
IV	Expanding Horizons	52
V	Of Ships and Cargoes	72
VI	Pirates and Privateers	92
VII	Codfish Aristocracy	117
VIII	An Obstacle Is Removed	131
IX	Thunderheads	144
X	First Blood	161
XI	Sons of Liberty	185
XII	British Flint and Boston Steel	205
XIII	Shots Heard round the World	235
XIV	Bunker Hill	259
XV	End of an Era	285
	Index	317

Illustrations

Facing page

The "Old State House" in King Street 80

A British ship of the line salutes Castle William on entering Boston
Harbor 81

Bostonians were determined not to be saddled with a bishop not of
their own choosing 81

From this point General Washington applied the final pressure
which drove Howe from Boston 168

The commission of a volunteer defender of Boston's South Battery 168

Paul Revere's famous engraving of "the Bloody Massacre of 1770"
was strictly for propaganda purposes 169

Old Faneuil Hall was the heart of Boston's Revolution . . . 208

The Green Dragon was the scene of secret meetings which furnished the heart's blood 208

The Boston Port Bill drew comment from all sections of the British
press. This cartoon is a Tory jibe 209

The climax of the Battle of Bunker Hill, as Trumbull pictured it 264

This rather fanciful view of the burning of Charlestown might be
entitled America's first amphibious operation 265

Boston

CHAPTER I

The Beginning

SATURDAY, 12 [of June 1630]. About four in the morning we were near our port. We shot off two pieces of ordnance, and sent our skiff to Mr. Peirce his ship (which lay in the harbor, and had been there several days before). About an hour after, Mr. Allerton came aboard us in a shallop as he was sailing to Pemaquid. As we stood towards the harbor, we saw another shallop coming to us; so we stood in to meet her, and passed through the narrow strait between Baker's Isle and Little Isle, and came to an anchor a little within the islands.

"Afterwards Mr. Peirce came aboard us, and returned to fetch Mr. Endecott, who came to us about two of the clock, and with him Mr. Skelton and Mr. Levett. We that were of the assistants, and some other gentlemen, and some of the women, and our captain, returned with them to Nahumkeck, where we supped with a good venison pasty and good beer, and at night we returned to our ship, but some of the women stayed behind.

"In the mean time most of our people went on shore upon the land of Cape Ann, which lay very near us, and gathered store of fine strawberries."

So wrote John Winthrop, their governor, describing in his

journal the arrival of the settlers of Boston in the New World.

It is mildly ironic that these people, who were to found the metropolis of New England, should so completely miss their ultimate destination as to land at what was, in later years, to develop into a rival port. Winthrop and his group landed at Salem, then known as Naumkeag. Some others went on shore at Charlestown. And at least one shipload was dumped, with scant ceremony, at Nantasket. But not until they were driven there by drought and pestilence did any of these founding fathers move to occupy the peninsula on which their town was to rise. By then it was already late in the season, and winter was just around the corner. There were no good venison pasties, and no good beer.

John Winthrop and his Puritan company were not the first to visit the shores of Massachusetts Bay. Indeed, by any standards, they were late-comers. Six hundred years and more before them white men had first sailed these waters.

Bjarne Herjulfson, the Norseman, voyaging in his high-prowed Viking ship from Iceland to Greenland, was the first to spy the new land in the west. A storm had blown him far to the southward, off his course, and he woke one morning to see the land lying low and blue and wooded on the horizon.

Bjarne did not land, but fifteen years or so later, about the year 1000, came Leif, the son of Eric the Red, seeking the land which Bjarne had said he had seen. He found the land and went on shore and built a house and spent a winter there. The place where he built his house he called Leifsbudir, and the land he named Vinland, for the grapevines which he found everywhere there.

After Leif came others: Thorvald, Leif's brother, and Thorfinn Karlsefne, and Gudrid, to whom was born Snorre—if the legend be true, the first white child to be born in the New

World. After that the Norse contact was more or less continuous for more than three hundred years, when it ended abruptly, probably about 1347, when the great plague swept Europe.

We are not certain just where Vinland and Leifsbudir were, though there have been those who have claimed that it was on the banks of the Charles. We do know, however, that it lay somewhere between Cape May and Cape Sable, and, if this were the case the waters of Massachusetts Bay must have been more or less familiar to the Norsemen.

But the visit of the Norsemen was only an interlude; nebulous, inconclusive, only half proven. A century and a half were to pass before the chain of discoveries and explorations, fishing and trading expeditions, and starry-eyed attempts at colonization that culminated in the settlement of Massachusetts Bay could begin. During those years there is no record of any European visit to the Western World, although there is a mass of confusing legend to hint the possibility. It was a day when literacy was a rare gift, rather than the common lot of every man. Those who could read and write their names were the exception rather than the rule, and it is not impossible that fishermen or other plain mariners, who had neither the incentive nor the knowledge to record their findings, might, from time to time, during that period, have been blown far enough to the west to sight our shores.

It was the Cabots, booming in from the fogbound banks and stumbling upon the frowning coasts of Nova Scotia and New England in 1497–98, who set the ball a-rolling once again. No one seems quite certain what sent the Cabots sailing westward. No doubt the discoveries of the Great Admiral, in more southerly waters, five years before, had much to do with it. But the rumors spread by less tutored voyagers, passed along from mouth to mouth, might well have had a share in it. In any event the Cabots sailed for the expressed purpose of discovery with the King's patent in their pockets "to discover new lands—and set up his ensign therein."

For more than a hundred years after the Cabots a bewildering stream of explorers passed this way; Cortereal, Verrazano, Estevan Gómez, John Rut, Master Hore, Thevet, Cartier, Roberval. Few of them so much as went on shore. None left an account sufficiently accurate to identify positively what land they saw.

But in the meantime, more important than these seagoing dilettantes was the ever increasing stream of French and English and Spanish and Portuguese fishermen to the offshore banks. These men came, not to look and see and go away again never to return, but rather to find good fishing and to go back to it after a successful voyage. Illiterate they might be, but it was their reports, whispered over a mug of ale or a tankard of wine, of fine fat catches and good profits that, passed on by word of mouth, brought others in their train.

Though they left us no records of their own, we know that these hardy sea dogs found their ways to the New World, for others have told us enough of them to let us draw our own conclusions. As early as 1527 an English captain, putting in at Newfoundland, found Norman, Breton, Basque, and Portuguese fishing vessels there. Later, in 1585, Queen Elizabeth sent ships of war into New England waters to drive away such vessels as might be found fishing there contrary to the rights of her subjects. It is a matter of record that many were found and some were captured. Only ten years before this, one hundred fifty vessels were at Newfoundland in a single season. In the year 1604 a French captain of the name of Savalet boasted that he had made no less than forty-two voyages to these waters.

That some of these reached the mainland, along the New England shore, and landed—to dry their fish, to trade with the natives, to feel solid earth beneath their feet, or perhaps, to cheat an Indian and thus sow the seeds of future discord—we know, for we have at least one account of them. Bartholomew Gosnold, sailing from Falmouth in 1602, was the first Englishman we know to have landed in Massachusetts. He also, so far as the record is concerned, discovered and named Cape Cod; and he came to anchor somewhere in the neighborhood of Cape Ann on the 14th of May in that year. Of what happened there he has this to say in his log:

. . . And standing faire alongst by the shore, about twelve of the clock the same day, we came to an anker, where six Indians, in a Baske shallop with mast and saile, an iron grapple, and a copper kettle, came boldly aboord us, one of them apparelled with a waistcoat and breeches of blacke serdge, made after our sea fashion, hose and shoes on his feet; all the rest (saving one that had a pair of breeches of blue cloth) were all naked. . . . It seemed by some wordes and signes they made that some Baskes or of St. John de Luz have fished or traded in this place. . . .

It seemed, too, that the savages understood the Englishmen better than the Englishmen understood the savages, and that they had some notion of map making as well, for Gosnold reports that they drew sketches of the coast in chalk upon the deck in response to his inquiries.

From this it would appear that the fisherfolk who landed on these shores took advantage of the opportunity to do a little trading on the side. In return for their iron grapples and copper kettles, their shallops and articles of clothing, they doubtless received such items of value on the European market as furs and sassafras—considered a potent panacea by the medical practitioners of the day—and similar forest products. As these began to come on the market in greater and greater quantities the interest of financial and commercial interests at home began to be aroused. Individuals and groups began to consider how they might go about the business of monopolizing both the fisheries and the trade.

Hitherto the expeditions which had been sent out had been in search of the riches of the East. They sought a quick route to India and China and Japan and the Spice Islands, with all their wealth of gold and precious jewels and spices. Consequently they had passed by these less exotic, more forbidding shores. The French, to be sure, had begun to tap the furry wealth of the St. Lawrence Valley. But it remained for more staid heads to realize the prosaic profits to be found in fish and sassafras and incidental furs.

To obtain the utmost from this business, efforts were made to establish stations, small colonies, upon the coast, to which the fishermen could take their catch for drying and curing, and from which the factors could deal with the natives. This was the purpose for which Gosnold had been sent, and though he did not succeed in establishing his station he did manage to return with such a cargo of sassafras as to turn the English market upside down with excitement.

On the strength of Gosnold's success Martin Pring sailed the next year, to discover the mouth of the Piscataqua, and to sail into Massachusetts Bay, which Gosnold, the year before, had overshot. Pring rested six weeks at the present site of Plymouth, trading with the Indians, entertaining them with the music of a "zitterne" when they behaved themselves, and threatening them with his two great mastiffs, of whom they were mortally afraid, when they showed signs of hostility. Like Gosnold he did not succeed in establishing a permanent station, but returned with a good cargo.

Some other attempts to settle were made along the coast in the years following. The Sieur de Champlain explored the coast from Cape Cod to the Bay of Fundy in 1605, drawing a map of it as he went, but his patron preferred the Saint Lawrence. In that same year Captain George Waymouth explored the coast of Maine and the mouth of the Penobscot, carrying off with him five Indians whom he had tricked on board one of his vessels. Waymouth's report inspired Sir Fernando Gorges and Sir John Popham to attempt a colony at that point, and accordingly, in 1607, two ships were sent out under Captain George Popham, brother of Sir John. The rigors of the winter, however, proved too much for the colonists. Captain Popham died, and the colony broke up the following spring. After that Englishmen appeared upon the coast in increasing numbers, but it was not until the appearance of Captain John Smith, the adventurer, that any further contribution to our knowledge or advance toward settlement was made.

It seems to have been accident, more than anything else, that brought John Smith to New England waters. In his own words:

In the moneth of Aprill, 1614, with two ships from London, of a few marchants, I chanced to arive in New England, a part of Ameryca, at the Isle of Monnahiggan. . . . Our Plot was there to take whales and make tryalls of a myne of gold and copper. If those fayled, fish and furres was then our refuge. . . . We found this whalefishing a costly conclusion: we saw many and spent much time in chasing them: but could not kill any. . . . For our golde it was rather the master's device to get a voyage that projected it, than any knowledge hee had at all of any such matter. . . .

If there was no gold to be had and the whales would not be caught, there were, at least, still fish in the sea and furs in the forest. Smith made his headquarters at "Monnahiggan" Island and set his men to catching a cargo of cod, while he, with eight members of his company, set out in an open boat to explore the coast and trade with the Indians.

Deep, narrow cove and marshy inlet, wide-mouthed bay and rocky headland, wooded isle and cape and river mouth—he explored them all between the Penobscot and Plymouth Harbor. Cape Ann he named for the Princess Tragabigzanda who, —so *he* said—had been kind to him when he was a prisoner among the Turks. He sailed into Boston Harbor—the first Englishman to record doing so—and found the French six weeks before him. He ignored the French and named the Blue Hills of Milton "Cheuyot," for the Cheviot Hills at home; the River of Massachusetts, the Charles, after the Prince of Wales. But it does not seem, from his description, that he penetrated very deeply into the harbor. Beyond Nantasket he had a narrow escape from the Indians, and at Plymouth he remarked the good land and the fine bay.

There is not space here to tell all his adventures, but Smith's little side journey had a number of important results. For one, it resulted in the best map of the region that had yet been produced; a map that was the standard for many years to come. For another, it inspired Smith to write *A Description of New England: Or The Observations and Discoueries of Captain John Smith (Admirall of that Country), in the Yeare of Our Lord, 1614,* a book that was to have a considerable effect on the shaping of New England's destiny. For a third, it so fired Smith himself with enthusiasm for New England's prospect that he spent the rest of his life promoting schemes for the settlement of the region.

England at that time had but just lately come into her own among the nations of the world. The defeat of the Spanish Armada had established her firmly as a power on the seas, and Richard Hakluyt, in his *Principall Navigations, Voiages, Traffiques and Discoueries,* had turned the eyes of Englishmen toward the possibilities of the world outside their own narrow isles. It was this that accounted in the main for the increase in British activity in American waters, and now John Smith came along, with his gift for glowing description and his stout promoter's heart, to give public imagination a further boost.

This is not to say that Smith's efforts were immediately effective. Conditions within England were not such as encouraged small and diverse enterprise in such matters. The Crown had a finger in every pie, and the repression of Parliament and the practice of currying the King's favor tended to the creation of monopolies in trade. Such a monopoly had already been set up in the East India Company, and the practice was at first extended to America. Two such companies were established for the colonization and control of American trade. The first, known as the Virginia, or London, Company, was given control over the territory lying between the 34th and the 38th degrees of latitude and was granted to certain "noblemen, knights and gentlemen" of London. It was under the direction of this company that Captain John Smith planted the colony at Jamestown, in Virginia, in 1607. The second company, known as the North Virginia, or Plymouth, Company, was granted to certain nobles, knights, and gentlemen of Plymouth, Exeter, and Bristol and controlled all the territory lying between the 38th and 45th degrees of latitude.

The affairs of the northern company did not prosper as did those of the southern. As Jeremy Belknap put it: "Either from the jarring interests of the members, or their indistinct knowledge of the country, or their inattention to business, or some other cause which does not fully appear, their affairs were transacted in a confused manner from the beginning." They made overlapping grants, laying the basis for controversies, some of which were not settled until long after the Revolution. They sent out halfhearted attempts at colonization and then failed to support them, with the result that by the time of John Smith's visit many of the members had lost interest and the company had all but ceased to exist.

There were two members, however, whose unflagging interest and tireless energy had served to keep the company alive. These were Sir Fernando Gorges and Captain John Mason, to whom several grants in the northern part of the territory had been made. These two, under the impetus of Smith's enthusiasm and, later, of the success of the Pilgrims at Plymouth—about whom more presently—were in a large measure responsible for the reorganization of the company in 1620, under the title of the "Council for New England."

In point of accomplishment the Council for New England was little more effective than the old company had been. It made several more conflicting grants, and under its aegis a few attempts at settlement were made. None of these attempts was successful in anything like a scale to dignify it with the title of colony, but, as each failed and broke up, the hardier remnants remained, leaving little pockets of civilization and individual settlers scattered at intervals all along the coast from Plymouth to the coast of Maine. A number of these clustered about the mouth of the Piscataqua. There were some at Cape Ann and Salem. William Blaxton lived alone on the peninsula of Shawmut, in Boston Harbor, where Winthrop and his followers were later to settle. Thomas Walford, a blacksmith, settled on the present site of Charlestown; Samuel Maverick at Winnesimmet—now Chelsea. David Thompson occupied an island in Boston Harbor and also had a hand in the settlement on the Piscataqua. A Captain Weston made a wholly unsuccessful attempt to establish a settlement at Wessaguscus, on the site of the present Weymouth. And Thomas Morton raised his Maypole at "Mare-Mount," in present Wollaston, and there held merry court until the elders of Plymouth and the other settlers on the coast, scandalized by his behavior and fearful of his influence upon the simple savages, took steps to drive him out.

All of these attempts at colonization were purely commercial in their intent. They could hardly be called successful. In the end it was religion that was to succeed where trade failed, and in order to understand this we must return again to England to examine the conditions there that were responsible.

The Beginning

The England of the first half of the seventeenth century was not a happy land. It was a nation in the throes of economic, political, and religious upheaval. Its economy was undergoing the drastic change from the feudal to the mercantile. Politically the Crown was fighting desperately to retain its feudal prerogatives in the face of growing popular sentiment. In matters of religion the Reformation had struck, and a great mass of Englishmen were no more inclined to look upon the King and his archbishops as the deputies of the Lord than they were the Pope. As usual in times of readjustment, it was not the very rich, nor yet the very poor, who bore the brunt. The rich had the means to weather the storm. The poor did not miss what they had never had. But the sturdy middle class, the small farmers and yeomen and tradesmen felt the full weight of it. An expanding wool market encouraged many of the great landholders to turn more and more of their acres to the pasturage of sheep. In consequence costs and rents soared. Men were turned off the land and out of work. The roads and lanes swarmed with "valiant rogues and sturdy beggars."

It was a condition calculated to make men turn their eyes longingly toward a land where the fields were green and to be had for the asking and for the labor that went into them. But oppression must be burdensome indeed before men will turn from the things they know to strike out into the unfamiliar. It took the Church to add the last straw to an already wearying load. It was James I who declared that he would make the Puritans conform to the Church of England or "harry them from the land." Small wonder then that in his reign they began to cast about for some other place to go. But first someone must show them the way.

The Pilgrims did this. The Pilgrims might be termed the radicals of the Reformation. They were out-and-out Separatists. That is to say, they favored a complete break with the Church of England. This was no part of the Puritan policy—not, at least, while they remained in England. Or, if it was, they were careful to conceal it. Reform within the existing Church was their evident aim.

It was for their Separatist leanings that the Pilgrims were among the first to feel the hand of the Crown. They *were* harried from the land, and went to Holland, where they remained for a time at Leyden.

To a man the Pilgrims were poor. They had not the means to buy comfort. The Dutch were kind, but as the years passed, the Pilgrims began to realize that not only was their general condition not improving but also that all that they stood for and hoped to be was likely to be obliterated by the fact that their children were growing up to be little Hollanders. It was not that they had anything against the Dutch, but, after all, they were still Englishmen, even in exile, and they hoped to remain such.

To shorten a long tale which concerns us only incidentally, they decided, if permission could be had, to go to America and there set up their own colony. Accordingly they applied to the Virginia Company for a charter or patent, which after some negotiation was granted. After a number of reverses which would have discouraged a less determined group—and which, indeed, did discourage some—they set sail in the ship *Mayflower*, and toward the middle of November 1620 they approached the shores of the New World.

It will doubtless always be a mystery why the Pilgrims landed at Plymouth. Their patent, derived from the Virginia Company, directed them farther south. In short they had no business to land where they did, and that they were well aware of it is borne out by the alacrity with which, the following year, they applied to the Council for New England for a new grant and permission to remain where they were. Land they did, however. And where they landed they stayed. In spite of hardship and privation and poverty their settlement throve and prospered as no other colony north of Virginia thus far had done. And at home, in England, their progress was followed with more than ordinary interest by more people than they knew.

One of those was Master John White, of Dorchester, an energetic Puritan pastor. White was deeply concerned with the plight of the fishermen of the neighboring coasts who each year crossed the ocean to the Banks for cod and ling. In the success of the Pilgrims he thought he saw an answer to his problem. Largely through his efforts a number of wealthy persons, mostly of Puritan leanings, were brought together to form what was called the Dorchester Company of Adventurers. The object of this company was to plant a colony of fishermen upon the coast of New England, there to build stages, tend the flakes, and help with the fishing when the fishing boats, manned only by crews sufficient to take them across the ocean, arrived on the grounds. Under their sponsorship a company of fourteen men was sent out, who settled on Cape Ann in the summer of 1623.

Like many another that had gone before, this attempt at settlement was a failure. The original group stayed only through the first winter, when all but a few returned home. Those who remained lived under the leadership of Roger Conant until the autumn of 1626, when they removed to Naumkeag.

In the meantime, however, matters had been moving backward and forward at home, and though the first effort at settlement was a failure, it was the germ from which a more successful venture was to spring.

In 1625 the Dorchester Company broke up, evidently in despair of ever planting a successful colony. One member, however, did not lose hope. Master White continued his efforts, and in 1627 he was largely instrumental in the organization of a new company to be called "The New England Company for a

Plantation in Massachusetts Bay." This company, in 1628, obtained from the Council for New England a grant to all lands in New England lying between parallels three miles north of the Merrimack, on the north, and three miles south of the Charles, on the south, and extending from the Atlantic, on the east, to the "South sea on the west parte."

This was an ambiguous grant, quite in keeping with the other fumblings of the council, for in time it not only gave rise to disputes between the Bay colonists and the Pilgrims on the south, but also set on foot a bitter controversy on the north, when the Massachusetts people interpreted their grant to mean three miles north of the *source* of the Merrimack, thereby including nearly all of New Hampshire within its limits. What was worse, however, it overlapped, and in one case completely included, lands already granted by the council to Captain John Mason, himself a member of the council and a man not likely to take these proceedings lightly.

The first move of the company was to send out colonists, under the theory that possession is nine points of the law. John Endecott, a member of the original company, was sent out with about fifty colonists and appointed to act as governor for the company. Endecott landed at Naumkeag and promptly elbowed the original settlers aside, appropriating their quarters for the use of his own people. Roger Conant must have been a very godly man indeed, for there is no record that he made any protest against this. But Endecott's own turn was soon to come.

The members of the company in England were quite aware of the insecurity of their position, and it was plain to them that immediate steps should be taken to solidify it. This was only to be done by a royal charter confirming their original grant. Even John Mason would hardly dare to quarrel with that. Moreover, money was needed if the project was to be successful, and money was what the men of Dorchester and the west had not.

The Beginning

Accordingly Master White set out for London, there to interest capital in his plans.

Master White was either a fine salesman or he was well equipped with rabbits' feet. In London he managed to interest a number of wealthy merchants and nobles, of Puritan leanings, prominent among whom were Matthew Cradock and Sir Richard Saltonstall. With the help of these, working through the Earl of Warwick, the associates obtained, in 1629, a charter from the King confirming their original grant in the name of the Massachusetts Bay Company. Further, this royal charter conveyed full powers of government to the company, and—here was the hidden joker—it failed to stipulate where the governor and assistants—that is to say, the chairman and board of directors —were to hold their meetings.

Whether this was an accident or done with malice aforethought, the result was auspicious. As John Smith had long since pointed out, the greatest stumbling block to success in the path of colonization was the fact that settlements were governed by remote control, as it were, across three thousand miles of ocean. The one successful colony thus far was proof in itself of the pudding, for the men of Plymouth were their own masters in matters of government.

The effect was immediate. There was no reason why the government of the company could not be moved bodily to Massachusetts, and this it was proposed to do. Puritans throughout the country sat up and took notice. This was something like it! New blood and new capital flocked to climb on the band wagon, and the result was the departure of Governor Winthrop, with the charter and more than a thousand colonists, well stocked, well manned, and well supported, for the New World. With him, or close on his heels, came the principal shareholders in the company, the directors and the assistants, or their representatives.

What were Governor Endecott's thoughts at being thus summarily superseded, we do not know. Like Roger Conant before him, he entered no protest. Winthrop, however, did not look with favor on Naumkeag as a site for settlement. Five days after his landing he walked around the bay as far as the site of present Charlestown and there decided to plant his banner.

The choice was not a good one. The water supply was insufficient, and the year was dry. But over on the peninsula of Shawmut, or "Trimountaine," as the settlers called it from the triple peaks of Beacon Hill, much higher then than they are now, where the hermit, William Blaxton, dwelt there was a good spring. In August, Blaxton, perhaps weary of his solitude, rowed across the Charles to extend his invitation to the settlers to join him there. Winthrop and his assistants were quick to accept, and on the 7th of September 1630 the Court of Assistants "ordered that Trimountaine shall be called Boston."

CHAPTER II

The Farmer Takes to the Sea

THERE are harbors which it is an adventure only to enter. There is Rio—which is the queen of them all—garlanded in bays and watched over always by her mighty guardian peaks. There is Sydney, with its rolling hills and cliffs and beaches; Capetown, with the anvil summit of Table Mountain floating ever in the sky above; San Francisco, with the narrow gut of the Golden Gate opening to the broad reaches of the bay beyond. Who would ever forget the purple hills of La Guayra, approached in the dawn; the narrowness of the harbor mouth at Valetta; the low, white spires and rounded domes of Cadiz, seen over the shimmering, sandy, sun-baked bar? Is there anything quite to match the picturesqueness of the red roofs and pink stucco walls of Charlotte Amalie, or the way the white houses march in tiers up the steep hillsides of Algiers? Even New York, with its man-made sky line, crowded and immense, has a certain flavor of its own. Even the smell of some harbors is distinctive.

But Boston is not one of these. The most ardent lover of Boston would scarcely contend that the city's seaward approaches are anything to fetch a traveler early from his bed. A vessel, butting in from the misty ocean, comes first to the Graves and the Brewsters, dark and forbidding, thrusting black, rocky fangs from a surly, leaden sea. Once inside this outer barrier we thread the channel, passing, now on the left, now on the right, low-lying, bare, bleak-seeming islands. Beneath us the water turns a muddy, viscous, foul green, aswim with slops and rubbish. North and south the bay opens momentarily in a broad green reach. Then the low flat lands close in on either hand, and the city looms ahead, dark and gray and grimy, bulking sullenly beside the thick water. The customhouse tower and the tarnished* dome of the State House are the only distinguishing features of the landscape. The rest is only rather drab, rather smoky, wholly uninspiring city. Across from the docks, as the ship warps in, big planes settle toward the flat of East Boston Airport. Up to the right blue-gray funnels and masts mark the location of Charlestown Navy Yard. But it is hard to make out now, at a glance, the mouths of the Charles and the Mystic under their cover of street and railroad bridges and fill. No, blessed neither with an equable climate nor fine surroundings, Boston's strength lies elsewhere than in its appearance.

The whole area of the harbor, from Winthrop to Nantasket, and inland to the upper reaches of the Charles, has changed a good deal since the day John Smith first laid eyes on it; since the day Governor Winthrop picked it as a site for his colony of Massachusetts Bay. You have to say that for those men who looked upon it and found it fair. If it still was not imposing in those days, it must have been a good deal pleasanter. The water was clean and clear, for one thing, and there was a good deal more of it. The mouths of both the Mystic and the Charles were wide and open. The islands in the bay were wooded—enough so to make the people of Boston dependent upon them for firewood while it lasted—and there were more of them. The hills all around were higher, and the bays were wider, deeper in the land.

*It is, too!—J. J.

The Farmer Takes to the Sea

"Stuff! Imagination!" you say?

Not at all. It is man's doing that Boston, like an aging dowager, has, with the years, increased her waistline and broadened her beam tremendously at the expense of her figure.

In times gone by the peninsula of Shawmut—that on which, as we have seen, Winthrop chose to plant his town of Boston—hung from the main by a tenuous thread of marshy ground, low-lying, and barely a quarter of a mile across. To the east of this strip lay the ragged indentation of South Cove and the shallows known as Dorchester Flats. On the west was the broad expanse of the Back Bay and Roxbury Flats, forming a deep pouch in the southern shore of the Charles. At low tide the flats on either side were frequently laid bare; and in moments of extreme high tide it was not unusual for the thin strip of marshy ground to be inundated, making the higher, lower end of the peninsula temporarily an island.

Beyond the narrow, swampy isthmus by which it was joined to the hills of Roxbury, Shawmut broadened and swelled, like an enormous, irregular raindrop. It rose, gradually at first, and then more abruptly, to the summits of three sharply defined hills: Copp's on the northeast, Beacon, in the center, and Fort on the east. Here, in turn, it dropped away sharply to the serrated, deepwater coves of the bay itself.

Over across the mouth of the Charles—much broader then than it is now—the hills of Charlestown rose much more sharply than they do today. And beyond that, in turn, the broad estuary of the Mystic swept down to split upon the bulk of Noddle's Island.

A glance at the modern map is enough to show that this is no longer the shape of the land today. Fort Hill is gone, and Copp's; and Beacon has had its pate so shaved that today it is no more than a single small nubble, almost lost beneath the welter of buildings. Over across the Charles the hills of Charlestown have disappeared so completely that we need a monument to remind us that they once existed, let alone mark the site of a great battle.

What has happened to these hills? They have been pushed off into the bay to make more land. The Back Bay and Roxbury Flats no longer exist, nor do the South Cove and Dorchester Flats. The mouths of the Charles and the Mystic have grown narrower as the fringes of Boston and Charlestown and East Boston have been filled in. East Boston and the airport have completely swallowed up Noddle's Island. On the other side of the Harbor Dorchester Neck and Dorchester Flats and South Cove have been filled to make South Boston, which, in turn, has reached out its arms to include Castle Island. And, tacking back across the lower harbor once again, there is no longer open water separating Deer Island from Pullen Point—or Point Shirley, as it has latterly been called.

These are the changes that man has wrought. But Nature, too, has had a hand in things. Bird Island has disappeared entirely, and all that remains of little Nix's Mate is a bit of retaining wall and a beacon. The rest has been washed away by the tide—the result, some say, of a pirate's dying curse. But more of that when we come to it.

But all of this is the shape of things to come. At the moment our interest lies in the peninsula as Governor Winthrop and his followers found it on that first hot August day when they rowed across from Charlestown and set foot upon it. Anne Pollard was a young, a "romping" girl, by her own description. When the first boatload touched the shore she was the first to leap out. In later years she described the place she found as "very uneven, abounding in small hollows and swamps, covered with blueberries and other bushes." It is the only description of Boston at the time that has come down to us.

So Boston was founded. So the first few hundred Puritan

The Farmer Takes to the Sea

settlers of the Bay Colony arrived. They were the forerunners of what was to be England's greatest colonial migration. Within the space of a decade nearly twenty thousand were to follow their example. But in the meantime what of those firstcomers?

The first winter was a miserable one. For all their care, for all their backing, for all their prudence and wisdom and shrewdness, it seems, Winthrop and his companions were still unable to foresee all the hazards of their undertaking. Even before the move to Shawmut, pestilence, the result of improper water at Charlestown, had taken its toll. Several had died, among them Isaac Johnson and his wife, the young Lady Arabella, for whom Winthrop's ship on the voyage out had been named.

Nor did matters improve with the removal across the river. It was too late in the season then to plant, even had the peninsula been suited to planting. Provisions were scarce—a fact curious in view of the care with which the project was undertaken. And the winter proved to be one of those early and severe ones which periodically visit the coast. Before it was over there were more deaths, and the records of Charlestown tell us that "people were necessitated to live on clams and muscles, and ground nuts and acorns." At the very darkest moment of despair, on the 22d of February, ever a lucky day for this land, a ship appeared laden with provisions, and a day of thanksgiving was declared—the first, incidentally, to be held in Massachusetts.

In view of all this we are led to wonder somewhat at the make-up of the colony. What manner of men were these, and what did they expect of the new land? Few evidently were farmers, else they would have had a better notion of the problems facing them. Nor would they, in such case, have hit upon the plan of settling on Shawmut, which was quite unsuited to such pursuits. We have it from one authority that they intended to farm, but if so they must have had the idea, common to city dwellers even today, that the business of wresting a living from the land is merely a matter of turning over the ground and putting down a few seeds! How often have we heard men who scarcely knew which end of a cow gave milk, men who could not drive a straight furrow to save them, men who would not know which way to mow around a field, declare fatuously that they have "bought themselves a place in the country" to which they can retire and "live off the land if worst comes to worst"! Gentlemen farmers, with no notion of reality! The record leads one to suspect strongly that there were many such among that first batch of Puritans who landed at Boston—merchants, city dwellers, tradesmen, clergymen, lawyers. A few farmers there may have been among them, but these sloughed off quickly and went to the more fertile areas near by, so that within a very short time there were the beginnings of other towns—Watertown, Mystic (Medford), Newtowne (Cambridge), Roxbury, Dorchester, Lynn—scattered about the region. Those who remained on the peninsula of Shawmut turned as quickly as they might to more familiar pursuits, and Boston never did go in heavily for agriculture.

Whatever the majority of the settlers may have had in mind for themselves, however, there is no doubt that some of their backers, as well as a few among the settlers themselves, had some notion as to which way the wind must blow. John Smith had long since pointed out the availability of the vast forests of the New World as a source of ship timber and naval stores, and the countless experiments along the coast had proved one thing, even though they failed in their immediate aim; namely, that there was profit in the fisheries if only a sound permanent base were established. Several such bases had secured a toe hold, but nothing so extensive as this had yet been attempted. Moreover, the firm establishment of the English in Virginia and at Plymouth and at Boston, of the Dutch at New York, and of all the little nuclei of colonies up and down the coast, began to suggest to some the possibility of intercolony trade upon our own coast.

It was doubtless with some such thoughts as these in mind that Matthew Cradock, the London merchant, prevailed upon certain others within the company to join with him in covering, as it were, a side bet. The first evidence of this we find in a letter to John Endecott, dated April 17, 1629, before the departure of Governor Winthrop and his companions, and bearing the general instructions from the company to their then governor:

We haue sent six Shipwrights, of whom Robert Molton is cheif . . . desiring that their labour may bee employed ⅔ for the generall Companie, and ⅓ for Mr. Cradock and his Assotiats. . . .

Moulton and his carpenters did not get around to building any ships before Winthrop arrived. They were kept too busy building houses evidently. And after the arrival of the colonists at Boston, doubtless, all who could wield a hammer were kept occupied with the primary problem of shelter for much of the first winter. There is evidence, however, that somehow someone among them did manage to find some time to knock together a few shallops. Whether it was Moulton and his fellows does not matter.

These shallops were easily the most popular and probably the most useful boats made for a long time upon these shores. Mention of them is constant in the early records. These are described as a "nondescript class of small boat, open or half decked, ranging from an ordinary ship's boat to a decked two master, something like the later 'Chebacco' boat out of Gloucester and Essex." Mostly they were lug-rigged, and were good sailers, used extensively in fishing and coasting.

That there were a number of these small vessels about, even before the Puritans' arrival, as well as during that first winter, is evident from Governor Winthrop's frequent mention of them. Even before they reached their destination they had sighted several of them. On the 11th of June, standing off and on between Cape Ann and the Isles of Shoals, he mentions seeing a ship "lie there at anchor, and five or six shallops under sail up and down."

In the next paragraph, that same day, he adds: "We took many mackerels, and met a shallop, which stood from Cape Ann towards the Isles of Shoals, which belonged to some English fishermen." Next day he speaks of meeting Mr. Allerton in his shallop, bound for Pemaquid, and as they bore into the harbor at Naumkeag they "saw another shallop coming to" them.

After the settlement at Boston, on the 24th of December:

Three of the Governor's servants, coming in a shallop from the Mistick, were driven by the wind upon Noddle's Island, and forced to stay there all that night, without fire or food; yet through God's Mercy, they came safe to Boston next day, but the fingers of two of them were blistered with cold, and one swooned when he came to the fire.

Still later:

A shallop of Mr. Glover's was cast away upon the rocks about Nahant, but the men were saved.

And still later:

Sir Richard Saltonstall and his two daughters, and one of his younger sons . . . came down to Boston . . . and the next morning, by seven of the clock, accompanied with Mr. Peirce and others in two shallops, they departed to go to the ship riding at Salem. . . . Mr. Sharp went away at the same time in another shallop.

One of the most exciting tales of the early settlement, as well as perhaps the best example of the extent to which these little craft were used and their seaworthiness, has come down to us in the adventure of Richard Garrett. Not all of it concerns us here, but because of its interest I retell it in full.

Richard Garrett was a shoemaker of Boston. On a day in late November, shortly after the establishment of the colony, he proposed, for some reason which the chronicler does not reveal, to sail in his shallop to Plymouth. With him he took his daughter, "a young maid," and four others.

It was not a day one would ordinarily choose for a pleasure jaunt. It was bitter cold, and weather was making. All Garrett's friends advised him against the journey, but either he was stubborn or his business in Plymouth was of such importance that he felt he must risk it. All went well until they were clear of the harbor and standing southward. But about Gurnett's Nose the storm that had been threatening overtook them and blew so hard from the northwest that they were forced to come to a killock* at twenty fathom. "But their boat drave and shaked out the stone and they were put to sea." The seas were mountainous and swept over the tiny craft, filling her with water. They bailed with everything at hand. But faster than they could bail it out more water came in, and almost as fast as it came in it froze, hard and fast. They gave themselves up for lost, but as luck would have it the set of the wind was such that in due time they had crossed the full width of Massachusetts Bay and come in sight of the tip of Cape Cod. With a superhuman effort one of the company managed to free himself from the ice and raise a part of their sail, and with its aid they drove among the rocks on the inside of the Cape, probably somewhere in the neighborhood of Provincetown. Some of the company managed to reach shore, but the others—the account does not say which ones— had their legs frozen in the ice in the boat so securely that they could not break free. As a result the others had to return and cut them out with knives, for they had no hatchet. This lack of a good cutting tool was a misfortune in another way, too, for having none they were unable to gather sufficient firewood to keep them warm. Consequently they were forced to lie the night through in the open, without cover or fire.

In the morning, supposing themselves to be no more than

*Killock—a rude anchor consisting of a stone enclosed within a frame of wood.

seven or eight miles from Plymouth, two of the party set out to walk there. Actually they were about fifty miles from their destination. On the way they passed two Indian squaws, who promptly told their menfolk of having met them. The Indians, realizing at once that they must have been shipwrecked—for there were no white settlers thereabout at the time—immediately went after them and fetched them back to their lodge and fed them and warmed them. The next day the Indians and one of the men went back for the others, but found them so weak they could not move.

The kindly Indians did their best for the company and sent messengers to Plymouth, whence another shallop was sent out with provisions. Garrett died, as did three others. The girl apparently came off best of them all, doubtless because the men cared for her most painstakingly. As for the boat, it was launched again from the spot where it had been driven, high above the high-water mark, evidently little the worse for its buffeting. It was sailed to Plymouth and there manned once more and returned to Boston in the teeth of another gale.

It seems evident from this that these shallops were sturdy as well as numerous. That they did some small amount of carrying between the various settlements up and down the shore is unquestionable. But they were hardly large enough to undertake long journeys in search of important cargoes. For the most they remained farm boats, useful for hauling marsh hay and firewood. Something bigger was needed for trade, however, and Samuel Maverick—he who was already settled at Winnesimmet when the Puritans arrived—had a pinnace, which is a small vessel, generally two-masted and pointed at both ends, sometimes decked, sometimes not, but running in size to as much as fifty or sixty tons.

Necessity was the mother of Boston trade in more ways than one. It was necessity which made Governor Winthrop dicker with Samuel Maverick for the use of his pinnace in September of that first year; the necessity for food. When the deal was made, the pinnace was sent out to trade with the Indians of Cape Cod for a cargo of corn and returned with eighty bushels. This was the first recorded trading voyage out of Boston Harbor.

The next spring there appeared at Salem a pinnace from Virginia laden with corn and tobacco. She was bound to the north, probably for fish, but foul weather forced her in and she disposed of her corn to the settlers at ten shillings a bushel. Whether or not the Virginians also found their fish there is not recorded. But the visit opened new channels of endeavor.

In the meantime Governor Winthrop had fetched Master Cradock's ship's carpenters to the banks of the Mystic, and, with admirable foresight, there set them to work, with the result that on July 4, 1631, was launched, on that river of ships, the first ship to be built in Massachusetts—the *Blessing of the Bay*.

The *Blessing* was not the first ship built in North America. But she was not far from it. In 1607 the ill-starred Popham colony at the mouth of the Kennebec had built the thirty-ton *Virginia*, which later made several voyages across the Atlantic. In 1615 or 1616 Adrian Block, at New Amsterdam, built the *Onrust*, in which he explored Long Island Sound and the shores of Connecticut, Rhode Island, and Massachusetts out as far as Cape Cod. About forty-five feet over-all, and of only sixteen tons burden, this little vessel was later sailed to Holland with a cargo of furs.

Other vessels of similar size may have been built. But if so the records have not told us. Hence the *Blessing of the Bay* becomes the third ship built in America, as well as the first in Massachusetts. She is described by Winthrop as a "Bark" and was of thirty to forty tons burden, built wholly of locust. The record of her activity, however, is meager. On August 31 she went to sea on her maiden voyage, probably to trade with the Dutch at

New Amsterdam. Again on October 4 she "went on a voyage to the eastward." In the next year she went again to the Dutch Plantation, and still later we hear of her being reconditioned for the pursuit of pirates. But of her end, or of the details of her life, we have no knowledge.

There were other vessels launched, however, and other voyages made, and though the accounts of them are as sketchy and fragmentary as those of the *Blessing*, still, by taking a detail here and a detail there, we are able to gather together enough bits to fit together a fair picture of the way in which, during the next decade, the Port of Boston slowly gathered her sea legs under her.

The *Blessing*, as we have seen, was built by carpenters sent out by Matthew Cradock. For this reason the yard from which she was launched became known as Matthew Cradock's Yard. The town that rose there was called Medford. The site was good for the purpose, and other yards were established, and the clatter of shipbuilders' hammers became the familiar music of the Mystic. For years afterwards the name of Medford stood well out in the front whenever men spoke of shipbuilding.

For all that she is not much mentioned after her launching, the *Blessing* must have proved a successful venture, for in the following year Winthrop records that a vessel of 100 tons was laid down at Cradock's Yard. This was a sizable ship for the times, but in the next year, 1633, still another ship of 200 tons was built. Also, in that year, Winthrop tells us: "a small ship of about sixty tons was built at Medford, and called the *Rebecca*."

But Cradock's was not the only yard. Others were quick to recognize opportunity. In 1636 the *Desire*, 120 tons, was launched at Marblehead. In 1637 Thomas Barker was building ships at Hingham. In 1640 a vessel of 300 tons was built by the Reverend Hugh Peter at Salem, and another of the same size was completed there the following year by Richard Hollingsworth. These were immense ships for the time, and good-sized vessels even so late as the 1820s. Their launching inspired the building of the *Trial*, 160 tons, by Nehemiah Bourne at his North End yard; the first vessel of any size to be built in Boston.

Once the ball was rolling, the shipbuilders flocked to these shores, despite efforts to keep them at home. The materials—timber, naval stores, deepwater coves, and room to expand—were here practically for the asking, and there seemed an almost insatiable demand. Shipyards sprang up one after another in Dorchester, Charlestown, Medford, Salem, Gloucester, Hingham, and Weymouth. Nor was Boston behindhand in the matter. Indeed, as the metropolis of the coast she became the ultimate destination of many who first settled elsewhere, and soon shipyards became thick around the North End. Benjamin Gillan and Company was one. It was from this yard, in the early forties, that Valentine Hill launched the ship *Welcome*, 300 tons. Captain Thomas Hawkins, in 1644, built at Boston the monster *Seafort*, 400 tons. This was the largest ship yet undertaken in the colonies, but like many another leviathan she came to an untimely end. On her maiden voyage she was loaded with fish and tobacco and salt for Malaga. But as she approached the Straits of Gibraltar she encountered foul weather and was driven on shore near Cadiz, a total loss.

But the business of shipbuilding not only sent ships to sea. It also fathered kindred industries, for which in itself it created a demand, and thereby helped in another direction the establishment of new occupations for the settlers. Ropewalks sprang up for the manufacture of cordage, and foundries and forges for the working of bog iron into chains and anchors. Sailmakers, working by hand on rough looms, used native hemp. And the inland forests yielded turpentine and pitch as well as timber for the building of ships. To be sure, the bulk of these necessary supplies at first had to be imported from England, but as rapidly as the means for making them came to hand the colonists moved toward the establishment of their own manufactories.

It is like asking which came first, the chicken or the egg, to speculate on whether it was the development of trade which produced shipbuilding in Boston, or vice versa. The truth is the two went hand in hand. If the development was seemingly slower, more deliberate, less spectacular, on the part of trade, it is only because the hazards were greater and the way less plainly defined. If it was less apparent, in that first decade of the colony's existence, than it later became, less striking, this trade development was present none the less for that.

We have seen that in the same year which saw the launching of the *Blessing of the Bay* there came a pinnace from Virginia with corn. In March of the following year the bark *Warwick* came from Virginia with corn, undoubtedly a voyage inspired by the success of the previous year's accidental venture. On the *Warwick's* return to Virginia, Samuel Maverick's pinnace accompanied her. That same year, in the following month, came a Dutch ship bringing 2,000 bushels of corn to sell at a price of four shillings sixpence a bushel. Small wonder, remembering the previous year's price of ten shillings per bushel charged by the Virginians, that the Dutch were before long looked upon as serious competitors. In the meantime the record shows a fairly steady stream of vessels arriving from England with new settlers, cattle, and supplies.

The year 1633 saw the arrival of more ships and small vessels from Virginia, widening that connection, as well as a number of Dutch traders. Massachusetts reciprocated in this coastal trade and sent vessels southward to Virginia with fish, and others out along the coast to eastward to trade for furs—thereby laying the groundwork for the first clashes with the French, who looked upon that area as their own particular bailiwick.

Welcome though it was, this growing maritime activity was

not without its headaches to the staid Puritans of Boston. Our indefatigable chronicler, Governor Winthrop, says that, on the 2d of June:

Capt. Stone arrived with a small ship with cows and some salt. The Governor of Plymouth sent Captain Standish to prosecute against him for piracy. The cause was, being at the Dutch Plantation [Manhattan], where a pinnace of Plymouth coming, and Capt. Stone and the Dutch governor having been drinking together, Capt. Stone, upon pretence that those of Plymouth had reproached them of Virginia, from whence he came, seized upon their pinnace, (with the governor's consent,) and offered to carry her away, but the Dutchmen rescued her; and the next day the governor and Capt. Stone entreated the master of the pinnace (being one of the council of Plymouth) to pass it by, which he promised by a solemn instrument under his hand; yet, upon their earnest prosecution at court, we bound over Capt. Stone (with two sureties) to appear in the admiralty court in England, etc. But, after, those of Plymouth being persuaded that it would turn to their reproach, and that it could be no piracy, with their consent, we withdrew the recognizance.

The good governor doubtless hoped that this would be an end of Captain Stone, but he was unduly optimistic. Stone either returned or remained in port, for on the 12th of September there is this entry in Winthrop's journal:

Capt. John Stone (of whom mention is made before) carried himself very dissolutely in drawing company to drink, etc., and being found upon the bed in the night with one Barcroft's wife, he was brought before the governor, etc., and though it appeared he was in drink, and no act to be proved, yet it was thought fit he should abide his trial, for which end warrant was sent out to stay his pinnace, which was ready to set sail; whereupon he went to Mr. Ludlow, one of the assistants, and used brave and threatening speeches against him, for which he raised some company and apprehended him, and brought him to the governor, who put him in irons, and kept a guard upon him till the court, (but his irons were taken off the same day). At the court his indictment was framed for adultery, but found ignoramus by the great jury; but for his other misdemeanors, he was fined £100, which yet was not levied of him; and ordered upon pain of death to come here no more, without license of the court; and the woman was bound to her good behaviour.

In the eyes of the Puritans retribution overtook the violent captain on his return voyage:

News came from Plymouth, that Capt. Stone, who this summer went out of the bay or lake, and so to Aquamenticus, where he took in Capt. Norton, putting in at the mouth of Connecticut, in his way to Virginia, where the Pequins inhabit, was there cut off by them, with all his company, being eight. The manner was thus: Three of his men, being gone ashore to kill fowl, were cut off. Then the Sachem, with some of his men, came aboard, and staid with Capt. Stone in his cabin, till Capt. Stone (being alone with him) fell on sleep. Then he knocked him on the head, and all the rest of the English being in the cook's room, the Indians took such pieces as they found there ready charged, and bent them at the English; whereupon one took a piece, and by accident gave fire to the powder, which blew up the deck; but most of the Indians, perceiving what they went about, shifted overboard, and after they returned, and killed such as remained and burned the pinnace.

On the first of June, of that same year, came in the ship *Thunder*, which had been sent out the previous fall to Bermuda. She brought with her corn and goats from Virginia, "for the weavils had taken the corn at Bermuda before they came there." This is the first mention we come across of other than coastwise trade, and is an indication that already the colonists were turning their eyes to more distant fields.

On the 29th of August arrived the *Dove*, from Maryland, a pinnace of about fifty tons, with corn to exchange for fish and other commodities. The Puritan elders made no secret of their disapproval of the Marylanders' Papist views, but evidently had no objection to trading with them.

In 1635 a Dutch ship put in at Marblehead with 140 tons of salt and 10,000 weight of tobacco from "Christopher Island," which we may take to be St. Kitts. And on the 11th of March, the following year, the *Rebecca* returned from Bermuda with

30,000 weight of potatoes, and oranges and limes, having first disposed of her cargo of corn in the West Indies.

In July of this same year the Pequot War opened with the murder by Indians of John Oldham, on board his pinnace, at the mouth of Narragansett Bay, another plain indication that the coastal trade was not without its hazards.

The year 1637 saw the return of a small pinnace which had set out eight months before for Bermuda, and which had been given up for lost. She had been driven from her course by gales, and brought up on the coast of Hispaniola, where the men in her did not dare to put in at any inhabited place for fear of the hostility of the Spaniards. For months they had frequented uninhabited spots, living on turtles, wild hogs, etc. But at last they had been forced into a harbor where lay a French man-of-war. They had thought their goose cooked at sight of her, but, as luck had it, the captain, one "Petfree," had lived at Piscataqua and knew the merchant of the pinnace, who was named Gibbons. "Whereupon," says Winthrop, "he used them courteously, and, for such commodities as she carried, freighted her with tallow, hides, etc., and sent home with her his prize, which he sold for a small price to be paid in New England." The pinnace also brought home an "aligarto" which was presented to the governor.

There were other voyages within this period without doubt, but these are sufficient to show the direction that New England's trade was generally to take. It was in the next decade that the great impetus was to come that was to send Boston skyrocketing to the forefront of New World ports.

CHAPTER III

Business in Great Waters

They that go down to the sea in ships, that do business in great
waters; these see the works of the Lord and His wonders in
the deep.

—Psalms, cvii, 23-24

BY THE end of the first decade of Boston's existence the tide
of the Great Emigration, whose start had been responsible
for her founding, had ceased to flow. The breaking of the power
of the bishops removed the driving force, and the outbreak and
continuance of civil disturbances in England occupied the
thoughts of Englishmen to the exclusion of such matters. Indeed, they led to an era of neglect which, had the circumstances on this side of the ocean been different, might well have
been fatal.

Boston, however, was by now well established. The Emigration had given her a considerable population, and the period of
being left to her own devices was rather beneficial than otherwise. Winthrop tells the story:

The parliament of England setting upon a general reformation both
of church and state, the Earl of Strafford being beheaded, and the arch-
bishop (our great enemy) and many others of the great officers and
judges, bishops and others, imprisoned and called to account, this called
all men to stay in England in expectation of a new world, so as few
coming to us, all foreign commodities grew scarce, and our own of no
price. Corn would buy nothing: a cow which cost last year £20 might
now be bought for £4 or £5, etc., and many gone out of the country,

so as no man could pay his debts, nor the merchants make return into England for their commodities, which occasioned many there to speak evil of us. These straits set our people on work to provide fish, clapboards, plank, etc., and to sow hemp and flax (which prospered very well) and to look out to the West Indies for a trade for cotton.

Boston was by now become a town of considerable proportions, complete with civic consciousness and an eye to power. More, she was by way of becoming the capital, so to speak, of New England; the chief town of all the colonies. Indeed, to the Puritans of Boston they themselves were New England, as is amply shown by Winthrop's sneering reference to the death of Captain John Mason in England, about this time: "As for this Mason," he says, "he fell sick and died soon after, and in his sickness he sent for the minister, and bewailed his enmity against us, and promised, if he recovered, to be as great a friend to New England as he had formerly been an enemy."

When it is recalled that Mason was the proprietor of New Hampshire, which, surely, was also a part of New England, and that his "enmity" for the men of the Bay Colony sprang from what he considered their encroachments upon his own territories and interference with his own colony, Winthrop's remark becomes more eloquent than its writer intended. Such an attitude could not but produce controversy.

With the intercolony disputes, however; with the difficulties of the colonists with the Indians; with the religious and political discussion which waxed and grew hot, we have no concern, save as they bore upon the maritime activities of Boston. On the whole they had little effect. The Boston merchants' eyes were upon the sea, and their thoughts were for the lining of their pockets, and other matters were not permitted to interfere with that.

The second decade of the town's existence was one of extraordinary expansion of trade. If, during the first ten years,

Bostonians had been busy finding their sea legs, during the second ten they stretched them with remarkable vigor. And in the stretching they found profit and adventure aplenty.

It has already been told that the ship *Trial*, 160 tons, was the first vessel of any size to be built in Boston. She was launched in 1641, but it was August of the following year before she was fitted and loaded with fish and pipe staves and sent forth to make her owners' fortune under the command of Thomas Coytmore, who was later to lose his life in the wreck of the monster *Seafort*.* Coytmore promptly set sail for Fayal, in the Azores, where he found "an extraordinary good market for his pipe staves and fish." There he took in wine and sugar and "sailed thence to Christopher's in the West Indies, where he put off some of his wine for cotton and tobacco, etc., and for iron, which the islanders had saved of the ships which were there cast away."

This iron which the islanders had saved, it appeared, was only a small part of the whole. There had been a number of wrecks about the island, and, if the tales were true, there was a good deal more of it in the shape of anchors and cable and pieces of ordnance, not to mention a quantity of gold and silver, still strewn about the bottom of the sea thereabout. Captain Coytmore listened to the tales and, putting on his thinking cap, determined to have a go at recovering them.

Now it happened that Captain Coytmore had an example of Yankee ingenuity already before him, which he needed only to follow to carry out his purpose. In the early spring of 1641 a vessel, the *Mary Rose*, had been blown up and sunk by accident, "with all her ordnance, ballast, much lead, and other goods," in the channel of Boston Harbor. Her owners were inclined to let her lie, and as she was an obstacle to navigation the Court of

---

*Coytmore's position on board the *Seafort* is not indicated, but he was probably sailing-master. The ship was commanded by Thomas Hawkins.—J. J.

Assistants were anxious to have her moved. One Edward Bendall, a merchant and owner of one of the new wharves which served the town, thought he saw how it might be done, and applied to the court for permission to attempt it on the condition that if he freed the harbor he would be entitled to all he might recover from her, but that if he failed to free it he should receive only half. His proposition was agreeable, and Bendall proceeded with his scheme.

He made two great tubs, bigger than a butt, very tight, and open at one end, upon which were hanged so many weights as would sink it to the ground (600wt.). It was let down, the diver sitting in it, a cord in his hand to give notice when they should draw him up, and another cord to show when they should remove it from place to place, so he could continue in his tub near half an hour, and fasten ropes to the ordnance, and put the lead, etc., into a net or tub. And when the tub was drawn up, one knocked upon the head of it, and thrust a long pole under water, which the diver laid hold of, and so was drawn up by it; for they might not draw the open end out of water for endangering him, etc.

This was undoubtedly the first use of a diving bell in this country, if not the first anywhere. Certainly it is the first recorded use of such an instrument, and doubtless Captain Coytmore was present when it was done, for it is precisely what he now set out to do at St. Kitts. With the permission of the island's governor he proceeded to rig his diving bell and was able to take "up 50 guns, and anchors, and cables, which he brought home, and some gold and silver also, which he got by trade, and so, through the Lord's blessing, they made a good voyage, which did much encourage the merchants, and made wine and sugar and cotton very plentiful, and cheap, in the country."

No one could suspect Captain Coytmore, apparently unbelievable as such profits might seem. But only a few months before his arrival, when one John Turner, who had gone out to the West Indies the previous year, returned with a small fortune in indigo and pieces of eight, there had been a good deal of headshaking and dark hints at piracy. Later such fine returns came to be looked upon as the rule rather than the exception.

Naturally others were not slow to follow the lead of the *Trial*. In the summer of 1642 five more ships were built in the neighborhood; three at Boston, one at Dorchester, and one at Salem. Toward the end of 1643 five ships set sail in one day from Boston. Two, of 300 tons each, and one of 160 had been built there, and one "was bound for London with many passengers, men of chief rank in the country, and great store of beaver." In 1644 the *Hopewell*, of Boston, sixty tons, traded at the Canary Islands. "The freight was wines, pitch, sugar, ginger, etc.," and, "she had her lading at Palma an island near Teneriffe." That same year the *Trial* traded to "Bilboa" with fish, "which she sold there at a good rate, and from thence she freighted to Malaga, and arrived here this day (March 23) laden with wine, fruit, oil, iron and wool, which was a great advantage to the country, and gave encouragement to trade." The narrator adds: "So soon as she was fitted she was set forth again to trade with La Tour (the Frenchman), and so along the eastern coast to Canada." Later still in that same year, two new ships of 250 and 200 tons were fitted and sent out to the Canaries. In 1645 "one of our ships, which went to the Canaries with pipestaves in the beginning of November last, returned now, and brought wine and sugar and salt, and some tobacco, which she had at Barbadoes, in exchange for Africoes, which she carried from the Isle of Maio (Cape Verde Islands)."

This is almost, but not quite, the first mention of an American vessel trading in slaves. In 1637 the *Desire*, out of Marblehead, Captain William Pierce, had carried a number of Indian captive slaves to the Island of Providence in the Caribbean, and returned the following year with "some cotton, tobacco, and negroes, etc., . . . and salt from Tertugos." Before the departure of the ship mentioned above in 1644 a number of Boston men, among them Thomas Keyser and James Smyth, had set out under joint articles in three ships, the *Blossome*, the *Seaflower*, and the *Rainbowe*, expressly for trading upon the coast of "Gynny" and there taking "neagers." They did not return until after the arrival above noted, but when they did they stirred up quite a tempest.

The said Mr. James Smith with his mate Keyser were bound to Guinea to trade for negroes. But when they arrived there they met some Londoners, with whom they consorted, and the Londoners having been formerly injured by the natives (or at least pretending the same,) they invited them aboard one of their ships upon the Lord's Day, and such as came they kept prisoners, then they landed men and a murderer (a small cannon), and assaulted one of their towns and killed many of the people, but the country coming down, they were forced to retire without any booty, divers of their men being wounded with the negroes' arrows, and one killed. . . .

For the matter of the negroes, whereof two were brought home in the ship, and near one hundred slain by the confession of some of the mariners, the magistrates took order to have these two set at liberty, and to be sent home; but for the slaughter committed, they were in great doubt what to do in it, seeing it was in another country, and the Londoners pretended a just revenge. So they called the elders and desired their advice.

There was a good deal of bickering back and forth, and Smyth and Keyser are lost sight of in the shuffle, but I believe the Negroes were sent home. Some pious folk are inclined to point smugly to this episode as an indication that Massachusetters never held with slavery from the outset, and so they may not. But the case of Smyth and Keyser is no proof of it, for from the petitions and records subsequent to their return it appears that what horrified the good people of Boston was not so much the trade itself as the fact that the Negroes were taken by violence, rather than bought, and that upon a Sabbath Day, which was worst of all!

There were other slave ventures in this period. Emmanuel Downing, Winthrop's brother-in-law, proposed that

if upon a just warre [with the Narragansetts] the Lord should deliver them into our hands, we might easily have men woemen and children enough to exchange for Moores, which will bee more gaynefull pilladge for us than wee conceive, for I doe not see how wee can thrive untill wee get into a stock of slaves sufficient to doe all our business, for our children's children will hardly see this great Continent filled with people, soe that our servants will still desire freedome to plant for themselves, and doe not stay but for verie great wages. And I suppose you know verie well how wee shall mayneteyne 20 Moores cheaper than one Englishe servant.

The ships that shall bring Moores may come home laden with salt which may bear most of the chardge, if not all of it. . . .

This proposal does not seem to have been acted upon. But other ships did go out upon that trade nevertheless. Among these were the *Fortune*, in 1649, and, ironically enough, in 1650, a ship named the *Gift of God!* But these early tentative fumblings with the slave trade are not to be confused, as some writers have done, with the later famous three-cornered "rum, niggers, and molasses" trade, which was not to develop until well on in the following century.

The general carrying trade, however, developed much more rapidly. Actual figures for the first two decades are not available, but an idea of the rapidity of its growth may be obtained from the fact that in 1666, thirty-five years after the founding of Boston, there were some three hundred vessels engaged in coastal and overseas trade in New England, most of them Boston-owned. Thirteen hundred smaller craft were occupied in offshore fishing. Thirteen years later, in 1679, Edward Randolph, newly created collector of the Port of Boston, called Boston the mart town of the West Indies, and in the six months from March 25 to September 29, 1688, 141 ships cleared from Boston, eighty-four bound for the West Indies, nearly all of these Boston-owned and Massachusetts-built. In the same period an approximately equal number of ships entered the port, eighty-nine of them with cargoes from the islands, thirty-seven from other American colonies, and twenty-one from England. For those times it was a considerable traffic.

All of this was not accomplished without obstacles, great and small, to overcome. And the course of colonial progress was not altogether serene.

For one thing there were the French, who, though they were not yet become a serious menace, were yet troublesome enough to be a nuisance. To a certain extent the colonists had themselves to blame for this, for, rather than leaving their neighbors to the north strictly to their own devices, they could not refrain from meddling in their affairs, with results that were discomfiting rather than anything more serious for the moment, though they had far-reaching effects.

It seems that there were two Frenchmen, La Tour and D'Aulnay, each of whom claimed to be governor of Acadia, as Nova Scotia was then called. Actually they were subordinate to another, the Chevalier de Rasilli, who, it appears, never came out from France, but who appointed La Tour to govern the eastern half of his holdings, as far west as the St. Croix River, while D'Aulnay was to govern those to the west.

The first English contact with this pair was in 1633, when La Tour's men descended upon a trading post which the English had established at Machias, on the coast of Maine, and drove them out. Two years later D'Aulnay made a similar descent upon a post at the mouth of the Penobscot. In the course of time, however, the two Frenchmen fell to quarreling among themselves, and D'Aulnay, repairing to France, got himself officially appointed governor of the whole area, ousting La Tour.

But La Tour was not to be so easily dislodged. He, too, had gone to France and as a result of D'Aulnay's machinations found himself proscribed. He left France one jump ahead of the authorities and came to Boston, where, enlisting their sympathies by pretending to be a Huguenot, he persuaded the elders and governor that he was the lawful governor and begged aid in ousting his usurping rival.

La Tour stayed a long time in Boston and made a profound impression with his salutes and courtesies, and with his soldiers whom he drilled, with the governor's permission, on muster day. Dazzled and somewhat flattered, the governor and council granted him the permission he asked to hire men and ships for his purpose, and this he forthwith did, and at length the expedition departed to the rolling thunder of many salutes and volleys. To make a long story short, the expedition burned a few haycocks and a mill and captured a pinnace loaded with moosehides and then returned home with a load of coal and limestone from Cape Breton, leaving La Tour to his own devices. La Tour tried again to get help from Boston, but was not successful, and shortly after his second visit D'Aulnay appeared with proof positive of his rightful claim.

Now the governor and council were embarrassed indeed. However, they dug up some ancient complaints against D'Aulnay and, by setting one against another, managed to patch up a peace between them. D'Aulnay departed happy, and that might have been an end to the matter—but for La Tour.

The latter had employed his time well while he was in Boston and had managed to make a number of friends. Now, after a short sojourn in Newfoundland, he returned to Boston in a state of destitution, and his former friends, taking pity upon him, rigged a ship and outfitted it for a trading voyage. The ship was manned with a crew part French and part English—men of Boston. The governor tells it briefly enough:

Monsieur La Tour being returned from Newfoundland in a pinnace of Sir David Kirk, was (by some merchants of Boston) set forth in the same pinnace to the eastward with trading commodities to the value of 400 pounds. When he came at Cape Sable, (which was in the heart of winter,) he conspired with the master (being a stranger) and his own Frenchmen, being five, to go away with the vessel, and so forced out the other five Englishmen, (himself shooting one of them in the face with a pistol,) who, through special providence, having wandered up and down fifteen days, found some Indians who gave them a shallop, and victuals, and an Indian pilot. So they arrived safe in Boston in the third month. Whereby it appeared (as the scripture saith) that there is no confidence in an unfaithful or carnal man. Though tied with many strong bonds of courtesy, etc., he turned pirate, etc.

This was not the first time Boston men had run foul of pirates. Nor was it the last. Piracy flourished on the high seas as long as private individuals were able, economically and otherwise, to fit out vessels of war. Only when naval armament was placed out of reach of individuals and wholly monopolized by governments—when naval efficiency was increased—did the game become unprofitable and die out altogether. The great heyday of the pirates was through the seventeenth and eighteenth centuries, and at the time of Boston's founding they were just coming into it.

Queen Elizabeth had gone to great pains to build up a formidable navy. And the wars in which she engaged went far to help toward this end. When James I acceded to the throne, however, he declared his intention of living at peace with the world, and made severe cuts in Britain's naval establishment. As a result many seamen were thrown out of work and left to rot ashore. Some took to begging, some to the pad. Some turned highwaymen. And it is not surprising, when one considers that a fast pinnace could show her heels to a lumbering ship of war, and that it was easy to obtain cannon and small arms and powder, that many and many a one took to robbery on the seas as a means of keeping body and soul together. More especially is it not remarkable when we remember how comparatively slight were the risks and how tremendous the profits.

The first pirate in New England waters appeared almost as soon as the Puritans in Boston. Dixey Bull came out from London in the year 1631 and took to trading with the Indians along the coast of Maine. In June 1632 he was trading in Penobscot Bay when D'Aulnay's men made their descent upon the trading post there, and, though Bull was not at the post, the Frenchmen came up with him a few days later and seized his shallop and entire stock of "ruggs, coats, blanketts, bisketts, etc."

As may be imagined, Bull was full of fury and a thirst for vengeance. He gathered about him fifteen others of a like spirit and added them to his crew. With these he set out in search of the French, but the French kept warily out of his way, and in due time Bull, being desperately short of provisions, took and plundered two or three small vessels belonging to other traders on the coast.

Having taken the first step, Bull and his comrades evidently now decided that they might as well go the whole hog. Their necks were in the noose anyway, and they might as well be hung for sheep as goats. Accordingly they fell upon Pemaquid and looted the trading station there of goods to the value of more than 500 pounds. This was too much for the authorities, and an expedition was sent out to overtake them. Four vessels with forty men sailed from the settlements on the Piscataqua, and one shallop was sent from Boston. But though they pursued him diligently, Bull managed to elude them and escaped to the eastward, where it was reported that he had "gone over to the enemy," by which undoubtedly the French were meant.

Bull did not return, and it was many years before New England's own home waters were again troubled by like marauders. More distant waters, however, held their share of danger. Pirates in the West Indies were growing ever bolder, and the pirates of

Barbary were always a menace to traders to Spain, the Azores, the Canaries, and the Guinea coast. When Captain Hawkins made his ill-fated voyage in the *Seafort* he carried with him a commission from the Great and General Court of Massachusetts "to take any ship that shall assault him, or any other that hee shall have certeine knowledge to have taken either ship or ships of ours, or to take any ship that hath commission to make any prize of ours." A similar commission was granted Captain Thomas Bredcake in 1644 to take Turkish pirates, by which was meant any Barbary corsair.

Winthrop does not record the taking of any Boston vessels by these pirates, but he does mention a fight between a New Haven ship and some Turks at Palma, in the Canaries, in which the pirates were beaten off, and it seems likely that Boston vessels must have encountered like difficulties. Later, in 1671, John Hull, the Boston mintmaster, records in his diary that a neighbor of his, one William Foster, was taken by the Turks on his way to Bilbao with fish and carried into Barbary, where he was ransomed and returned home safely in 1673.

There were others that were troublesome besides these. Winthrop, in his journal, mentions a Boston ship that was attacked at sea by an "Irish man-of-war." And in those turbulent times it was sometimes difficult to tell friend from foe. Especially was this true during the period of the civil wars in England, when both the King's ships and the Parliament's roamed the seas. Both sides traded where they willed, and both seized upon vessels which they suspected of favoring the other. In Boston this gave rise to several peculiar situations and entanglements.

One of these occurred in 1644 when a London ship and a Bristol ship happened to be in Boston Harbor simultaneously. Ships from London, at that time, sailed under the colors of the Parliament, while those from the western ports were manned, in general, by the King's men.

Boston: Cradle of Liberty

In the case in point a vessel out of London, Captain Stagg, of twenty-four guns, hove into Boston Harbor and found there, lying before Charlestown, a Bristol ship of 100 tons, laden with fish for Bilbao. Captain Stagg, it seems, recognized an opportunity when he saw it. Although a natural hostility between the two vessels was to be expected, Stagg pretended to ignore the west countryman until such time as he had disposed of his principal business in the port, which was the discharge of his cargo, made up in the main of wine from Teneriffe. Neither did he reveal the fact that he held a letter of marque from Parliament commissioning him to seize such hostile ships as he might encounter. As soon as he had completed his business, however, he cleared his ship for action and moved it up so as to lie between Charlestown and the Bristol man, when, with his enemy under his guns, he called upon him to surrender or be blown out of the water, allowing him a turn of the half-hour glass in which to make his decision. The Bristol man, being a discreet individual, although it is said that some of his crew would have preferred to fight it out, surrendered peaceably enough, and there might have been an end to the matter but for the fact that word of Captain Stagg's intentions had somehow leaked ashore and a great crowd had gathered upon Windmill Hill to watch the outcome.

Now it happened that there were a number of persons present who had an interest in the Bristol ship, among them one, a merchant of Bristol, whom Winthrop—obviously a Parliament man—calls "a very bold malignant person." These "began to raise a tumult," whereupon some of the people present seized them and dragged them before the deputy governor, who placed them under arrest and then sent constables to disperse the crowd.

Stagg was then summoned and commanded to show by what authority he had carried out the seizure in the port. In response he showed his commission, which was apparently in good order, and though there was quite a tempest raised over the affair it does not appear that he had to relinquish his prize.

Not long afterwards, in September of the same year, a ship out of Dartmouth, also a King's port, came into the harbor. There were several London ships present at the time, and apparently the master of the Dartmouth vessel had some fears for the safety of his ship. Moreover there were some merchants of the town who, having had a ship seized by the King's people in Wales only a short time before, now sought to have the Dartmouth ship seized in retaliation.

The governor and council were petitioned, and the master of the Dartmouth ship was summoned. To him it was proposed that he place his ship in custody of the council until a trial could be held in the matter, and to this he agreed readily as the only alternative to seizure by the London men. A guard was set aboard, and it was considered that the matter was closed for the time being.

The Londoners, however, were evidently not satisfied with this solution, and one, Captain Richardson, having a commission from the Lord High Admiral, prepared to seize the ship, "notwithstanding that he had been forbidden over night by the deputy governor to meddle with her." Moreover the Dartmouth ship so lay that in the event of any action the town itself must be endangered by the gunfire. An order of the governor and magistrates was sent to Richardson, commanding him to desist, but he had already gone too far to withdraw. He ignored the order and proceeded to board the Dartmouth man. Next Richardson was commanded ashore, but this he refused to do, and a warning shot was fired from the battery which came so close as to cut a rope in the head of Richardson's ship.

As may be supposed, all this while excitement, both ashore and on board the two ships, was mounting. At the shot of warning from the shore one of Richardson's men, without any command, ran down to the gun deck to fire upon the battery. "But," says Winthrop, "it pleased God that he hurt himself in the way, and so was not able to go on." At the same time a stranger ashore, having gotten someway into the battery, touched off another piece which hit the cutwater of the Dartmouth ship but evidently did little damage. The whole matter was resolved when a strong force was sent out from the battery to seize Captain Richardson and fetch him ashore. The captain, seeing the jig was up, "acknowledged his error, and his sorrow for what he had done, yet withal alleging some reasons to his excuse. So we only ordered him to pay a barrel of powder, and to satisfy the officers and soldiers we had employed—and dismissed him."

Not all the problems of this period were so tangible. In 1647 a plague broke out in the West Indies which resulted in the first crude attempts at establishment of a quarantine in Boston. Some ships slipped through, however, by various tricks, being unwilling to lie outside and having no other place to go. A few people were stricken in the town, and some died, but on the whole Boston escaped lightly this time.

In addition to this came troubles of a supernatural order, which were matters not to be taken lightly in those times. Two vessels were blown up by accident in the harbor, the men of one being, by all reports, a particularly dissolute crew. About two weeks later came reports of apparitions in the bay which Winthrop regarded as sufficiently serious to be soberly reported in his journal. He says:

About midnight three men, coming in a boat to Boston, saw two lights arise out of the water near the north point of Town Cove, in form like a man, and went at a small distance to the town, and so to the south point, where they vanished away. They saw them about a quarter of an hour, being between the town and the governor's garden. The like was seen by many, a week after, arising about Castle Island and in one fifth of an hour came to John Gallop's Point. . . .

The 18th of this month two lights were seen near Boston, (as is before mentioned,) and a week after the like was seen again. A light like the moon arose about the N.E. point in Boston, and met the former at Nottles Island, and there they closed in one, and then parted, and closed and parted divers times, and so went over the hill in the island and vanished. Sometimes they shot out flames and sometimes sparkles. This was about eight of the clock in the evening, and was seen by many. About the same time a voice was heard upon the water between Boston and Dorchester, calling out in a most dreadful manner, boy, boy, come away, come away; and it suddenly shifted from one place to another a great distance, about twenty times. It was heard by divers Godly persons. About fourteen days after, the same voice in the same dreadful manner was heard by others on the other side of the town towards Nottles Island.

These prodigies having some reference to the place where Captain Chaddock's pinnace was blown up a little before, gave occasion of speech of that man who was the cause of it, who professed himself to have some skill in necromancy, and to have done some strange things in his way from Virginia hither, and was suspected to have murdered his master there; but the magistrates here had not notice of him till after he was blown up. This is to be observed that his fellows were all found, and others who were blown up in the former ship were also found, and others also who have miscarried by drowning, etc., have usually been found, but this man was never found.

The charge of witchcraft in those days was a serious one. But in this case there was nothing to be done about it, since the devil seemed to have claimed his own—a matter which, incidentally, seemed to the Puritan elders to be sufficient proof of the pudding.

One, however, was not thus spirited away. At a session of the General Court in June 1648, one Margaret Jones was tried for witchcraft. It appeared that she was possessed of some slight knowledge of simples and healing, as well as a neighborly spirit, but little patience. Some whom she had tried to persuade to take her remedies had refused, and she, foolishly enough, had told them that if they did not take them they would die. And so it fell out.

It is questionable whether they would have recovered under her care. It is still more questionable whether her simples would have effected the cure even had they recovered. But the fact that they died after she had predicted their deaths made it look black for Margaret. She was accused of having the malignant touch, such as made persons she touched with affection fall victims to deafness, vomiting or other "pains and sickness." She was accused of having secret speeches and spells, etc., and it was said of her that "in the prison, in the clear light of day, there was seen in her arms, she sitting on the floor, and her clothes up, etc., a little child, which ran from her into another room, and the officer following it, it was vanished."

Other ridiculous charges were brought and solemnly pondered, and Margaret, being, as I have said, a woman of no great patience, apparently told the magistrates what she thought of them: "Her behaviour at her trial was very intemperate, lying notoriously [doubtless in denying the charges] and railing upon the witnesses and jury, etc."

Margaret was convicted, sentenced, and hanged, and it was recorded in all seriousness: "The same day and hour she was executed there was a very great tempest at Connecticut, which blew down many trees, etc." Such was the naïveté of the day.

The sequel to the story is that Margaret's husband, as well he might in the circumstances, determined to leave Boston forever and seek a new life in the West Indies.

The Welcome, of Boston, about 300 tons, riding before Charlestown, having in her eighty horses and 120 tons of ballast, in calm weather, fell a rolling and continued so about twelve hours, so as though they brought a great weight to the one side, yet she would heel to the other, and so deep as they feared her foundering. It was then the time of the county court at Boston, and the magistrates hearing of it, and withal that one Jones (the husband of the witch lately executed) had desired to have passage in her to Barbados, and could not have it without such payment, etc., they sent an officer presently to apprehend him, one of them saying that the ship would stand still as soon as he was in prison. And as the officer went, and was passing over the ferry, one said to him, you can tame men sometimes, can't you tame this ship? The officer answered, I have that here, that (it may be) will tame her, and make her be quiet; and with that showed his warrant. And at the same instant, she began to stop and presently staid, and after he was put in prison, moved no more.

What happened to poor Jones, the records do not tell. This is the only instance I have been able to find of witchcraft in connection with the port and shipping of Boston.

CHAPTER IV

Expanding Horizons

THE two decades of comparative neglect which almost immediately followed her birth were a distinct benefit to Boston. While the eyes of Old England were turned inward upon her own troubles, the people of New England were, perforce, feathering their own nests. Like neglected children cast out upon the world and left to shift for themselves, the settlers were forced to make their own way, and those who succeeded drew strength from the struggle. It was a case of survive or die.

It is seriously to be doubted if such survival—at least on such a scale—could have been accomplished without the help of the lowly codfish. Not for nothing do Massachusetts men worship at the shrine of the sacred cod. That rather flabby, coarse-fleshed, soft-boned but nonetheless succulent fish lies at the very root of their existence, and all their wealth and trade has stemmed directly from the fisheries. The land was cold and often bleak and inhospitable. The pockets of tillable soil were infrequent and quickly taken up. The rest of the countryside was woods, or where it was not wooded it was rocky. No farmer would pick such land from choice. Only necessity could drive men to till such ground.

But there was always the sea and all the teeming life that was

in it. It was fish that drew the firstcomers—the first solid comers
—to these shores, and when all is said and done, religious freedom and politics to the contrary notwithstanding, it was fish
that kept them after they arrived. It was fish that brought the
first traders in from other settlements, creeping along the shore
in their tiny shallops and pinnaces, carrying grain and tobacco
and livestock, necessities of life ashore, to exchange for cod. It
was fish that set the shipyards going. As soon as men realized
the profits to be made from the fisheries, they set about building the vessels necessary to go out and catch the fish. And then
they began to build slightly larger vessels to carry the fish to
their customers. In time they took to building still larger ships
to carry the product of their front-yard waters to distant seas.

It was a cargo of fish that the first New England trader carried down the coast to sell for corn and tobacco and goats and
indigo. And as that market was developed they reasoned that,
if Virginia wanted fish, so might the West Indies. The great
numbers of Basque fishermen that appeared every year upon the
Banks attested the Spaniards' taste for bacalao, and contacts with
Spaniards and Portuguese in the islands confirmed the hunch.
Ergo ships were fitted out to carry fish to those countries.

We have seen already how the trade of Boston developed during those first two decades of the colony's existence. That trade
was based upon fish as the main staple of exchange. But, though
fish remained as the foundation of Boston's maritime activity
for many a year, toward the middle and the end of the second
decade a new development began to take shape and flourish—
the carrying trade.

As Boston men grew more and more sea-minded they began
to cast about for other means of profit than the simple business
of supplying their own needs and those of their immediate
neighbors. It was this urge that gave rise to the various varieties
of three—and sometimes more—cornered trade.

Boston: Cradle of Liberty

This was carried on in this way: A Boston vessel would load at home with fish for the West Indian market, say. On arrival at the islands the master would sell his cargo and load with island produce—sugar, molasses, tobacco, salt. These would be carried to England, to Spain, or to Portugal, or perhaps even to France, where they could be sold for a higher price than they would bring on the home market. Then, once again, the shipmaster would load with goods in high demand at home and return to Boston with a pretty penny's profit to show for his dickering along the way. Sometimes the process would be reversed, and the ship would sail with fish for London or Bilbao or Lisbon or Cadiz or the Azores or the Canaries. There the master would load with trade goods and brandy—not rum, for rum, only then being discovered—or should one say invented?—in the West Indies, had not yet become the article of trade that it was later to be. That development was to wait upon the growth of New England's great distilleries. Thence he would sail to the Guinea coast and there take on gold dust, "elephant's teeth," mahogany, and slaves. These were carried to the West Indies and there exchanged for products in demand in New England.

So long as Old England continued in a state of upheaval, New England was left to her own devices. With the coming of comparative peace, however, this situation was changed.

The civil wars in England were an expression of a changing world; a world emerging from feudalism to a state of broader individual freedom. This change gave rise to mercantilism and the ascendancy of commercial interests on a broader plane than ever before, replacing the concentration of such interests in the hands of a very few of great wealth and noble birth. So long as the wars went on, this growing merchant class was occupied with domestic matters. But with the coming of peace they began to realize that they were faced with overseas competition, and, what was more, that that competition constituted a pinch that hurt.

The upshot of the scream of pain and rage which this pinch produced was Cromwell's Navigation Act of 1650.

This first Navigation Act of 1650 was not aimed solely, or even primarily, at New England. Ever since the days of James I there had been growing competition between Dutch and British on the seas. When the English became involved in their own troubles, the Dutch seized the opportunity to grab the world's carrying trade. By the time the English realized what was happening, the Dutch were firmly in the saddle. Their ships were better-built and roomier. Their skippers were shrewder bargainers. And they were unhampered by any restrictions. They were everywhere, even in British ports, plucking prize cargoes from under the noses of irate British skippers and walking away with the trade of the seven seas.

Far behind the Dutch came the New England traders. Few as yet took them very seriously as a potential menace. Yet there were enough who felt the sting of their competition to see that there were clauses in the Navigation Act which would restrict their seagoing activities to a more subservient level. Consequently, though it was at the Dutch that Cromwell primarily aimed, New England, too, stood in the line of fire.

It is food for thought, therefore, that the first of a long series of repressive measures, ultimately destined to play such a great part in driving the colonies from the English fold, was instituted, not by the Crown, which was later to become a symbol of oppression, but by the very party for whose principles of religious and political freedom the settlers of Boston themselves stood!

As a matter of fact, however, despite their intent the Acts of Trade and Navigation meant little to the colonists—at least during the seventeenth century. In the concluding years they became a nuisance rather than anything else; something to be taken much in the way the Puritans' descendants were to take prohibition almost three hundred years later. They caused some acrimony and some bitterness and set the stage for later, more serious quarrels. In themselves they were peculiarly ineffective, although the Act of 1660 (which was the work of Charles II and his counselors and, therefore, a much more heinous offense), as well as the Orders in Council which related to it, was much more stringent.

Actually the acts were a benefit rather than a deterrent to New England's trade. There were no agencies of enforcement that were effectual, and no one took them seriously. But they did serve to eliminate the Dutch from English ports up and down the coast and in the West Indies, as well as in England itself. And the Dutch, with their base at New Amsterdam, had hitherto been a source of competition to be seriously considered.

Boston traders on their own account, as has been indicated, went merrily on their way. In trade between their home port and other British ports, since they sailed under the British flag, they were presumably protected by the act. But in trade with foreign ports, or with such trade as that between the West Indies and Britain, from which they were supposedly excluded, they simply went their own course and did as they pleased. Thus, in a sense, they all became smugglers, and when the finger of scorn is pointed at John Hancock and others of his ilk it should be remembered that they came from a long line of such lawbreakers who only regarded their transgressions as their inalienable right!

This is not to say that the colonists favored free trade altogether. Never let it be said that Bostonians ever held with such notions! On the contrary there was a sort of crude customs and system of levies from the beginning. But—and here lay the fundamental point—they were levied and collected by the governor and council and administered, supposedly, for the general benefit of the community. Regulation from a distance without proper regard for local interests is what Massachusetters have always objected to.

In 1632, only two years after the town's founding, a duty was placed upon beaver pelts fetched into port by those traders who went out to deal with the Indians up the coast. Peltry, however, never formed a large part of Massachusetts trade. In 1634 duties were placed on imports of fruits, spices, sugar, wines, liquors, and tobacco, and in 1645, or thereabout, a tonnage duty was levied for a year or so against all ships entering the port. This was apparently dropped, but it was revived again in later years, toward the end of the century, and applied against vessels not owned and registered in the colony. By 1678, when the Crown finally got around to doing something about enforcing the acts, while there were no export duties in force by the colony there was an import duty on all goods entering the port, except wool, salt, fish, and a few similar staples, amounting to a penny a pound. Wines and spirits paid a higher tax ranging from two shillings sixpence on a hogshead to ten shillings on a pipe. In addition all vessels entering paid a small port fee toward the maintenance of harbor fortifications.

Though the royal customs were consistently ignored, these local taxes appear to have been paid without protest. Just what the machinery was for their collection, however, is obscure, for Edward Randolph, who was sent out about that time as collector of customs for the Crown, reported that "there is not any form of a custom house" at Boston.

This Edward Randolph set the fur to flying. He was not popular in Boston. Until his coming Boston's trade had flourished without molestation, much as it had done during the first two decades, but with greater and ever expanding prosperity. This was due mainly to the fact that no adequate machinery of enforcement had been set up with the Acts of Trade and Navigation. To be sure, the colonial governors were empowered to grant licenses and collect duties, but they, knowing well on which side their bread was buttered, found it convenient to ignore the mandate. By 1670, however, colonial trade had grown to such proportions that the muttered protests of old country shippers and merchants had increased to screams of alarm. Inquiries were set on foot, and it soon became apparent that, from the viewpoint of the Crown, at least, something must be done. In 1672 the complaint was lodged with the Privy Council that the traders of Massachusetts

boldly employ two or three hundred Sail of Ships yearly, trading to and fro, from several plantations and most parts of Europe . . . and this without being under the Restrictions of such Laws, as put our Merchants to vast charges, either by customs, or otherwise, which enabled them to undersell our English Merchants 50 percent at least, to the unspeakable prejudice of the King's customes, and the decay of our Manufactures, as well as an infallible Bait to all our Manufacturers to remove thither, where People trade with such advantage over their fellow Subjects.

The result of all this was that the new created Committee of Trade and Plantations, to whom the matter was referred by the Privy Council, determined to take steps to curb the abuses. A threefold plan was decided upon which it was hoped would have the desired effect. A special commission was to be sent to each governor to authorize him to enforce the acts—and, incidentally, to see to it that he did. Special customs officers were appointed for New England—the most serious offender—and the ports were to be blockaded if any resistance was offered. In addition the captains of all His Majesty's naval vessels in American waters were ordered to stop suspected vessels and seize and bring offenders to trial.

Only the second of these provisions seems to have been seriously attempted. If the commissions to the governors came to the colonies, there is no record of it. Perhaps the officers of the Royal Navy had a sneaking sympathy with the colonials. Or perhaps the New England ships were a bit too sharp and too handy to be easily caught. At any rate it was to be years before the Navy showed its teeth. But the collectors descended upon the coast in numbers and remained to become a pest and a plague to Yankee shippers.

Randolph's task in itself was enough to make him unpopular in Boston. He was in the position of the "revenooer" amongst the Kentucky mountaineers, or of a prohibition snooper in more recent times. Nevertheless it seems apparent, from what he himself has to say, that he came to Boston with a chip on his shoulder; that he brought with him, already established firmly in his own mind, a definite prejudice against the people and the country and all that they stood for. He was a king's man to the core, and he made no bones about it. Whatever else one may say about him, however, it cannot be denied that he was faithful to his charge. He saw his duty and he did it to the full extent of his power. If that power was inadequate it was not the fault of the man. What he could do he did, and if the results were not all he looked for, still his efforts were not entirely without effect. Some of his activities, at least, bore evil fruit for Massachusetts, as we shall presently see.

By 1676 Boston had become a considerable town, yet descriptions of it are hard to come by. In 1650 Johnson described it in his *Wonder Working Providence:*

Invironed it is with the Brinish flouds saving one small istmos which gives free accesse to the Neighbour Townes by Land on the South side; on the North-west and North-east two constant Faires [ferries] are kept for daily traffique thereunto. The forme of this Towne is like a heart naturally scituated for Fortifications, having two Hills on the frontice part thereof next the Sea; the one well fortified on the super-ficies thereof with store of great artillery well mounted, the other hath a very strong battery built of whole Timber and filled with Earth at the descent of the Hill [Copp's] in the extreme poynt thereof; betwixt these two strong armes lies a large Cove or Bay on which the chiefest part of this Town is built, overtopped with a third Hill; all three like overtopping Towers keepe a constant watch to foresee the approach of forrein dangers, being furnished with a Beacon and lowd babling guns to give notice by their redoubled eccho to all their Sister-townes. The chief Edifice of this City-like Towne is crowded on the sea bankes, and wharfed out with great industry and cost, the buildings beautifull and large; some fairely set forth with Brick, Tile, Stone, and Slate, and orderly placed with comly streets, whose continuall inlargement pre-sages some sumptuous city. The wonder of this Moderne Age, that a few yeares should bring forth such great matters by soe meane a hand-full. But now behold, in these very Places where at their first landing the hideous Thickets in this place were sich that Wolfes and Beares nurst up their young from the eyes of all beholders, where the streets are full of Girles and Boyes sporting up and downe.

Some fifteen years later the King's commissioners were not so complimentary. "Their [Bostonians'] houses," said they, "are generally wooden, their streets crooked, with little decency and no uniformity." But Josselyn, who spent some years in Boston, and left in 1671, left this description of the town at his departure:

The houses are for the most part raised on the sea banks and wharfed out with great industry and cost [one sees here the influence of John-son!]; many of them standing upon piles, close together on each side of the streets, as in London, and furnished with many faire shops. Their materials are brick, stone, lime handsomely contrived, with three Meet-ing houses or Churches, and a Town-house, built upon pillars, where the Merchants may confer. In the chambers above they keep their monethly courts. The town is rich and populous. On the south there is a small but pleasant common, where the Gallants, a little before sunset, walk with their Marmalet-madams, as we do in Morefields, till the nine o'clock bell rings them home to their respective habitations; when presently the Constables walk their rounds to see good order kept, and to take up loose people.

Expanding Horizons

If Randolph saw the "Girles and Boyes sporting up and downe" or noticed the "Gallants" squiring their "Marmalet-madams" on the Common, he did not mention it. He did, however, observe the ships which came into the harbor and reported that "they violate all the Acts of Trade and Navigation—by which they have engrossed the greatest part of the West India trade, whereby your Majesty is damnified in the customs 100,-000 £ yearly, and the Kingdom much more." In that same June he wrote that in a single week,

a Bostoner from Nantes, 100 tons . . . laden with 50 butts brandy and French commodities; a pink of Boston from France, of 70 tons, with 12 tun of wine, brandy, etc., a Scotsman, 130 tons, from the Canaries, with 80 pipes of Canary, a Bostoner, 80 tons, from the Canaries with 50 pipes of Canary, this day a ketch of Southampton from Canary, the contents and burthen I do not know,

had all arrived in port without the payment of a single farthing of royal duty. He was further incensed by the fact that the Bostonians continued "a private trade with the French and Indians and openly keep on their fishing on the coast of Arcadia, though forbidden by the French King's Lieutenant." "The Boston Government," he goes on to say, "impose on the French and encourage an interloping trade, causing to the inhabitants dread of a French invasion, and they look at the French with an evil eye, believing that they had a hand in the Indian wars."

For that piece of discernment alone he deserved honorable mention. In the long struggle that was brewing between the two nations the English were scarcely more lily white than the French, whatever airs they gave themselves. But we could scarcely expect the gentlemen of that day and time to make such an acknowledgment.

The truth was that, even had he not come upon such an obnoxious errand, Randolph arrived at a time when Bostonians' nerves were badly frayed. During the Rebellion and the Commonwealth they had been loud, quite naturally, in their support of Cromwell and the Parliament. With the coming of the Restoration, however, their scramble to regain the other side of the fence had been both undignified and unsuccessful. Of the two it was the former that stung the most. But on the practical side of the ledger, their behavior had involved them in an acrimonious dispute with the Crown. Then there were the Quakers. A few of these had come out in the '60s and '70s, and the cruelty with which they were treated and the persecutions with which they were hounded to the gallows in Boston and elsewhere in the colony were enough to make even that cruel age raise its hands in horror. Advanced the Puritans may have been in coming to the New World in search of religious freedom and the chance to raise their voice in politics. Contact with the outer world through trade may already have begun to exert a broadening influence, a general heightening of their appreciation of the rights of others and of the delights that they themselves might enjoy in the good things of this world. But they were neither advanced enough nor broad enough yet to accord to others that same freedom of religion and political thought which they themselves had sought, or to look upon the beliefs of others with the same tolerance which they themselves demanded.

They were still smarting beneath the censure of England for having indulged in a sort of colonial auto-da-fé, and on top of that had come King Philip's War, the last serious Indian threat to the seaboard colonies. Now came this wasp, this Randolph, whose buzzing was an infernal nuisance and whose sting was far from fatal, yet sufficiently sharp to produce a howl of anguish, to add to the burden of their woes. Small wonder that they looked upon him with a bilious eye!

Randolph did what he could to stem the swift race of trade and put a stop to the open flouting of His Majesty's laws, while, on their side of the mill dam, the colonists used every means in their power to sweep away the infinitesimal chips with which he tried to raise the dike. Even those who had no connection with his objective, and many to whom he might reasonably have looked for aid, seemed to delight in putting obstacles in his way.

In his first reports Randolph complained that he had no power, and suggested that

three frigates of 40 guns, and three ketches well manned, lying a league or two below Boston, with express orders to seize all shipping and perform other acts of hostility against these revolters, would bring them to the King's terms, and do more in a week than all the orders of King and Council in seven years.

His vehemence bore fruit. In 1678 he returned to England to press his point, and upon listening to his report the Lords of Trade decided that more drastic action must be taken. At Randolph's own suggestion he was given a commission as collector and surveyor of the customs in New England, with power to appoint deputies, to enforce the Acts of Trade, collect duties, receive oaths and bonds, inspect ships and seize those engaged in smuggling activities. He was to keep account of monies received and spent, and make his reports at least twice a year. He was to reside in Boston, and he had the right to appoint assistants in other ports upon the coast. Of all this the government of Massachusetts were informed in no uncertain terms, and they were strictly enjoined to assist him in any way possible.

One of Randolph's first acts on his return to Boston in 1679 was an attempt to seize the Boston pink, *Expectation*, which had been engaged in illegal trade. The results of the action were typical of the sort of opposition with which he found himself face to face at every hand. The master of the vessel, instead of submitting tamely, turned about and had Randolph arrested for exceeding his powers and disturbing the peace. When the col-

lector was brought before Governor Bradstreet, instead of upholding him the governor required him to give personal bond
of £800 before releasing him. In court he was denied an attorney
and was granted only the rights of a private individual and an
informer, without official status whatever. He was unable to
bring any real evidence, "everyone appearing for me being accounted an enemy to this countrey." By his own account his
case against the *Expectation* was clear, and he had three sound
counts against her. Yet the case was lost because the passengers
gave "perjured testimony," and the jury, being composed of
Boston merchants and shipmasters, would have found for the
defendant anyway!

Nor was this one instance the whole of his difficulties. On one
occasion his servant, who was guarding a warehouse for him,
was severely beaten. Again one of his deputies was chased from
his home. Randolph himself was threatened several times, and
once, when he was going out into the harbor to seize a vessel,
the master had the audacity to fire upon the royal flag he bore.
For this the master was fined £10, but insofar as the charge of
illegal trading was concerned, the case was dismissed.

This sort of opposition must itself have been enough to give
stomach ulcers to an angel, and to a man of Randolph's irasci-
ble disposition it must have been pure gall and wormwood. It
was the worse for the fact that the Boston traders were waxing
fat and prosperous with their flouting of the King's laws. Boston
ships were everywhere, and cargoes of all descriptions were
piling up on Boston's wharves. Randolph himself reported that
"some vessels had been sent as far as to Guinea, Madagascar—
and some to Scanderoon [Alexandretta] laden with masts and
yards for ships." And the colonial governors reported that
"there are two or three Merchants worth £18,000 apiece; he is
counted a rich man who is worth £1000."

Viewing all this, it is scarcely strange that such a degree of resentment was aroused in Randolph that he became determined that by one means or another he would have revenge. The cause in which he worked was by the very force of the opposition by now become an absolute fetish, to be accomplished by one means if not by another. The King's laws must be obeyed, whatever the cost to the colony, and, by the Lord, if the authorities would not co-operate with him, then he would see what he could do to remove them and have other, more compliant persons put in their place! In 1681 he returned once more to England and presented twelve charges against Massachusetts, the bases of which were evasion and non-enforcement of the Navigation Acts. It was his recommendation that, by way of punishment, the charter of the colony be revoked, and in 1684 this advice was followed.

The change, appalling though it was to Bostonians, did not have the immediate effect for which Randolph hoped. It was at first intended, while plans for the government of the new Dominion of New England were being completed, to permit the governor and company of Massachusetts Bay to continue to rule the colony. Randolph, however, protested vigorously against this, and in the end his suggestion was followed. Joseph Dudley, the son of a former governor, was named president of the council which was to exercise authority for the time being.

Randolph, who had been influential in having Dudley appointed, expected much of this council, but he was doomed to further disappointment. The trouble was that although the president and the council represented a moderate element, they were yet New Englanders with New Englanders' views of Randolph. To them he was a troublesome outsider interfering in matters which were none of his affair, and consequently they ignored him much as the former government had done.

They took steps, however, to put the commerce of the colony on a more legal-seeming basis, without, at the same time, doing anything so drastic as might harm it. Under their rule Boston's trade continued its merry way. Indeed, if the truth were told, it even enjoyed a considerable boom, much to Randolph's disgust.

The rule of the council was at best only a temporary expedient, however, and could not last forever. Still it was not until 1685 that the King finally announced that the plan of government was complete and that the first royal governor would be Colonel Percy Kirke.

New England stood aghast at the announcement. Colonel Kirke had not then gained the notoriety which was subsequently to be his as the leader of the brutish, swashbuckling, rapacious Kirke's Lambs. Still he had already sufficient reputation as a disciplinarian to give sinister point to the announcement. There is reason to believe that even Randolph was appalled, for when Charles II suddenly died and the appointment of Kirke was thus automatically ended, his advice to the new King James was: "Whoever goes over Governor with expectation to make his fortune, will dis-serve his Majesty, disappoint himself and utterly ruin the country." What was more needed, he averred, was "a prudent man to reconcile," rather than "a hot heady, passionate soldier to force." In 1687 King James announced the appointment of Sir Edmund Andros as governor of the Dominion of New England.

It is altogether to be doubted if Sir Edmund was quite so black a villain as some of our history books have been at pains to paint him. He was a soldier and an old servant of the King. He was not unacquainted with the colonial picture, having served James once before as governor of New York, at the time when the former, as Duke of York, had been one of the proprietors of that province. Whatever the New Yorkers might have thought of him, his work had evidently been satisfactory to his employer, and now his choice as governor of New England was a logical one. There is no question that he was honest, that he was able, that he was a good soldier. But he had no sympathy with the democratic notions of the colonists, nor had he the patience to learn. He was a martinet accustomed to absolute and instantaneous obedience from the soldiers under him, and he had the misfortune to come at a time when the colonists were in a naturally rebellious mood, owing to the removal of their charter, and were in a frame of mind to look with hostility and distrust upon any governor that might be sent them. That that governor should have been Andros only served to make the situation worse.

The story of Andros's rule in New England is too well known to need repeating. There were many examples of his ineptitude in the situation, and, indeed, only as a soldier, in his campaigns against the Indians, did he have any chance to prove his real ability. As a governor he was a failure because any governor, at that time, was doomed to failure. But only one phase of his administration concerns us here. This was the effort under him to regulate trade.

Proposals to establish a currency—essential if trade was not to be altogether crippled—were brushed aside. The frigate *Rose* was stationed outside the Port of Boston with strict orders to enforce the Acts of Trade, particularly with reference to foreign commerce. The trade with the continent of Europe and with the French and Spanish was entirely shut off, and as these were the greatest sources of Boston revenue many Boston ships were perforce laid up. Nor was anything constructive suggested to take the place of the business so arbitrarily disrupted.

The result was depression, swift and severe. It lasted two years and, more than any other single factor, drove the colonists to the brink of revolt.

How far the colonists would have gone had James II remained on the throne is problematical and somewhat beside the point, for an event occurred in 1688 which changed the entire picture. This was the landing of William of Orange at Torbay on November 5.

Rumors of this occurrence and of William's progress toward the throne reached Boston during the winter, creating a good deal of unrest. But absolute confirmation of the fact waited until spring. It was on the 4th of April 1689 that John Winslow arrived from Nevis with definite word of the accomplished fact. The governor, suspecting his news, had him at once brought before him and demanded his news and his papers. These Winslow stoutly refused to surrender, and the governor remanded him to Justice Bullivant, who also demanded them with the same results. Winslow was then imprisoned for "bringing into the country a traitorous and treasonable libel." Nor was he granted his liberty on bail, although he offered £2000.

It was too late, however. The news was out. Winslow had taken such opportunity as he had been granted to see to that, and the people were now aroused to the fever pitch of resentment by the highhanded actions of the authorities. Matters came to a head a few days later, on the 18th—ever a portentous date in Massachusetts history—when some mutinous companies were brought back from the frontier. On that same day Cotton Mather was ordered arrested for certain incendiary writings. If both the troops and the reverend gentleman were to be saved from arrest by their friends, immediate action was imperative. In some way the alarm was given, and men sprang to arms throughout the town and the surrounding countryside. What happened then is described by an anonymous eyewitness:

I knew not anything of what was intended until it was begun, yet being at the north end of the town, where I saw boys running along the streets with clubs in their hands, encouraging one another to fight, I began to mistrust what was intended; and, hasting towards the Town Dock, I soon saw men running for their arms, but before I got to the

Red Lion, I was told that Captain George and the Master of the frigate [the *Rose*] were seized and secured in Mr. Colman's house at the North End; and when I came to the Town Dock, I understood that Bullivant and some others of them were laid hold of, and then immediately the drums began to beat, and the people hastened and ran, some with and some for arms. Young Dudley and Colonel Lidget with some difficulty attained to the Fort. The Governor immediately sent Dudley on an errand, to request the four ministers, Mr. Joyliffe, and one or two more, to come to him at the Fort, pretending that, by them, he might still the people, not thinking it safe for him to go to them. They returned for answer, that they did not think it safe for them to go to him. Now, by this time, all the persons whom they concluded not to be for their side were seized and secured, except some few who had hid themselves, who afterwards were found, and dealt by as the rest. The Governor, with Palmer, Randolph, Lidget, West, and one or two more were at the Fort. All the companies were soon rallied together at the Town House, where assembled Captain Winthrop, Shrimpton Page, and many other substantial men, to consult matters; in which time the old Governor [Bradstreet] came among them, at whose appearance there was a great shout by some of the soldiers. Soon after the Jack was set up at the Fort, and a pair of colors at Beacon Hill, which gave notice to some thousand soldiers on the Charlestown side that the controversy was now to be ended, and multitudes would have been there, but that there was no need. The Frigate, upon the news, put out all her flags and pendants, and opened all her ports, and with all speed made ready for fight, under the command of the Lieutenant; he swearing that he should die before he was taken, although the Captain sent to him that if he fired one shot, or did any hurt, they would kill him, whom they had seized already; but the Lieutenant, not regarding, kept those resolutions all that day. Now about four of the clock in the afternoon, orders were given to go and demand the Fort, which hour the soldiers longed for; and had it not been just at the nick, the Governor and all the crew had made their escape on board the frigate, a barge being sent for them, but the soldiers being so near, got the barge. The army divided, and part came up on the back side of the Fort, part went underneath the hill to the lower battery or sconce, where the redcoats were, who immediately upon their approach retired up to the Fort to their master, who rebuked them for not firing on our soldiers, and, as I am informed, beat some of them. When the soldiers came to the battery or sconce, they presently turned the great guns about and pointed them against the Fort, which did much daunt those within; and the soldiers were so void of fear that, I presume, had those within the Fort been resolute to have lost their lives in fight, they might have killed an hundred of us at once, being so thick together before the mouths of the cannon of the Fort, all laden with small shot, but God prevented it. Then they demanded a surrender, which was denied until Mr. West and another should go first to the Council, and, after their return, we should have an answer, whether to fight or no. Upon their return, they came forth from the Fort, and went disarmed to the Town House, and from thence some to the close Jail, and the Governor, under a guard, to Mr. Usher's house. The next day they sent the two Colonels to demand of him the surrender of the Castle, which he resolved not to give; but they told him if he would not give it presently, under his hand and seal, he would be exposed to the rage of the people, and so left him; but he sent and told them that he would, and did so; and they went down and it was surrendered to them with cursings, and they brought the men away, and made Captain Fairweather commander in it. Now, by the time the men came back from the Castle, all the guns, both in the ships and batteries, were brought to bear against the frigate, which were enough to have shattered her in pieces at once, resolving to have her. It is incident to corrupt nature to lay the blame of our evil deeds anywhere rather than on ourselves, so Captain George cast all the blame now upon that devil Randolph; for had it not been for him, he had never troubled this good people; earnestly soliciting that he might not be constrained to surrender the ship, for by so doing both himself and all his men would lose their wages, which otherwise would be recovered in England, giving leave to go on board and strike the topmasts, and bring the sails on shore, and so he did. The country people came armed into the town, in the afternoon, in such rage and heat that it made us all tremble what would follow, for nothing would satisfy them but that the Governor must be bound in chains or cords and put in a more secure place; and that they would see done before they went away, and, to satisfy them, he was guarded by them to the Fort.

Thus, in less than two days, the revolution was begun and ended without bloodshed. A provisional government was set up following closely the lines of that under the old company, with the old governor, Bradstreet, at its head.

Submission and assurances of allegiance were promptly dispatched to William and Mary and an immediate and approving response was looked for. This was some time in forthcoming, however, and by the time it finally arrived the members of the provisional government were near to being nervous wrecks. This was due in large measure to the treatment of the rebels of New York as traitors by the home government, and some of the ringleaders of the Boston affair, notably Cotton Mather and several of his close companions, were preparing for flight when word came that all was well.

The old governor, Andros, and his friends lay in prison for many months. Andros made several attempts to escape, but was recaptured each time, and ultimately he was sent to England with Dudley and Randolph, there to stand trial and finally to be released.

Massachusetts, on its part, slipped quickly back into its old ways. Trade revived and increased and so ended an era.

CHAPTER V

Of Ships and Cargoes

THE reversion of Boston—and of the rest of New England—to the *status quo ante* Andros, during the last decade of the seventeenth century, was not altogether complete. Much as we may suspect that the Mathers, the Winthrops, the Bradstreets, the Stoughtons, the Ushers, the Hulls, et al., would have liked to see it so, that was not possible. Too much water had flowed over the dam for that. Time Marches On! Progress waits on no man, and all that sort of thing. Certain changes had taken place which no one could undo: changes in the political scene, and in the social and political outlook, as well as the beginnings of a less rigid, more relaxed view of life in general. Then, too, there was the fact that both sides, the Crown and the colony, had toyed with fire, and both had been scorched. Both, remembering the scorching, were in a frame of mind to accept compromise and give thanks—in secret—that matters were no worse.

The Crown—and Parliament with it—clung stubbornly to the theories of control that had been advanced since mid-century and had been laid down in the Acts of Trade and Navigation, in the Orders in Council, and in the creation of the Dominion. On the other hand, the colonists, having tasted self-government and the sweets of free trade, were equally anxious to regain them. Yet all sides saw the need of concession, and the new charter, now drawn up and adopted, was, to great extent, the expression of this realization. To be sure, it restricted the colonists considerably and heightened the royal control beyond that of the old company charter. But at the same time it did grant the colonists a greater measure of self-rule than had existed under the Dominion plan. Moreover the new king, in permitting Increase Mather, who was the colony's agent in London, to propose the new governor together with some members of his council, went a long way toward conciliating the old theocratic party in Massachusetts, which was the most anxious to see a return to the old system.

To be sure, the charter itself dealt a death blow to the theocratic system. But the Crown's concession permitted it to die a lingering death. The old religious fanaticism died hard, and flared evilly in its death throes in the witchcraft scare. But thenceforward it dwindled, and there was a marked advance in the liberalism of the colony's religious views.

If the colony forfeited a measure of its self-rule, both Parliament and the Crown made concessions in regard to trade. The right of control was rigidly maintained, but the impossibility of enforcing the acts and orders by highhanded methods was recognized. Duties, levies, and penalties were so lightened as to be but slight burden, and the merchants of Boston and of the other New England ports, remembering the horrors of the Dominion days, were glad enough to accept them as the lesser evil. To be sure, the old notion of free trade, prevailing before the Dominion, was as dead as theocracy. But it produced a virile ghost which walked often. In short, under the royal charter royal control was tightened, but it was not so strongly exerted as to inhibit trade. The result was happy.

With the death of the Dominion and the removal of the uncertainties inherent in the provisional government, Boston's trade began to revive by leaps and bounds. There were few changes in the type of goods imported. Spain, Portugal, France, and the Azores and Canary islands continued to send ever larger cargoes of wine and brandy, fruit, oil, silk, laces, and fine linens, as well as salt. England still provided the bulk of manufactured goods, such as cloth and clothing, rigging, refined sugar, lead, paper, and glass. But as colonial manufactures increased and the trade with Europe grew, this dwindled appreciably. From the West Indies came raw sugar, salt, spices, and molasses. The last took a tremendous jump after the Peace of Utrecht, when the French islands were opened to New England vessels, and it was this that gave impetus to the unsavory three-cornered trade, as we shall see presently.

On the export side of the books fish remained the great staple. From the beginning the produce of the sea had been divided into three grades for export purposes. The first, called "dunfish," was prepared by alternately drying and burying the larger cod until it reached a degree of ripe mellowness suited to the tastes of southern Europe. This was almost entirely sent to Spain, Portugal, and southern France, where it brought the highest prices. The second grade, the middlings, were fish dried in the ordinary way and somewhat smaller. These were easy to transport and formed the basic article of commerce for the Azores and Canaries, as well as for the coastal trade. They were also a favorite winter staple for the colonists themselves. The third and lowest grade of fish—the smaller dried cod as well as the pickled mackerel, bass, and alewives—practically all went to the West Indies, which were evidently not so particular.

This trade continued, with all its old vigor, but with one exception: gradually the Boston fishing fleet dwindled in size and that of Gloucester grew and replaced it. So that, in time, the fishermen of Boston did little more than supply the local market. For purposes of export the Gloucestermen became the producers, so to speak, while the Boston traders devoted themselves wholly to the business of carrying.

Important though fish remained as the grand old man of Boston trade, however, it gradually receded somewhat from the foreground as other, newer articles of export rose to take their place beside it. Whale oil and cod-liver oil became important factors in the game, as, in time, did whalebone, masts, boards, staves, shingles, clapboards, naval stores, potash, horses and livestock, pickled beef and pork, beeswax and rum. Even ships themselves became an item of export, to the vast despair of English shipbuilders who, in 1725, protested to the Lords of Trade that they were being ruined by Massachusetts competition.

An offshoot of all this was by way of portent—a sort of shadow showing the shape of things to come. This was a tendency on the part of Boston skippers to explore new avenues of trade. In a later era this adventurous spirit was to sustain Boston's commerce through trying times and ultimately to fetch the port into its golden age. But now it was only just appearing. Boston seamen and Boston ships poked their ways now into a good many remote and hitherto obscure spots, in search of trade, and by their curiosity they uncovered many a hidden vein of untapped ore. The coast of Honduras and Central America disclosed valuable stores of logwood and mahogany, in great demand in London, and in return were glad to receive fish. At Dutch Surinam, on the coast of South America, Boston traders found themselves able to exchange fish and New England products for those of the Dutch East Indies without the necessity of voyaging all the way round Africa. And we have already heard Randolph reporting that Boston ships put in at such distant ports as Scanderoon, the Guinea coast, and Madagascar, the pirate rendezvous.

Huge profits and quick turnover were the baits that lured men on these voyages. The risks were great, of course, but if a man chanced to uncover virgin territory his chances for sudden wealth were excellent. We have a concrete example of this in the voyage of Captain Henry Atkins in 1729.

Atkins was a coastal trader, and in that year, on what was strictly a hunch, he voyaged northward, past Newfoundland and far beyond Labrador to "the esquimeaux coast." He touched at several points near Davis's Inlet, but the sight of his ship, which was evidently something such as they had never before beheld, appeared to frighten the natives. With some difficulty he managed to persuade them to come and trade with him, and on his return he reported that he had found a vast wealth of fish and seal, and great forests of pine, alder, birch, and hazel. Apparently the natives had no notion of the value to white men of the seal and beaver skins in which they dressed—indicating that they had never been visited by traders—and they seemed anxious to exchange them for the white man's products. At one place Atkins exchanged trifles—files, knives, and other such trade goods—to the value of ten shillings, for a quantity of whalebone which he later sold in Boston for 120 pounds sterling! Small wonder that Boston skippers liked to ferret out new routes and markets!

Nor was it remarkable, in such circumstances, that the mercantile class grew swiftly and soon came to dominate, almost entirely, the society of the town. Other trades, if not so abruptly lucrative, were equally profitable by virtue of their steady regularity and greater extent; and two or three of these deserve a glance in passing.

Most important, unquestionably, both in its own right and in its repercussions, was the trade in molasses with the French West Indies already mentioned. For one thing, it became on the import side of the ledger what fish was on the export side. For another, it mothered two rather unsavory brats, which in themselves became big business. And for a third, it played a large part in fostering that animosity for the mother country which was ultimately to be responsible for the colonial break and the creation of an independent American state.

That may seem a considerable charge to lay at the door of a sticky but innocent, innocuous black syrup, whose sole offense consists in being the base of rum. Yet it is true, and it is precisely because it was the base for rum that it was true.

Rum, for all we may think to the contrary, is a comparatively modern tipple—and I speak here of rum in its true sense, rather than in its popular use to cover the entire field of intoxicating liquor. Just where the name came from is obscure. The Britannica suggests that it might have come from the Malay—or, on the other hand, it goes on, it may have originated in the Romany gypsy term for "queer." But they don't seem certain about it, and probably they just don't know. Webster is not more illuminating. "Short for rumbullion," he says. "Cf. Rumbooze." Both of these refer the reader back to rum, and there you are. Perhaps Charles Taussig is right when he says the name is American; an abbreviation of a "West Indian word"—rumbullion. Wherever the name came from, however, it has only one true meaning. It refers to the liquor distilled from sugar cane.

Rum was definitely of West Indian origin. White men were familiar with sugar cane before the discovery of the islands, but apparently none had ever before thought to distill its juice. Perhaps the Indians of the islands, before the whites killed them off, showed them how it was done. Perhaps the blacks brought the idea from Africa. At any rate it did not put in its appearance much before the middle of the seventeenth century. What the British seamen used for grog before that time is anybody's guess, but it was about then that travelers returning from the West Indies took to mentioning in their diaries a new and potent tipple they had found there. That the drink was popular and took quick hold is indicated by the following, from an old book on

Barbados written in 1676: "The chief fudling they make in the island is Rumbullion, alias Kill-Divil, and this is made of sugar canes distilled, a hot, hellish and terrible liquor."

Hitherto brandy had been the chief article of alcoholic exchange. But that, owing to French monopoly, was comparatively expensive. Here was a drink which possessed all the potency and fire of brandy, and which yet could be made almost literally for a song. In New England, to be sure, after it had been introduced and become popular there, it cost a little more: just under two shillings a gallon, it is said! But in the islands themselves—and I speak now of the bulk of the trade rum, not the better grades—it cost little more than the sweat of a black man's brow, for it was made in the main of the dregs and castoff refuse of the grinding mills.

It was a seafaring man, beyond question, who first thought to introduce this island product to the other parts of the world. And seamen, French, Spanish, Dutch, and Portuguese, as well as British, were quick to help. Some went to New England and became instantly popular as a substitute for the more expensive French brandy—which was slightly disfavored as a Papist tipple, anyway—and as more efficacious than the somewhat less potent hard cider or, more difficult to obtain, applejack. It went to England and found immediate popularity with the Navy, which spread it about the land. It went to Guinea direct from the Indies, and in its rawer forms proved more popular than the better French liquors with the simple blacks, who, like all primitive peoples, appeared to think that the more of the lining of the throat a drink removed in passing, the better it must be. Good rum, of course, was another story; a smooth, well-blended, expertly distilled liquor, worthy of popularity in any land. Perhaps it was some of this that found its way to France and was received with such enthusiasm as to alarm that nation's brandy barons.

Of Ships and Cargoes

Hitherto the rise of rum's popularity has followed more or less conventional lines. But now the economists step in to do a little of that juggling with the trends of nature which so often produces results quite different from those that they pretend to foresee. Economists, of course, in that day had not become the terrible brood they are today. I speak now of the late seventeenth- and early eighteenth-century forebears of the present tribe.

France was at war, not only with England, which was quite the usual state of affairs in those days, but also with Holland and Spain and Austria. In those times the French islands in the West Indies were more numerous than they are at present, and in the matter of sugar production they equaled the British. The British and the Dutch and the American colonies, however, were the sugar eaters of the world, and it was quite natural that, in order to curtail her enemies' food supplies to as great an extent as possible, the French Government should forbid the re-export of sugar and sugar products from her ports. Under the mercantile laws of the day French ships were forbidden to trade with foreign ports without first touching at a French port, and though they might have been able to maintain themselves with an illicit trade with the colonies on the American mainland, who never seemed averse to that sort of thing, they had no place else to go except a few small Baltic ports. There was no market to amount to anything for sugar in France, and as a consequence the price of sugar in the French islands took a sharp drop.

There was still hope, however, in rum, which was just beginning to be well received at home. But when the French authorities, lending their ears to the brandy barons, forbade the importation of rum into France the sugar market in the islands simply dropped out of sight. With no place to sell their sugar it became scarcely worth while for the French planters to grow it. Still, probably because they did not know what else to grow, they continued to raise cane and clung, year by year, to the feeble hope that something would happen to ease their plight.

It did.

Peace came in 1714, and with it the French and Dutch and Spanish islands of the West Indies were thrown open to English—and colonial—trade. Now doubtless certain canny Yankees, by virtue of flags of truce or other such devices, had already found out that sugar and molasses were obtainable in the French islands for a mere fraction of their cost in British ports. At any rate the peace was scarcely announced before the rush was on. New Englanders flocked to Martinique and Guadeloupe and Saint Domingue and carried away all of the sweetening they could carry. For their part, the French planters, amazed to find that suddenly a product which had seemed to have so little value was overnight become a thing for which men would exchange lumber and livestock, provisions and good New England products, hastened to extend their acreage in sugar.

The result was a swift pyramiding of interlocking trades, with the importation of raw sugar and molasses as the broad base. Just when the first New England distilleries were placed in operation is not altogether certain. Henry Hill seems to have opened one in 1714, according to Winsor, but it seems highly probable that there were others before that elsewhere in New England if not in Boston itself. If this were not so it would be difficult to account for the sudden increase in the demand for molasses.

Be all that as it may, however, the fact remains that by 1750 there were sixty-three distilleries in Massachusetts. In 1731 Boston alone imported 20,000 hogsheads of French molasses and from them distilled 1,260,000 gallons of rum, which was marketed at two shillings a gallon. By 1744 sugar production in the French islands had reached 122,500 hogsheads, while the British islands in the same year produced only 60,950 hogsheads. And

The "Old State House," in King Street. This is the building referred to in the text as "the Town House," since it was so known during the period before the Revolution. It is still standing at State and Washington streets.

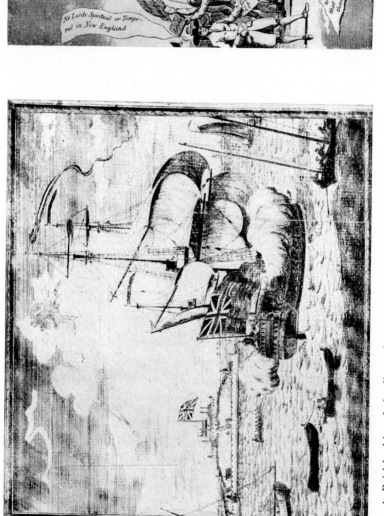

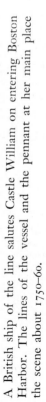

Bostonians were as determined not to be saddled with a bishop not of their own choosing as they were not to take tea with the East India Company. Above is a commentary from the British press upon that

A British ship of the line salutes Castle William on entering Boston Harbor. The lines of the vessel and the pennant at her main place the scene about 1750–60.

even before that, in 1740, the amount of molasses brought into American ports was more than eight times the total of that commodity produced in the British West Indies! By 1760 two thirds of all the molasses brought into Boston was French, and in the following year that figure increased to three fourths!

We may be sure that all this was not accomplished without opposition from abroad. Where once only the merchants of Britain had complained that they were being ruined by Yankee enterprise, now the shipbuilders of London, whose labor was being drawn off by the renewed activity of New England's yards, added their voice to the hue and cry; and to top the lot came shrieks of rage from the British planters of the West Indies, who, seeing themselves forced to lower their prices to compete with the French, were determined that someone must suffer for it.

The result was the Molasses Act of 1733, levying prohibitive duties on molasses imported from other than British possessions. Overnight it became Boston's turn to protest, and protest she did, for strict enforcement of the provisions of the act would have utterly ruined her. It would have put a tight stopper upon her rum trade and her distilleries. It would have closed off one of the greatest outlets for her fish. And it would have plugged entirely her one source of specie. Small wonder that, from Boston's point of view, it was unjust, outrageous, out of the question.

But protests were ignored. Customs officials were sent to see the act enforced, and everyone waited for the explosion.

None came. The customs officials proved "reasonable men," willing to wink and look the other way provided it was made worth their while. The trade continued and prospered, until it reached, in 1761, the proportions described above. Even in wartime it prospered, when Britons once again fought Frenchmen, for, as was inevitable with a business at once so profitable and so illegitimate, it was impossible to escape the attitude that the trade was illegal anyway—what difference did war make? Hence we have the paradox of New Englanders dying beneath the guns of Louisbourg, while their cousins in Boston lined their pockets with the profits of their illicit trade with the French West Indies!

The Molasses Act was a British blunder, typical of the blunders that Britain was making in that muddled, blundering time; and it was a serious one. Even the British could see that it was unenforceable, for it was not until the late 1750s that any serious attempts were made to enforce it. In the meantime it was permitted to stand upon the books, gathering dust and contempt and heightening the New Englanders' notion that smuggling was a small matter. Had it been wiped from the books and reasonable duties imposed, this attitude could have had no grounds for existence. But because it was permitted to stand, neither strictly enforced nor expunged from the record, the taint was removed from smuggling under it—and by degrees from all smuggling—with the result that it became the accepted notion that a man might damned well trade and exchange his goods where he pleased; a right, please notice, rather than a privilege.

The whole consequence was that when, in 1756, it was suddenly decided that the acts must be enforced, and revenue cutters were assigned to the Boston station to see that it was enforced, the men who by strict interpretation of the law were actually smugglers became persecuted martyrs, "pillars of commercial propriety," and men of great moral and political strength. The British, then, seeing only that they were up against a stubbornness as great as their own, turned stubborner still, as Britons will, and attempted to force their measures. In 1760–61 the collectors of the customs were granted the right to use writs of assistance—"extraordinary search warrants which authorized the holder to seize suspected goods anywhere and without notice, even to break into homes to search for contraband." And though these were not immediately put to use, in 1763 British naval commanders were authorized to act as customs officers and were permitted to retain a certain percentage of profits from all they seized as reimbursement. Still the smuggling continued—nay, even increased—and in time the writs were called into active use. What happened then belongs to another chapter.

In the meantime the Molasses Trade's stepchild had been born, waxed mighty, and flourished. The slave trade out of Boston, to be sure, never reached the proportions which it did in some of the other colonies. Nevertheless fortunes were made in it, and it was sufficiently extensive to warrant attention.

It is interesting—if futile—to speculate on why Boston should have been less active in the infamous three-cornered trade than, say, Newport. She was larger, more important as a trading center, and her commerce was much more far-flung. It would be safely conservative to estimate that three ships sailed out of Boston Harbor for every one that left the Rhode Island port, and it would be natural to assume that, all other things being equal, such a leader of colonial trade would take the lion's share of this as well. Yet the fact remains that she did not—or, at least, so it appears from the record. Of the Carnegie Institution's *Documents Illustrative of the History of the Slave Trade to America*, volume III: *New England and the Middle Colonies*, edited by Elizabeth Donnan, an exhaustive—and, I might almost add, exhausting—collection of documents, reports, letters, news items, advertisements, etc., pertaining to the slave trade from the earliest days of the colonies down to the nineteenth century, 104 out of 512 pages are devoted to Massachusetts, while 296 are devoted to Rhode Island, which appears to have been the greater participator in the trade in about that ratio. Further, it appears from a study of the documents that Boston's share in the trade was little, if any, greater than that of Salem or Marblehead or Newburyport, despite her relatively greater importance as a port.

It seems unlikely that the reasons for this were moral; that Boston men were any better or more advanced in thought than their neighbors. To be sure—to give the devil his due—the first articulate protest against the trade on moral grounds came out of Boston. Samuel Sewall, in a pamphlet entitled *The Selling of Joseph, a Memorial*, protested against the trade with considerable scriptural reference to back up his arguments in 1700. But this was answered in a similar pamphlet by John Saffin, in which the author drew equally upon the Scriptures in extenuation of the trade. And Sewall himself admitted that he drew upon himself "Frowns and hard Words . . . for this undertaking."

But there is further ample evidence that Bostonians accepted the prevailing view of the times with regard to the traffic in human beings. The first New Englanders to engage in the trade—long before any of their neighbors—were Boston men. We have already read the letter of Emmanuel Downing, Governor Winthrop's brother-in-law, proposing that Indian captives be exchanged for "Moores." And good old Cotton Mather himself, on "September, ye, 15, 1682," wrote a letter "To Ye Aged and Beloved Mr. John Higginson," in which he set forth a snide and startling proposal:

There is now at sea a ship called the Welcome which has on board an hundred or more of the heretics and malignants called Quakers, with W. Penn who is the chief scamp, at the head of them.

The General Court has accordingly given secret orders to Master Malachi Huscott, of the brig Porpoise, to waylay the said Welcome, slyly as near the Cape of Cod as may be, and make captive the said Penn and his ungodly crew, so that the Lord may be glorified, and not mocked on the soil of this new country with the heathen worship of these people. Much spoil can be made by selling the whole lot to Barbados, where slaves fetch good prices in rum and sugar, and we shall not only do the Lord great service by punishing the wicked, but we shall make great good for his ministers and people.

But perhaps better evidence of popular acceptance of slavery as a natural order of things is contained in the many advertisements appearing in Boston newspapers, from 1700 onward, offering Negroes for sale. Of these there are a great number to be found, and I shall quote only a few, picked at random, to give an idea of their general tenor:

June 1, 1704—from the Boston *News Letter:*

Two Negro men and one Negro Woman and Child; to be Sold by Mr. John Colmon, Merchant; to be seen at Col. Charles Hobbey, Esq. his House in Boston.

June 10, 1706—from the Boston *News Letter:*

Three Negro Men Slaves, and three Negro Women, to be Sold; Inquire of John Campbell, Postmaster, and know further

November 10, 1712—Boston *News Letter:*

A young negro girl born in Barbadoes that speaks good English, to be sold by Mr. Grove Hirst, merchant, and to be seen at his house in Trea-mont Street, Boston.

(Grove Hirst was Samuel Sewall's son-in-law.)

September 13, 1714—Boston *News Letter:*

To be disposed of by Mr. Samuel Sewall [!] Merchant, at his Ware house near the Swing-Bridge in Merchants Row Boston, several Irish Maid Servants, time most of them for Five years, one Irish Man Servant who is a good Barber and Wiggmaker, also Four or Five likely Negro Boys.

September 1, 1726—Boston *News Letter:*

To be Sold; A Parcel of Negros, Just Arrived, viz. Men, Women, Boys and Girls; they are to be seen at Captain Nathaniel Jarvis's House near Scarlett's Wharff.

Boston: Cradle of Liberty

November 17, 1726—Boston *News Letter:*

Several choice Gold Coast Negroes lately Arrived. To be Sold at Mr. Bullfinch's, near the Town Dock, Boston.

October 7, 1740—Boston *News Letter:*

Just imported from the Coast of Africa, and to be Sold by Mr. John Jones on board the Brigantine Poultney, now lying at Clark's Wharff, a Parcel of likely Young Negroes, Men, Women, Boys and Girls; to be seen on Board said Vessel.

An entire volume could be filled with such notices, but the foregoing should suffice. It should be remembered that in general the slaves were not imported directly to Massachusetts by the vessels engaged in the trade. Generally the ships carried rum to Africa, which was there exchanged for a human cargo. Followed the infamous Middle Passage, about which so much has been written. Such slaves as survived were then unloaded and sold in the West Indies, or, occasionally, the southern colonies. The vessel was then again loaded with raw sugar or molasses and returned to Boston. On this final leg a few Negroes, generally a picked lot, either born or trained as house servants in the islands, would be carried northward as an extra item of profit. Massachusetts itself was not an extensive user of slave labor, nor was any part of New England. Economic conditions made it generally impracticable. But some were imported as household help and similar workers.

Just how many of these were brought in, it is impossible now to say. William Weeden quotes an article in the Boston *News Letter*, published in 1766, which accounted for 23,743 Negroes imported into Massachusetts in the decade just preceding, but believes that this must have included those brought into Newport as well. At the other end of the scale Professor Hart, in his *Commonwealth History of Massachusetts*, says that a census of Negroes taken in 1764–65 showed a total of 5,779, few of them free. Doubtless many of those mentioned in Weeden were re-exported to the southern colonies. But the report of a French Protestant refugee in Boston, written in 1687, is interesting. He says: "You may also own negroes and negresses; there is not a house in Boston however small may be its means that has not one or two. There are those that have five or six, and all make a good living."

So much for Bostonians' attitude toward the institution of slavery. Why, then, did not more Boston skippers take part in the trade? Some did, of course, and a list of the names of those merchants of Boston who engaged in the business would read like an eighteenth-century *Social Register*. But on the whole Boston's part was not large.

It is impossible, of course, at this date, to say definitely why this was so, but one may hazard a shrewd guess. Perhaps it was because, having been first in the trade, Boston men were the first to discover its drawbacks and consequently the first to abandon it. However, a much more likely reason lies in the risks involved.

This is not to say that Boston men shrank from risk and danger. They proved themselves in this respect many times over in later, as well as in earlier, years. But they were shrewd and calculating, and they were in business for profit rather than adventure. There were huge profits to be made from a successful voyage in the Middle Passage, but the odds against such a successful voyage were high by comparison. Cargoes sickened and died. Occasionally the natives in Africa rose and attacked the trading vessels, slaughtering, or at least decimating, their crews. The kind of men willing to take a hand in such a game, which was full of hardship quite apart from any considerations of humanity, were not the most trustworthy that a shipowner could desire, and more than one case of mutiny and seizure of the vessel is on the record. And, again, the dread and little-known diseases and fevers of the coast, often as not, struck, carrying off half the cargo and the crew as well, and there was small profit in that.

No. It is this writer's guess that Boston merchants and Boston seamen, in the bulk, having sound, if less spectacular, trade elsewhere, and having fish to export to the West Indies in return for the molasses they brought back, were content to take the slower, steadier, but in the long run equally great, profits and leave the slave trade to those who liked it.

There is ample ground for such an assumption. The records of ships that sailed out of Boston were often in themselves enough to discourage the most optimistic investor. Why they did not discourage more is the great mystery. The Boston *News Letter* of September 6, 1733, gives the following extract from a letter from Captain Moore, written at Santiago, in the Cape Verde Islands, July 20 of the same year:

On the 17th of June last, as we were coming down the River Gambia, at Twelve o'Clock in the Night, the Natives fired at us, upon which began a very smart engagement, which lasted till daylight: Mr. Lowder was most of the Time in the Cabbin loading Small Arms, some of our People not having Discretion to do it themselves, till by an unhappy contrary Wind, the River narrow, and the Vessel not answering her Helm, we fell along the Shore, the Natives rush'd on in great Numbers in order to board us, but were so received that they thought proper to Retreat: In which Conflict Mr. Lowder came upon Deck, and (being in a Consternation) was shot thro' the Body; He went immediately down, and had all imagineable Care taken of him; He being in the Height of Action, his Wound was with great Difficulty stop'd bleeding. He liv'd Twenty four Hours, sensible of his approaching Dissolution, and spent his little Time in making his eternal Peace.

On July 10, 1739, the schooner *Mermaid* appeared off Boston in a rather sad state. The selectmen's minutes report what followed:

John Robinson, Master of the Schooner Mermaid from the Coast of Guinea, being sent for appear'd . . . and being Examin'd, on oath, Declares . . . That he came from the River Gambo, two and forty days ago, with Eleven White Men on board and Fifty Slaves; That they had the Small Pox, on board, five Months ago, for about Ten Weeks, one Hundred and Forty Leagues up the River Gambo; that he buried Two Whites and one Black; that afterwards he burnt Brimstone in the Vessel and Cleansed her with all possible care Vizt. in February last, Since which no Person has been Sick of that Distemper, but that they have had the Measles and the Flux on board, that the Flux continues among the Slaves, but the Measles is not now among them, that they have lost fifteen Slaves of the Flux, in the said River and in their Passage and that they buried two in sight of Cape Cod, Yesterday; That 3 Whites and 4 Blacks have had the Small Pox, that all the White men on board have had the Small Pox; That the Negroes are all young under Twenty years of age; That he took out all his Water Casks and Cleansed them, but the Ballast had not been shifted.

They considered this report and decided that it would be best, until a committee, which was to include a doctor, could go down the harbor and inspect the vessel, for the *Mermaid* to remain where she was. The committee went and saw, and reported "as follows, Vizt.":

That they found about Twelve of the Slaves on board Sick of the Fever and Flux, and that there is a very dangerous Stench on board, and 'tis their Opinion, It is necessary for the Safety of the Town, that the said Vessell be not permitted to come to the Wharf, for the present, but that she be sent down to Rainsford Island, or some other Convenient place, in order for the Airing and Cleansing the Vessell, and Shifting her Ballast, and for Airing and taking Care of the Slaves, and that they put on Shore all their Casks.

One of the most prominent Bostonians to take a hand in the three-cornered trade was Peter Faneuil. One of his ships—owned jointly with two others, John Jones and Captain Cutler—was the *Jolly Batchelor*, snow, of Boston. One day in August, 1743, the *Jolly Batchelor* limped into Newport, Rhode Island—which must have been the last port into which old Peter, or rather his heirs—for Faneuil himself had died while the snow was away—would wish to see her sail. In command of her was not Captain Cutler, who had taken her out of Boston, but a

Captain Charles Wickham, of Newport. Half her Boston crew were gone, and their places were taken by Rhode Islanders, and the story of her adventures was one of the sorriest and most complicated that ever came out of Africa. The Boston *Evening Post* reported it as follows, on August 15, 1743:

We now have certain Advice, that Capt. John Cutler, late Commander of a Snow belonging to this Town, who sailed for Guinea some time ago as he was trading in the River Sierra Leona, was murdered, with 2 or 3 of his Men, by some Portugese who are settled on that River. They rifled the Vessel, and took away his Slaves, etc., but by the Assistance of an honest English Man who is settled in those Parts, some of the Slaves were recovered, and the Vessel again fitted for the Sea, and last Friday she was brought into Newport by Captain Wickham of that Place, who had himself been taken by a Spanish Privateer on the Coast of Guinea some time before.

There were statements and depositions by Wickham and Mackenzie, one of his men, and a long letter full of crocodile tears, from George Birchall, the "honest English Man," all of which are too long to be quoted here. Birchall's letter is particularly interesting, for though the Englishman admits that Cutler had tried to cheat him and he had tried to cheat Cutler, still they had been very good friends, and all that he had done to recover the ship

I did it to serve my deceased friend, his Friends and family, whose virtues and honour, the Unfortunate Deceased used often to mention to me, with so much Satisfaction, that we used often to wish our Selfs with you, to whome he had Promisd to interduce me, in my way to old England, this makes me Mellancholly, therefore I must conclude this Subject . . .

"Mellancholly" or no, Birchall did not hesitate to libel the snow and her cargo, claiming "a Third of all" for his share, and declaring that "when that is done I do Ashure you I shall be a looser."

The court awarded his claim and ordered the vessel and her

cargo sold to satisfy it, whereupon Captain Wickham and his lads brought further claims against her. And where was the profit for Peter Faneuil in all that?

Perhaps it was as well that the old rogue was dead, for he might well-nigh have died of apoplexy had he lived to see the outcome of his fine venture in the *Jolly Batchelor!*

CHAPTER VI

Pirates and Privateers

NED LOW was a Boston man. Ned Low was a pirate.

There are those who think of pirates as romantic, swashbuckling, reckless, devil-may-care fellows. They labor under a misconception. The plain truth was that your pirate was a rat; a loud-mouthed, foul-mouthed, flannel-mouthed, bullying, sadistic, evil, and cowardly rat; generally without even that rodent's saving grace of being willing to fight when backed into a tight corner. Boston bred pirates other than Ned Low, but as his career as a buccaneer of the top flight is reasonably average, he becomes a logical choice for an example.

In the year 1719 Ned Low was living in Boston. By trade he was a ship rigger, and as this was a time when shipyards were booming, he had no lack of employment. In 1714 he had married Eliza Marble, which was apparently a good thing for him, for he was, by all accounts, a wild young fellow with a savage and ungovernable temper, and, whether through affection for her or because, as so many women will, she managed to dominate him entirely, he had kept pretty well out of trouble since.

It is curious how remote a cause may prod a man into his ultimate niche. Eliza Low, in 1719, gave birth to a daughter, Elizabeth, and shortly thereafter died. Now if Ned Low ever had a redeeming trait it was that he often expressed great affection for the young daughter he left behind him in Boston, as was attested by members of his crew as well as by captives, and that he would not force a married man to join him. Both of these would seem to indicate a deep and abiding love for his wife, intense grief at her loss, and unbounded reverence for her memory. Had he been of sterner stuff this might have served to keep him honest. But like many a weakling before and since, he found himself unable to cleave to that course, for the sake of the dead, that the living would most have desired.

That, at least, is the look of things on the surface. In later years, however, Low was possessed of another characteristic which was to make him especially dreaded by Boston skippers. This was a bitter and persistent hatred of New Englanders. Never a one fell into his hands but he treated him with the utmost cruelty and harshness, and the simple sight of a New England vessel was enough to make him fall into a tantrum. This may have been simply the result of a sense of guilt upon a weak and certainly diseased mentality. In short he may have been conscious of having been first at fault upon his native heath, and so cherished an enmity for those who first saw him for what he was. On the other hand, the beginning of his downward career certainly dates from the death of his wife, and this leads one to wonder at the circumstances surrounding that event. Were neighbors unsympathetic? Was the event itself due to some community neglect? Or was there in connection with it one of those manifestations of man's inhumanity to his own kind that are not uncommon even today? The fact seems unlikely. Yet it is not impossible. It makes an interesting point of speculation. But it can never be anything more, for the truth is lost now, buried in the sepulcher of time.

So much for the background. We do know that following his wife's death, Low was not long in returning to his former quarrelsomeness. As a result he was soon after discharged from his post at the shipyard, and a little later shipped as foremast hand on board a vessel bound to the Bay of Honduras for logwood.

Honduras in those days was claimed by Spain, and people of other nations were forbidden to cut logwood. In other words the trade, in which New Englanders played such a large part, was altogether contraband and illegal. It was the custom for vessels, once they had arrived off the coast, to send their boats ashore, with crews fully armed, to mark out and cut the most salable timber. If they chanced to be caught by one of the coasters or Spanish privateers who abounded in those waters, there was likely to be a fight.

One day Low was sent ashore with the boats. The day was spent in hard work, cutting and skidding out the timber and loading it upon the boats, and toward dinnertime the boat in which Low was sent pulled back to the ship fully laden.

The men of the boat were tired and hungry and proposed to stay on board the larger vessel and have dinner before returning ashore for another load. The captain, however, was evidently nervous about the Spaniards in the vicinity and wished to complete his loading as quickly as possible. Accordingly he ordered them ashore again immediately.

High words followed, and the upshot of it all was that Low, quarrelsome as ever, finally, in a rage, snatched up a loaded musket and fired at the captain.

Perhaps the captain ducked. Perhaps Low's aim was poor. At any rate the shot went wide and killed a sailor who happened to be standing near by. At that Low turned and flung himself down into the boat in which his twelve companions were already seated, and they promptly pulled away from the ship, hoisted sail, and stood away among the islands that fringe the coast.

With such a start it is not strange that they should decide to turn pirates. They were all deserters, hard men, and one, at least, was a murderer. It was natural, too, that he who was the greatest criminal amongst them should take command.

Their luck was in, for on the very next day they fell in with a small vessel, probably a ketch or a shallop, which they promptly fell upon with savagery and captured. They thereupon cleared away from the coast and shaped their course for the Cayman Islands, lying to the southward of Cuba and west of Jamaica, which were noted as a pirate rendezvous.

At Grand Cayman, Low fell in with one George Lowther, a more experienced pirate who seemed to take a fancy to him and his fellows, and the long and short of it was that presently they joined forces, Lowther retaining command and Low becoming his lieutenant. The little vessel which they had taken in the Bay of Honduras was destroyed, and the whole company, shipping together on Lowther's ship, the *Happy Delivery*—quaint name for a pirate—set sail once more for the Honduran coast, where they fell to plundering everything that came within their reach. For several months they remained there, taking and plundering in that time, besides others, eight Boston vessels, including the ship *Greyhound*, Benjamin Edwards, master. All of these they burned "because they were New England men," according to the report, and their crews were cruelly whipped, beaten, and cut, and several were forced to serve in the pirates' ship.

But like everyone else the pirates had their downs as well as their ups. By now they had a fleet consisting of four vessels: Lowther's ship and two large sloops and a small one. With this complement they put up for Port Mayo, in the Gulf of Matique, where it was intended they should careen and clean the fouled bottoms of their craft. On arrival they all moved ashore, taking with them all their stores and sails, which were used for tents, and the ship, which was the largest of the fleet, was hauled up and hove down. Just as they were getting down to work, however, the local Indians, who, it seemed, made few distinctions, attacked them in force and with great suddenness, so that they were forced to flee to the other vessels in the harbor which had not yet been careened, and get away as best they might.

Shorthanded, now, and short-provisioned, and shorter-tempered still for the state in which they found themselves because of their own carelessness, they all went aboard the largest sloop, abandoning the other vessels, and turned toward the West Indies. Near the Island of Discade (?) they were put in a better humor by the capture of a brigantine, laden with such supplies as they stood most in need of. After transferring the cargo to their own vessel they then destroyed this vessel and turned north, heading up the American coast. On the 28th of May 1722 they overtook the brigantine *Rebecca*, of Charlestown, James Flucker, master, out of St. Kitts for Boston. This was in latitude 38 degrees, somewhere between the Virginia and Delaware capes, and here Low and Lowther parted company. Lowther had evidently a bellyful of Low and his quarrelsome ways, for he now proposed that Low take the brigantine and such men as he wanted and strike off on his own account.

Low was quick to accept the proposition, and that very day, with forty men who chose to sail with him, he parted company with his erstwhile commander.

Our hero now embarked upon a career that was as bloody and as violent as that of any pirate who ever roved the seas. His first act was to draw up a set of articles, by which he and his pirate crew were to be governed. This was customary among those who "took to the account," and is interesting as an indication that even thieves must have laws among themselves. Low's articles were published in the Boston *News Letter*, August 8, 1723, and were as follows:

1. The Captain is to have two full Shares; the Master is to have one Share and one Half; the Doctor, Mate, Gunner and Boatswain, one Share and one Quarter.

2. He that shall be found Guilty of taking up any Unlawfull Weapon on Board the Privateer or any other prize by us taken, so as to Strike or Abuse one another in any regard, shall suffer what Punishment the Captain and Majority of the Company shall see fit.

3. He that shall be found Guilty of Cowardice in the time of Engagements, shall suffer what Punishment the Captain and the Majority of the Company shall see fit.

4. If any Gold, Jewels, Silver, &c, be found on Board of any Prize or Prizes to the value of a Piece of Eight, & the finder do not deliver it to the Quarter Master in the space of 24 hours he shall suffer what Punishment the Captain and the Majority of the Company shall think fit.

5. He that is found Guilty of Gaming, or Defrauding one another to the Value of a Ryal of Plate, shall suffer what Punishment the Captain and the Majority of the Company shall see fit.

6. He that shall have the Misfortune to loose a Limb in time of Engagement, shall have the Sum of Six hundred peices of Eight, and remain aboard as long as he shall think fit.

7. Good Quarters to be given when Craved.

8. He that sees a Sail first, shall have the best Pistol or Small Arm aboard of her.

9. He that shall be Guilty of Drunkenness in time of Engagement shall suffer what Punishment the Captain and Majority of the Company shall think fit.

10. No Snapping of Guns in the Hould.

With this attended to, Low shaped his course northward for the waters lying between the tip of Long Island and Nantucket, where, off Block Island, he fell in with a sloop out of Amboy, New Jersey, which he plundered of all its provisions and let go. Later in the same day he brought to another sloop, owned and commanded by James Cahoon, of Newport. Cahoon was severely cut in the scuffle, and Low, after plundering his vessel of everything of value, took away his mainsail, water and provisions, chopped off his bowsprit and cut away all his rigging and threw it overboard, after which he turned him adrift and stood away to the southeast.

As well he did, for Cahoon, despite his plight, managed to make Block Island about midnight. At once a boat was dispatched to the governor with the news that a pirate was in those waters. By sunset the next day two of the best sloops in Newport Harbor were armed and fitted out and manned and sent out in pursuit. But though Low's vessel was still in sight from Block Island at the moment of their sailing, yet he managed to elude them in the night and they were forced to return after several days of fruitless cruising without so much as catching sight of him.

Meantime word had been carried to Boston, where a proclamation against the pirate was immediately read, and, by beat of drum, more than one hundred men were enlisted to sail against him. These sailed in a ship under command of Captain Peter Papillion, but had little better luck than their Newport neighbors. Ned Low appeared to have disappeared entirely from the sea. However, they did have the good fortune to fall in with the brigantine *Rebecca,* which Low had abandoned at Port Roseway, Nova Scotia, and turned over to Captain Flucker.

Actually Low had for a time gone to ground at the mouth of Buzzards Bay, where it was his intention to take on fresh water for a cruise to the Bahamas. He remained there for a time, stealing sheep from the various islands and plundering whale-boats out of Nantucket. But presently this palled and he put to sea once more.

Instead of heading south, however, he turned north toward the Banks, where at this time of year there was an abundance of small and comparatively defenseless vessels and plenty of provision. Putting into Port Roseway on a Sunday, he found about thirteen fishing vessels at anchor there. Pretending to be an innocent trader just arriving from the West Indies, he deliberately sailed in and cast anchor among them. As night came on, however, boats, each carrying three or four men, put out from the brigantine and passed to the other vessels, the men going on board simply as though they came on a friendly visit to ask after the news and give their own stories.

Once on deck these parties instantly drew cutlasses and pistols and demanded the surrender of the vessel they were on, and such was the finesse with which the trick was carried out that not one of the fishermen was sufficiently able to recover from his surprise to offer resistance. All thirteen of the vessels in the harbor were taken, and all were presently plundered.

Among the vessels taken was the schooner, *Mary*, of Marblehead, eighty tons, new, of clean lines and a good sailer. Low took a fancy to this vessel and decided to transfer his activities to her, renaming her, appropriately enough, the *Fancy*. After plundering the rest of the ships and forcing a number of men from among them—as well, it is to be suspected, as picking up some willing recruits—he placed Captain Flucker in the brigantine and ordered him to make sail for Boston. Thereupon he, in the *Fancy*, now armed and fitted for his purpose, sailed out of the harbor and once again disappeared.

He next turned up at the mouth of St. John's Harbor in Newfoundland. There was a misty fog hanging upon the harbor, and through it Low made out a large vessel riding at anchor which he took to be a fish trader. He determined to run in and cut her out, and accordingly ordered all but a few of his men below hatches, that no undue suspicion might be aroused, and stood in toward her. On the way, however, he met with a fisherman coming out who hailed him, demanding whence they had come. Low answered that they came from Barbados with a cargo of rum, and in turn asked the name of the large ship riding near by. When the answer came that it was the *Solebay*, man-of-war, Low was quick to put over his helm and take to his heels, losing himself in the fog before the warship could slip her cable and stand out after him.

A little farther along the coast, a few days later, Low appeared suddenly out of the fog and fell upon the little town of Carbonear, which he plundered and burned. From there he passed on out to the Grand Banks, where he took and plundered several vessels, including a French banker, a huge vessel of nearly four hundred tons and two guns. Then, learning that the *Solebay* was prowling about in search of him, he turned southward once more and headed for the West Indies.

It is not the purpose here to trace, step by step, the entire career of the pirate. The foregoing is enough to give some idea of how such a one obtained his start and of the way in which he operated, and a good deal of what remains would have little bearing upon the story of Boston Port. Low did not discriminate in his choice of victims. He fell upon Englishman, Frenchman, and Spaniard alike whenever opportunity offered. But, as has been pointed out, he seemed to reserve a special animosity toward Boston men, and some of the gratuitous and deliberate cruelties he practiced upon those who fell into his hands are almost unbelievable.

On one occasion Low and his crew captured a great Portuguese ship, the *Nostra Senhora da Victoria*. Suspecting that she was richly loaded, and being unable to find any trace of gold, Low tortured several of her men to make them tell where the money was. At last one of them confessed that the captain had put it all in a large bag and hung it out a stern-cabin window, standing by to cut the rope if it seemed likely that the ship was to be taken. When that, at last, became apparent, he had chopped through the rope with his cutlass and eleven thousand gold moidores—about fifteen thousand English pounds—had plunged to the bottom of the sea.

When Low learned of this he was so enraged that he ordered the captain lashed to the mast. He then sliced off the unfortunate man's lips with his cutlass, had them broiled before the galley fire, and then forced the Portuguese mate to eat them hot before the captain's eyes. Captain and crew were then further tortured, until the pirates, tiring of the sport, put them all to death, slaughtering in that one orgy a total of thirty-two persons.

On another occasion Low came upon a fleet of five vessels, sailing together for safety's sake, bound north around the western tip of Cuba. He fell upon them furiously, took and plundered them, and the sequel is told in the *American Weekly Mercury* of June 13, 1723:

They cut and whiped some and others they burnt with Matches between their Fingers to the bone to make them confess where their Money was. They took to the value of a Thousand Pistoles from Passengers and others. . . . They are commanded by one Edward Low. The Pyrates gave us an account of his taking the Bay of Hondoras from the Spaniards, which had surprized the English, and taking them and putting all the Spaniards to the Sword Excepting two Boys; as also burning the King George and a snow belonging to New York, and sunk one of the New England Ships, and cut off one of the Master's Ears and slit his Nose; all this they confessed themselves. They are now supposed to be cruizing off Sandy Hook or thereabouts.

Still later they fell in with the ship *Amsterdam*, merchant, Captain John Welland, bound from Jamaica for Boston. Low cut off the captain's ear, slit up his nose, and cut him in several places, "because he was a New Englander."

The list might be continued indefinitely, but there would be little point in so doing. For several years, at least until 1724, Low continued to terrorize the shipping of New England and the West Indies and then disappeared from the scene. What actually happened to him is somewhat uncertain. There was a rumor that, having quarreled with his companions, he was marooned on an uninhabited island—a rumor that persisted for several years. But the most reliable account of his fate tells of his capture by the French at Martinique and of his quick dispatch there upon the gallows. Poetically just as it might be to have him captured by a New England vessel and carried to Boston, there to be gibbeted in chains, it is yet to be feared that the French account of his end is more accurate.

But Ned Low was not the first, nor the only, pirate to plague New England shipping. We have already glanced at the career of the redoubtable Dixey Bull, who in 1632 had the dubious distinction of becoming New England's very first own pirate. But there were others who delighted in making the sea unsafe for Boston ships. Few of them hailed originally from Boston. Either Boston men had not the stuff (*sic*) to become leaders in this desperate game, or few of them went on the account. A number, however, ended their days in Boston.

Previous to the rise of Dixey Bull no one in Boston appeared to have thought of passing any laws aimed at the suppression of piracy. The expeditions sent out to intercept him were based upon necessity, the common law, and the theoretical adherence to old English law which prevailed in the Bay Colony when convenience indicated. Following Bull's disappearance, it was many years before the threat of piracy again reared its ugly head, and the matter seems to have been forgotten.

With the inauguration of serious attempts to enforce the Acts of Navigation, however—which, it must be remembered, were intended to apply to other British colonies as well as New England—and with the resistance and evasions which this attempt fostered, there came a noticeable increase in lawlessness on the high seas. This was not altogether remarkable. It was only natural that simple seamen, seeing the merchants who hired them grow fat with lawbreaking, should attempt to emulate them after their own fashion. It is not to be expected that they should take into account the niceties of the law. To them it was much the same if you seized a vessel from a master who was harsh or if you cheated a greedy king of the duties that the law allowed him. To cheat the Crown was the prerogative of masters and owners, but to cheat masters and owners was a sailor's right. From such reasoning it was but a short step to mutiny, and beyond mutiny there was little left but piracy, for those were harsh days and the law exacted harsh penalties from those that transgressed.

It was just such a case as this that was responsible for the passage of the first anti-piracy law in Boston—which is to say, in the Bay Province. There was a ship—the *Antonio*—owned in England and manned by Englishmen, which, sometime in the year 1672, was proceeding about her lawful business somewhere off the coast of Spain.

It is not known exactly what was the cause of the dispute that arose between the master and the crew. Perhaps it was ill-usage, perhaps it was bad food. Both were frequent causes of such happenings in those days. But one thing is certain: such a dispute arose, and in the end the crew took matters in their own hands and, rising against the captain, set him and some of his officers adrift in the ship's longboat "with a small quantity of provisions." The mutineers—"pirates" they were called in the bill of indictment—then shaped their course for Boston, where they arrived in due course of time and were sheltered by a merchant of the town, by name, Major Nicholas Shapleigh.

Now it happened, whether through adverse winds or from some other cause, that the captain and his companions, too, bore westward, and they, also, in time came to Boston. To quote Cotton Mather, who wrote an account of the business:

By a surprizing providence of God, the Master, with his Afflicted Company, in the Long Boat, also arrived; all, Except one who Dyed of the Barbarous Usage. . . . The Countenance of the Master, was now become Terrible to the Rebellious Men, who, though they had Escaped the Sea, yet Vengeance would not suffer them to Live a Shore. At his Instance and Complaint, they were Apprehended; and the Ringleaders of this Murderous Pyracy, had sentence of Death Executed upon them, in Boston.

The upshot of this affair, besides the hanging of the three ringleaders and the fining of Major Shapleigh, was the passage of a law by the General Court providing for the death penalty for acts of piracy.

In the course of time other pirates were caught and hanged under the stipulations of this act. In 1689 Thomas Pound, who had been pilot of the frigate *Rose*, which had been sent to Boston to support Governor Andros, together with Thomas Hawkins and some others put to sea in Hawkins's boat on the account. After a brief career and a merry one, Hawkins deserted and made his way to Boston, while the remainder of the crew were overcome in a pitched battle in Tarpaulin Cove, on the south side of Naushon Island in Vineyard Sound. They were carried to Boston and there dealt with variously. Pound, who was a friend of Randolph, was sent to England for trial, where he was acquitted and died a gentleman in bed. Hawkins was also sent to England, but on the way the vessel in which he was held prisoner engaged in a running fight with a French privateer and Hawkins was killed. Others of the company were let off with varying penalties. But one Thomas Johnson, who was known as "the limping privateer," was found guilty and hanged. This was in 1690.

In 1703 several merchants of Boston fitted out a ship, the *Charles*, brigantine, of eighty tons, at Marblehead, to act as a privateer, preying on the French shipping off the coast of Acadia and Newfoundland. The captain of this vessel, Daniel Plowman evidently, after signing them on, felt some misgivings concerning the character of his crew, for he fell ill on the eve of sailing and wrote to the owners in Boston to come at once to Marblehead to "take some speedy care in saving what we can." One of the owners went, as requested, but found Plowman too ill to see him. Some correspondence followed in which the owner proposed to his associates that a new captain be chosen and the ship sent to sea, and Plowman protested that it would not do "with these people" to send her out. He hinted that the sooner she was disarmed the better it would be for everyone.

Before any action could be taken, however, on this proposal he went on board, having recovered sufficiently by this time to take command, was promptly seized by the crew and locked in his cabin. His lieutenant, John Quelch, was then elected captain in his place, and the anchor was weighed and the vessel put to sea. Sometime after that Captain Plowman was brought on deck and thrown overboard. But whether he was then alive or dead is not now known.

Captain Quelch now headed south, instead of north, as the owners intended, and in due course of time arrived off the coast of Brazil, where he plundered a number of Portuguese vessels.

It has been said, in extenuation of Quelch, that he may well have been unaware of the treaty of amity between Great Britain and Portugal, which had been signed in May 1703. But this would hardly excuse him, as the ship had been commissioned expressly for the purpose of harrying the French, with whom England was at war. At any rate the long and short of it was that Quelch, almost a year after his departure, sailed boldly into Marblehead and reported a successful cruise. However, the circumstances of her departure, the fact that they had heard nothing from the vessel in all that time, and the fact that she had gone south instead of north, apparently aroused the suspicions of the owners, and they lodged a written "information" with the authorities, with the result that a warrant for the arrest of

Quelch and his fellows was sworn out and served by Paul Dudley, the attorney general and son of the governor.

The pirates were already partly dispersed, but of the lot some twenty-four were taken and lodged in jail in Boston. There was some delay in bringing the case to trial, occasioned mainly by the necessity of catching them up by ones and twos and threes up and down the countryside and here and there along the coast. But folk were impatient, and Cotton Mather even went so far as to hint that the governor sheltered them for his own purposes, which, of course, was nonsense.

In time all of them received the death sentence, but only nine were hanged. The rest were lodged in prison for the space of a year, when they were released by the Queen's "most gracious pardon." Three others, who had surrendered themselves voluntarily, were let go on the grounds that they had been forced against their will and had turned state's evidence. Seven of the pirates were hanged at once on a gallows set up on a point of land just under Copp's Hill, and it is said that when the trap dropped there was such a screech set up by the women among the spectators that it was heard a full mile upwind of the place. According to the custom of the time the bodies were left hanging where they were until they rotted away, to serve as a warning to all who might have in mind a like career.

Six other pirates, survivors of Samuel Bellamy's ship, the *Whidaw*, wrecked at Wellfleet on Cape Cod, were hanged "near the Charlestown Ferry" in 1717. The bodies of these men were afterwards removed to Bird Island, which has long since disappeared, there to hang until they rotted as a warning to others. In 1726 William Fly and three others were also hanged at the Charlestown Ferry and their bodies afterwards removed to hang in chains on Nix's Mate; a circumstance which destroys an old-time legend about that island, for, according to the tale, Fly was hanged there protesting his innocence and declaring that in witness of the fact the island would presently be washed away. The island has since disappeared, save for a retaining wall and a small monument containing a warning beacon. But the fact remains that Fly was a pirate and that he met his end at the customary place of execution.

Other, and perhaps better-known, pirates were lodged in Boston's jail, but were transported to England for trial. James Gillam was one of these, as were also Joseph Bradish, Cambridge's own pirate, and Tee Wetherley. But undoubtedly the most famous of all was Captain William Kidd.

William Kidd was a native of Scotland who had gained some reputation as a privateersman. In 1696 a company was formed which had as its avowed purpose to take advantage of the expressed desire of the Crown to rid the waters of the New World of pirates. Heading this company was the Earl of Bellomont, presently to become the second governor of Massachusetts under the new charter, and associated with him were Lord Somers, the Lord Chancellor; the Earl of Orford, First Lord of the Admiralty; the Earl of Romney and the Duke of Shrewsbury, Secretaries of State; Robert Livingston, Esquire, of New York; and William Kidd. By the terms of their agreement Livingston and Kidd were to pay one fifth of the cost of fitting and sending out the *Adventure Galley*, 287 tons, thirty-four guns, while the balance of the cost was to be divided among the other members. Kidd was to command actual operations, and of the "goods, Merchandizes, Treasure and other Things . . . taken from the said Pirates" one fourth was to go to the crew, while the balance was to be divided in five equal shares to be distributed amongst the company.

Kidd found difficulty raising a crew in England, and accordingly he sailed in April 1696 for New York, where he anticipated the matter would be simpler. In his pocket he carried the King's commission to apprehend Thomas Tew, of Rhode Island,

Thomas Wake and William Maze of New York, John Ireland, and "all other Pirates, Free-booters, and Sea Rovers, of whatever Nature soever . . . upon the Coasts of America or in any other Seas or Parts." He also held the King's commission to prey upon the French as a privateer. En route to New York he captured a French ship, which he brought in, and which undoubtedly served as a valuable advertisement for his project, for in September he sailed from that port with a crew of 154 men—fifty-four more than his contract required—and promptly headed for Madagascar, then the favorite rendezvous of the most formidable pirates.

It was three years before he returned.

In the meantime a number of things had happened. One, the Earl of Bellomont had come to occupy his new jurisdiction. Another, Kidd appeared to have turned pirate on his own account.

Whether or not this was his intention when he sailed, or even whether it was his intention at all in doing what he did, remains a mystery to this day. At any rate some facts are clear, and chief among these is that, not long after his arrival at Madagascar, Kidd attacked and captured the *Quedah Merchant*, and another vessel belonging to the Great Mogul, both heavily burdened with booty.

Now the Indian trade was the monopoly of the mighty East India Company, a combine that did not scruple about seizing the vessels of independent traders but which protested vigorously against any interference in its own enterprise. It was to the interest of the East India Company to remain on good terms with the Great Mogul, and accordingly it snatched up the cudgel in his behalf and complained loudly that Kidd was a pirate preying upon the vessels of a friendly nation. As a result, when, in December 1698, the Crown extended a general pardon to all pirates who would surrender themselves, William Kidd and Long Ben Avery, whose operations out of Madagascar had also become a stench in the nostrils of the East India Company, alone were excepted from the Act of Grace.

The sequel to all this is even more confused. In April 1699 Kidd arrived in the West Indies in the *Quedah Merchant* and there for the first time learned of his proscription. Leaving the *Merchant* secure with most of her booty in a lagoon on the island of Saona, southeast of Haiti, Kidd embarked with forty of his men in the sloop *Antonio* and sailed northward for New York. Arriving in those parts, he did not put into the Hudson, but instead went in to Oyster Bay, and there took on board one Joseph Emmot, a New York lawyer who specialized in Admiralty cases. From Oyster Bay he ran across to Rhode Island, and from there sent Emmot as a messenger to Bellomont, seeking a safe passage to Boston.

The governor appeared uncertain as to what he should do. He sent oral word to Kidd that he might safely enter the port, but Kidd and his crew, which by now was reduced to sixteen, would have none of this, and Emmot was sent back again to demand written permission. This was presently forthcoming in rather veiled fashion, the governor writing:

> I assure you on my Word and Honour I will perform nicely what I have promised though this I declare beforehand that whatever goods and treasure you may bring thither, I will not meddle with the least bit of them; but they shall be left with such persons as the Council shall advise until I receive orders from England how they shall be disposed of.

In the meantime Kidd had put across the Sound once more and placed his treasure in the hands of John Gardiner, owner of Gardiner's Island, for safe keeping.

Taking the governor's promise at its face value, Kidd and his companions then proceeded to Boston. When he arrived the governor was ill with the gout and could not see him, but on

July 3 Bellomont met with the council and Kidd was summoned for questioning.

He behaved himself here with the utmost dignity and begged permission to make a detailed report of his activities in writing. It was on this occasion that he declared that the *Quedah Merchant* and the other vessel sailing for the Great Mogul were sailing under passes issued by the French East India Company, and that this automatically made them enemy vessels and fair prey under his commission. Lawyer Emmot bore him out in his statement that he had already forwarded the captured passes as evidence to the governor. Emmot should have known, for it was he who carried them.

Kidd was given a day in which to write his report, but it may be that he was not facile with the pen as was the governor, for when he was summoned the next morning and questioned further he begged for more time. It was granted, and finally on the 6th he was again summoned, and returned word that he would have his report finished by afternoon.

Apparently he was suspected of stalling, for some discussion ensued, and it was at this point that the governor revealed to the council that he had orders to arrest Kidd as a pirate.

From that point there could be no further question. Warrants were immediately sworn and constables sent in search of Kidd. They came upon him near the governor's house, and when they went to seize him he ran, eluding them, into the house and went straight, with the constables at his heels, to the governor's study. There can be no question but that he meant to demand the governor's protection in accord with his "Word and Honour." But he soon discovered what they were worth, for he was seized and thrown into prison.

Kidd lay in jail in Boston for six months, until H.M.S. *Advice* arrived with orders to convey him to England for trial. The balance of the story is well known. Captain Kidd was tried, sentenced, and hung in chains in London. To the end he protested his innocence, and had he been able to produce the French passes taken from the Mogul's ships he might well have been able to prove it. As it was, the documents were never presented. What became of them is a mystery. Whether, as some say, Lord Bellomont, for his own reasons, did not forward them to England with the rest of the evidence, or whether, at the instance of the East India Company, they were suppressed by the Lords of Trade, it is impossible to say. One thing is certain, however: they did not appear at the trial of William Kidd for piracy and murder on the high seas.

So much for the individual sea marauders who either plundered Boston shipping or lodged in Boston's new stone jail. There were others, of course, for it was a time when lawlessness on the seas flourished, and scarcely a stranger stopped at an inn at night along the coast but he was viewed with suspicion until he had given good account of himself. The opening chapters of Stevenson's *Treasure Island* were in no way exaggerated in that respect and might as easily have applied to New England.

There is not space here to look into the career of every pirate that ever entered Boston Port or plagued her ships. But we may spare a moment for a glance at a school for pirates that produced an astounding number of graduates.

It was not extraordinary, considering the times, that a port with such a wealth of shipping as Boston should feel the pinch of piracy. The more wealth flowed in and out of a locality, the more that locality became a magnet to those who lived on plunder, and its ships became fair game in all parts of the world. As ants cluster about the honey pot, so did pirates gather about Boston.

We have already seen that the idleness of peace and the reduction of the Navy, in the time of James, threw many seamen on the pad, the highway, and the account. But war, too, proved a pirate breeder. The Navy itself turned out many a sea rover, and this was scarcely to be wondered at. It was a harsh life, little better than slavery, on most ships. It was underpaid and ill-fed, and many times a man would not even be aboard voluntarily, but was rather the victim of a press gang sent out to pick up likely-looking hands by force when the ship chanced to find itself short and in port. To be sure, the crews of naval vessels received a share of such prizes as they made. But such shares were infinitesimal when compared with those of a privateersman, and they shrank to nothing by comparison with the ill-got, easy gains of the freebooter.

No, navy men in those days had little incentive to stay honest, and many of them yielded to temptation. But the most prolific incubator of pirates was not the Navy, but the privateers, as may, perhaps, already have been noticed.

Privateers were a sort of legalized pirate. They were privately armed vessels, sent out to plunder the shipping of an enemy nation, under a commission issued by their own local authorities, for the profit of the owners. In later years all privateers were lumped under one head, but in the beginning there were two varieties: those with letters of marque, and privateers proper. A merchant vessel with a letter of marque was primarily engaged in trade, but was armed for its own defense and commissioned to take such enemy vessels as it might encounter in the course of its voyage. Such a commission was that carried by the mighty *Seafort*, which was wrecked on the Spanish coast, near Cadiz, in 1644. A privateer, on the other hand, was no more, no less than a privately armed vessel of war. She carried no cargo, and she did no trading. She was fitted out and heavily armed for the express purpose of playing hob with the enemy's shipping, and this was indicated in her commission. Such a vessel was Kidd's *Adventure Galley* and Quelch's *Charles*, and the end to which they came was not unusual.

There were profits to be made in privateering—vast profits—and it is hardly to be wondered at that many a pursy merchant turned from honest trading and equipped his ships for this legalized form of plunder, or that many an honest seaman signed articles on board for the sake of his share of the prize money.

The difficulty with the business, however, was that the habit, once taken, was difficult to break. When peace came it was hard for seamen and skippers to return to the prosaic world of trade. Having found the ease with which riches might be taken, it was hard to be satisfied with the lesser, slower profits of honesty. By the same token, even while war continued, when the enemy's ships grew wary and were hard to catch, it was simpler and often more profitable to fall upon the unsuspecting vessels of friendly nations. The temptation was not always resisted, as witness the career of John Quelch!

Thomas Tew, of Newport, was another example of a privateer who turned pirate. He went to Bermuda and was there commissioned commander of the privateer sloop *Amity*. But scarcely was he out of sight of land before he announced to his crew his intention of turning pirate, and, as the crew were not the least reluctant to follow where he led, set his course around the Cape of Good Hope and bore up into the Red Sea, where he encountered immediate good fortune.

Captain Thomas Cromwell of Boston obtained a commission as a privateer in 1645 from the Earl of Warwick, Lord Admiral of the Long Parliament. He sailed in the ship *Separation* for the West Indies, and after taking several rich prizes there turned northward, toward Massachusetts Bay. On his arrival there strong northwest winds forced him to take refuge in Plymouth Harbor, where he lay for some two weeks. Bradford, in his *History of Plymouth Plantation*, wrote of his visit that his crew "did so distemper themselves with drinke as they became like madd-men; . . . they spente and scattered a great deale of money among the people, and yet more sine than money." By all accounts his crew was about ready to turn pirate, if, indeed, they had not already done so. But Cromwell was one of the rare wise skippers. From Plymouth he sailed for Boston, where he disposed of his vessel and retired on shore—not neglecting, in doing so, to pay his respects to the governor by presenting him with a sedan which had been sent as a present by the viceroy of Mexico to his sister and had fallen into Cromwell's hands by capture.

Edward Hull was another Boston privateer with a rather shady career. He was the brother of John Hull, the mintmaster, and the vessel, *Swallow Frigott*, in which he sailed was owned by his father and his brother. His commission also derived from the Long Parliament, and he made a number of rich prizes before he overstepped the line. This occurred in Rhode Island waters, when he sent some of his men on shore to raid the house and store of Captain Kempo Sebada of trading stock to the value of about one hundred pounds. No doubt he realized that retribution, if it could catch up with him, would be swift, for he promptly thereafter sold his vessel and went away to England. It is interesting to note that, in the suit which Sebada afterwards brought against the Hulls of Boston, Edward Hull is named pirate.

These accounts of privateers who gave way to temptation, however, are not meant to imply that there were no honest privateers. Unquestionably there were many. Captain Thomas Hawkins, who commanded the *Seafort*, had no chance to prove his honesty, for he was wrecked before he could get into action. But there is no reason to doubt his good intention, even though he was the grandfather of that Thomas Hawkins who in later years turned pirate in Boston.

In the same year that it issued a commission to Hawkins the

General Court commissioned Captain Thomas Bredcake, of Boston, for twelve months, to take Turkish pirates—meaning Barbary corsairs—who were thick about the coasts of Spain and the Canaries.

In 1695 Captain Robert Glover ranged the eastern coast in a privateer sloop, the *Dragon*, and took several rich prizes from the French. In the mouth of the St. Lawrence he took a French ship, the *Saint Joseph*, with a cargo valued at 15,000 pounds. Captain Cyprian Southack cruised against the French out of Boston in 1691, and with him also cruised Captain Leonard Walkington and Captain William Kidd. Southack sailed again in 1702, in the *Province*, and in the same year Captain Peter Lawrence went out in the sloop *Charles* and met with success.

All through, the eighteenth-century privateering was a profitable game, for there was scarcely a year but there was war somewhere. Of all the privateers that sailed out of Boston during the first half of the century, however, the most famous was the ship *Bethel*.

Strictly speaking, the *Bethel* was not a privateer, but a letter-of-marque ship, sailing between Boston and an unnamed European port. She belonged to the Quincy family, was armed with fourteen guns, and carried a crew of only thirty-eight men. This fact, however, did not daunt her master, Captain Isaac Freeman, when off the Azores he fell in with a large Spanish ship carrying twenty-four guns. With typical Yankee ingenuity Freeman promptly had his carpenter rig six more dummy guns of wood and ordered the men to stuff their spare clothing and scatter the resulting dummies about so that their true strength might not be seen. He then waited until dark, hoisted lanterns all about his ship, and closed with the enemy. He wrote in a letter to his owners describing the affair—

After a serenade of French horns and trumpets . . . we demanded from whence she came and whither bound. When—after a few equivocations—she announced she was from Havana for Cadiz—we gave them a hearty cheer, and ordered . . . her Captain on board immediately. He begged we would tarry till morning . . . but we threatening him with a broadside which he much feared, he complied. By daylight we had the last of the prisoners secured, (there were 110 of them) who were ready to hang themselves on sight of our six wooden guns, and scarce men enough to hoist topsails.

The prize, as it turned out, was valued at near one hundred thousand pounds sterling, and this no doubt had much to do with the *Bethel's* fame!

CHAPTER VII

Codfish Aristocracy

IN THE first fifty or sixty years of its existence Boston grew from a struggling settlement to a thriving town. It had survived at least two great fires, in 1676 and 1682, and, what was more difficult to overcome, considerable opposition from home. It had outlived the Indian wars and come face to face with the French menace. The witchcraft superstition, but for one last dying fling, had run its course, and pestilence had several times been cheated of a clean sweep. To be sure, its *raison d'être* during this period, or for most of it, at least, was chiefly religious, but now a change began gradually to creep in. Religion receded reluctantly into the background, and trade began, slowly at first and then more rapidly, to edge forward.

Boston, by 1690, was scarcely more than a village in present-day terms, boasting no more than five thousand inhabitants—figures previously given have referred to the entire colony of Massachusetts Bay—and perhaps two thousand houses. Yet it was one of the four great colonial centers, and it now began its rapid rise to first place among them all.

Descriptions for a given year are difficult to find and are inclined to the particular writer's point of view—whether biased or otherwise. Nevertheless some notion of the town in each period may be gained from each of them. Jasper Dankers, writing in 1680, said:

The city is quite large, constituting about twelve companies. It has three churches, or meeting-houses, as they call them. All the houses are made of thin, small cedar shingles nailed against frames, and then filled in with brick and other stuff; and so are their churches. For this reason these towns are so liable to fires,—as have already happened several times; and the wonder to me is that the whole city has not been burnt down, so light and dry are the materials. There is a large dock in front of it, constructed of wooden piers, where the large ships go to be careened and rigged; the smaller vessels all come up to the city. . . . Upon the point of the bay on the left hand there is a block house, along which a piece of water runs, called the Milk Ditch.

In 1686 John Dunton merely contented himself with reiterating the descriptions already given by Johnson and Wood, and quoted elsewhere. Edward Ward, in 1699, was obviously disgruntled, yet his account is amusing:

The houses in some parts joyn, as in London, the Buildings, like their women being Neat and Handsome; and their Streets, like the Hearts of the Male Inhabitants, are paved with Pebble. In the Chief or high Street there are stately Edifices, some of which have cost the owners two or three Thousand Pounds the raising; which I think plainly proves Two old Adages true,—viz., That a Fool and his Money is soon Parted, and Set a Beggar on Horseback he'll Ride to the Devil,—for the Fathers of these men were Tinkers and Peddlers. To the Glory of Religion and the Credit of the Town there are four Churches, built with Clapboards and Shingles after the Fashion of our Meeting-houses, which are supply'd by four Ministers, to whom some very justly have apply'd these Epithets,—one a Scholar, the Second a Gentleman, the Third a Dunce, and the Fourth a Clown. . . . Every Stranger is invariably forc'd to take this Notice, That in Boston there are more Religious zealots than Honest men, more Parsons than Churches, and more Churches than Parishes; for the Town, unlike the People, is subject to no Division. The Inhabitants seem very Religious, showing many outward and visible Signs of an inward and Spiritual Grace; but tho' they wear in their Faces the Innocence of Doves, you will find them in their Dealings as Subtile as Serpents. Interest is Faith, Money their God, and Large Possessions the only Heaven they covet.

Poor Ward! One wonders what happened to him in Boston to make him so bitter. Both he and history are silent about that.

Some notion of Boston's rate of growth during this period is to be gained from Captain Nathaniel Uring's description, penned in 1721:

The town is near two miles in length, and in some places three quarters of a mile broad, in which are reckoned 4000 houses; most of them are built with brick [here was another sign of progress] and have about 18000 inhabitants. The streets are broad and regular; some of their richest merchants have very stately, well built, convenient houses. The ground on which the town stands is moderately high, and very good water is found all over it; it is much the largest of any in America under the British Government. They have built several wharfs, which jut out into the harbour, for the conveniency of shipping, one of which goes by the name of the Long Wharf, and may well be called so, it running about 800 feet into the harbour, where large ships with great ease may both lade and unlade; on one side of which are warehouses almost the whole length of the wharf, where the Merchants store their goods which they unlade, and those they ship off, and where more than 50 sail of vessels may lade or unlade at the same time with great conveniency; and the town altogether is most excellently situated for trade and navigation. It is very populous and has in it 8 or 9 large meeting-houses, and a French Church, and but one English [the captain here means Anglican, or Church of England] and that built of wood; but I am informed since I was in that country they have another building with brick.

Captain Uring, no doubt, allowed his enthusiasm to run away with him somewhat, for in the next year John Bonner published the earliest engraved plan of the town. This notes forty-two streets, thirty-six lanes, and twenty-two alleys; and though these may have been wide for the times, even a Londoner of the day could scarcely have thought them regular. In addition Bonner notes on his margin, "Houses, near 3000; 1000 brick, rest Timber. Near 12,000 people." Meetinghouses and other public buildings are noted, and in the last edition, published in 1769, there is also a list of the nine great fires which swept the town between 1631 and 1760, as well as a list of the seven epidemics of smallpox suffered between 1640 and 1730. It is interesting also to note, on the edition of 1722, that there are thirty-eight named wharves jutting from the south, east, and north sides of the peninsula, and as many more unnamed. In addition there are five wharves and stillhouses combined on the southeast side, facing Dorchester, and one on the north facing Charlestown. There are also two stillhouses and a sugarhouse on the Mill Pond, about where the North Station stands today—"sugarhouse" in this case evidently meaning a refinery. Thirteen shipyards, fringing the north and east shores, give some hint of the extent of Boston's shipbuilding activity at this time, and while no gallows is shown near Charlestown Ferry, there is one marked as being set up on Roxbury Neck. Perhaps this is where they hung highwaymen.

Probably the most outstanding development upon the waterfront at this time, if not, indeed, the most outstanding in the city, was the Long Wharf, which so excited Captain Uring. Certainly it was the most eye-filling sight to a newly arrived traveler, for prints of Boston made just before and after the Revolution show it thrusting out into the harbor and practically overshadowing the town behind. This was built by Oliver Noyes and several associates in 1710, when the town granted them leave to "build a wharf with sufficient common sewer from Andrew Faneuil's corner to low water mark, to be of the width of King Street." There was to be a public thoroughfare thirty feet wide along one side of it, and a space sixteen feet wide in the middle for the convenience of ships loading and unloading. In effect it was simply a continuation of King Street, extending it out into the harbor, for one side of it quickly became lined with shops, counting rooms, and warehouses, the passageway teemed with traffic, and the great ships shadowed the whole with their outstretched yards. Twenty years after Captain Uring described it the wharf was doubled in length, and later it was extended still further, for by the time of the Revolution it was described as "a noble pier 1800 or 2000 feet long."

Views of Boston from the harbor, made before the Revolution, show as the most prominent landmarks, aside from the steeples of the meetinghouses, which were by then very numerous, and the eye-filling Long Wharf, several other wharves which may be identified as Scarlett's, Clarke's, Rowe's, and Apthorp's on Bonner's map. Also prominent in the waterfront pictures were the North and South Batteries, standing respectively where Atlantic Avenue turns into Commercial Street today, and just under Fort Hill Square.

Not so prominent in the old views, but nonetheless there, were the shipyards. The boom in Boston shipbuilding during the first half of the eighteenth century kept pace with the boom in trade. From the turn of the century to 1740 there was a terrific increase in the activity of the shipyards, but following that, owing to restrictions in trade imposed by the home government, there was a sharp decline. In 1760 the business experienced a revival, which continued to mount until by the end of the century it had reached new heights of prosperity. In the year 1710 fifty-six vessels were built in the province, having a total tonnage of 3,520. Of this number, twenty-one, with a tonnage of 1,530, were built and launched in Boston, and it is probable that the bulk of the remainder were fitted there. By 1723 the province rate had jumped to a total of 700 vessels. In 1738 it was reported that forty-one ships were built in Boston with a total tonnage of 6,324, and in 1741 John Oldmixon reported that there were, on Boston ways, forty vessels with an aggregate tonnage of 7,000.

In 1724 Lieutenant Governor John Wentworth, of New Hampshire—not the John Wentworth who was governor of the province at the outbreak of the Revolution, but his grandfather—reported querulously to the Lords of Trade in London that he had it on good authority that his neighbors to the south were building a 1,000-ton ship, truly a leviathan in those days, to engage in the trade in contraband lumber with Spain and Portugal. The complaint is curious when one remembers that John's son Benning, who was later to become governor in his own right, all but lost his shirt in that very trade, and by his complaints to London of the dirty dealing of the Dons became one of the instigators of the War of Jenkins' Ear. However, it appears that the lieutenant governor was either misinformed or was starting at shadows, for the largest ship launched in Massachusetts during this period was a 500-tonner, built at Clark's yard in Boston in 1732.

Like everything in which the Bostonians prospered, this boom in shipbuilding elicited cries of rage and anguish in Britain. In 1724–25 London shipwrights protested that they were being systematically ruined by the competition from Massachusetts and demanded that limits be placed upon the size of vessels built in the colonies. They pointed out that ships could be built in Boston for eight pounds a ton, whereas in England the cost of building ran between fifteen and sixteen pounds. The difference had enabled Boston builders to build, not only for New England, but also for export, and many a fine ship had sailed out of the harbor with instructions to her master to dispose of both ship and cargo as conveniently as possible abroad. It was a long time, however, before the Lords of Trade got around to doing anything about it, and by that time other causes had brought about a natural decline in the building rate, so that their measures were largely nullified. In the meantime Boston shipbuilders merrily followed their own bent and flooded the sea with sails.

With such increases in shipbuilding and trade, it is scarcely strange that Boston, soon after the beginning of the century, should become more than ever aware of the hazards of the sea. Nor was it necessary to voyage half around the world to encounter them. Boston's own dooryard had as dangerous waters as any in the world. It was a "stern and rockbound coast" indeed. From Cape Ann to Brant Rock the sea soughed and gurgled in the rocky crevices and caverns of the shore, even in fine weather. In stormy times it bellowed with the voice of wrath. At low tide jagged upcroppings of rock dried and bristled all along the coast offshore. When the tide was high they became vicious traps for the unwary or storm-tossed mariner. When the wind howled out of the north and east; when the snow swirled thick; when the fog lay dank upon the bosom of the sea—God help the poor sailor who wasn't absolutely dead certain of his bearings. In times like these the entrance to Boston Harbor was the worst of all, for then its guardian bank of islets and reefs foamed and bristled like the teeth of a ravening shark.

Many a storm-tossed seaman went down to a cold, wet end fairly within sight of home. In 1702 the brigantine *Mary*, with logwood from Campeachy, went ashore and broke up on the rocks off Marblehead. The next year the *John of Exon*, carrying wine and salt from Lisbon and Fayal, drove on the fangs of George's Island, at the very entrance to Boston Harbor. In 1715 the *Hazard*, one of His Majesty's sloops, went on the rocks off Cohasset. There were others, of course, and in increasing numbers as Boston's trade increased. But in 1713 Boston's merchants decided that something must be done about it. In that year they suggested to the General Court that it might be a good idea to build a "light Hous and lanthorn" at the harbor mouth.

The building of a lighthouse in those days was a considerable undertaking. This was especially true of that type of structure known as the "wave-swept light"—which is to say, those built on rocks or shoals exposed to the action of the sea. To be sure, there had been beacon towers as far back as 660 B.C., but most of these were at some point ashore, marking the coast, but not within reach of the water. Of the type marking the more dangerous shoals and rocks and reefs on which shipping might drive offshore, there were very few, even in Europe. The New World had none.

Hence, it was a matter for serious consideration, this proposal of the merchants. The General Court did not hurry themselves over it, and it was not until 1715 that the body passed "An Act for Building and Maintaining a Light-house upon the Great Brewster (called Beacon Island), at the extreme of the Harbour of Boston." Apparently the colony fathers felt that some explanation of this evident extravagance was called for, for they further declared that the want of such a light "hath been a great discouragement to Navigation, by the loss of the lives and estates of several of His Majesty's subjects." The light was to be built upon the southernmost part of Great Brewster Island, and was "to be kept lighted from sun-setting to sun-rising." Still further, all vessels entering the port, except coasters, were thereafter to pay duty of a penny a ton towards its maintenance.

The building was completed and put into operation in September 1716, but though it survived the great storm of that year, in which Captain Bellamy's great ship, the *Whidaw*, was wrecked on Cape Cod, its first few years were not auspicious. Captain George Worthylake was the first tender. One evening in November 1718, when he was coming up the harbor in his skiff with his wife and daughter, a sudden gale of wind arose and overset them near Noddle's Island and the entire family was drowned. Worthylake's mishap inspired thirteen-year-old Ben Franklin's first literary effort, "The Lighthouse Tragedy"—a doggerel ditty "in the Grub Street Ballad style," which he persuaded his brother to print for him while he hawked it about the streets.

Codfish Aristocracy

Captain Saunders, Worthylake's successor, met with an equally grim fate, being drowned before he could even take over his new duties. With such a start it might be imagined that it would be difficult to find a third incumbent, and a few years earlier it might have been so. By this time, however, the men of Boston were become toughened. They feared not the devil nor all his henchmen. Captain John Hayes came forward and accepted the post, which he held for several years, guiding ships in and out of the harbor. Ultimately he retired safe ashore, and his place was taken by Captain Ball.

Boston Light was a mark of progress surely. But it was more than that. It was an indication of the kind of men Bostonians were now becoming, as well.

It is a mistake—a mistake frequently made—to assume that Bostonians of the eighteenth century represented the purest of English stock. This was most emphatically not true. At the risk of shattering an illusion fondly held by many a Boston bluestocking, one might venture to say that the Bostonian of the middle eighteenth century was likely to be of as mixed racial stock as the Bostonian of today. Religious rather than racial prejudices held the center of the stage. And even before the mass migrations of the late seventeenth and early eighteenth centuries, individuals of foreign extraction had come to settle about the shores of Massachusetts Bay. Some were Dutch. Some were Portuguese. Quite a number were French. So long as they were not Papist, so long as they were willing to accept the doctrines and the teachings of the Church, little more was asked of them, and they were regarded with only slight suspicion.

To be sure, the colony had had a sound, solid English Puritan foundation, but as trade flourished and external interests grew, this original stock was leavened with additions from outside. This is not to say that the resulting strain was any less sound or solid than the original, but it was certainly broader. Some strains apparently were not acceptable. Spaniards, for instance, evidently were always viewed as Papists, as were the Irish in general. Scotsmen were accepted. But if they had come through the North of Ireland by way of Londonderry, they were open to suspicion, as witness the group which came in 1719 and, finding themselves looked upon as Irish in the Bay Colony— and hence unable to obtain land—moved to New Hampshire, where they settled the town of Londonderry, on the Merrimac—later to become Manchester—and produced such figures as John Stark, Robert Rogers, and Daniel Webster.

A good number of Germans apparently came in the first part of the eighteenth century, as did a few Dutch, though these last were not popular—elephant-memoried Bostonians not having forgotten the competition the burghers of New Amsterdam had given them so many years before. There were a number of Welshmen, too, who came. But far and away the greatest influx was that of the French Huguenots.

Toward the end of the seventeenth century, Louis XIV, King of France, decided to rid his dominions of non-Catholics. From the year 1598 Protestants in France had been protected and allowed certain civil rights, under Henry IV's Edict of Nantes. On October 17, 1685, however, Louis XIV repealed the edict and began that purge of Protestants in France which has not been without its modern European counterpart.

It has been said that, by the repeal of the Edict of Nantes, France opened her own veins and permitted much of her best blood to flow from her. The simile is apt, and the modern counterpart is clearly visible today. Just as Hitler, in modern times, attempted the persecution of any individual even remotely suspected of Semitic ancestry who might fall beneath his power, so did Louis prey upon anyone who was even vaguely thought to entertain heretic notions. The result was a great emigration which numbered among its participants many of the foremost mercantile families of France.

But France's loss was Boston's gain, for then, as more recently, a great many of the refugees sought shelter in the New World. Charleston received her share, as did Philadelphia and New York. But the great bulk of them came to Boston, were absorbed, and gave to the city such names as Bowdoin, Blanchard, Faneuil, Oliver, Sigourney, Johonnot, not to mention Revere.

Whether the parallel between the ancient and the modern movement ends at that point is a matter for interesting speculation. The records do not tell us. Still we might be pardoned for wondering if those old Frenchmen and Dutchmen and Scotsmen and Irishmen who brought so much to Boston in those early days were looked upon with the same suspicion and mistrust and resentment with which so many German and Austrian and Jewish refugees have lately been received.

It would be a mistake, however, to assume that these newcomers were all refugees—immigrants—in the somewhat derogatory sense which those words have presently come to assume. That is to say, they were not necessarily poverty-stricken or helpless or stupid. We may trust the town fathers to see that they were not. Naturally there were laws which governed the matter of who might land and who might not. And there was a property clause in these that required that a prospective settler should prove that he was not likely to become a public charge.

As a matter of fact a good many of the newcomers were wealthy merchants, who arrived in their own ships, bringing their own silver and carrying their own families, prepared to set up shop in the city of their choice and carry on their business and their life in considerable style. These men were shrewd. They picked Boston, not for its climate or its hospitality, but rather for its commercial possibilities, and they prospered ex-

ceedingly. Their prosperity created a sort of a colon
mercial round robin. As Boston's trade grew, more n
from all parts of the world were attracted to it. An
merchants were attracted to it, so Boston's trade and
creased. The result was an ever expanding mushroom
which continued its upward progress until British jealousy began to focus upon the port and Philadelphia snatched the initiative. This was toward the middle of the eighteenth century.

That, however, was only the commercial, the trade, result.
The social effect was equally profound. The influx of new blood
brought a leavening, a softening—not of the brain, but of the
manner—to the old stock. Intermarriage and intermingling made
for broader and more gracious ways, and the Winthrop and the
Bradstreet and the Mather of the mid-eighteenth century was a
very different fellow from his great-great-great-grandfather.

By the middle of the eighteenth century travelers were re-
marking upon the comfort of Boston inns—the Bull, the Bunch
of Grapes, the Green Dragon, the O. Cromwell's Head. They
were gasping with admiration at the magnificence of such public structures as the Long Wharf, Faneuil Hall, the old State
House—the Town House then—King's Chapel, and the various
churches. A never ending source of wonder seemed to be the
fact that houses could be both wooden and gracious! They remarked upon the dress and manners of Bostonians, saying that
in point of fashion one might as easily imagine himself to be
in London as in the provinces when one walked the streets of
Boston. Young bloods carried swords and fought duels on the
Common and had their own version of the Hell-Fire Club, no
less raucous or in the spirit of the age than their Old World
models. Cards—oh, horrors!—were openly advertised in
the newspapers of the day and were used in every salon. And
there was even talk of a theater. Tea was a favorite drink
among the ladies, who dressed in the height of London fashion,

provided, of course, at a later date, that no duty had been paid upon it—and even then one suspects a black market. Among the gentlemen rum, sack, and Canary were the favorites, and oranges, lemons, and limes from the West Indies were much in demand for the fragrant punches which were so popular everywhere. Manners were elaborate in public and somewhat revolting in private, if all accounts be true. It was a curious age. An age tinged with all the harshness and hardness and cruelty of the Middle Ages, yet touched with the namby-pambyism of the nineteenth century, and yet, at the same time, an age in which men thought more for themselves and came to more far-reaching conclusions than many an era before or since.

Trade was responsible for most of this, of course, certainly for much of it. And trade had its minor ramifications and branches. The slave trade was one of these. The Spanish trade was another. The West Indian and South American trades and the trade to the Mediterranean—these were all a part of it. Even privateering was a form of trade; a form in which the most respected merchants and the best families took a hand. But the broad base and firm foundation upon which all of this was built was fish. Directly or indirectly fish was primarily responsible for the prosperity of Boston and Bostonians. Apthorp and Amory, Boylston, Faneuil, Adams, Clark, Rowe, Quincy, Oxnard, Boutineau, Hull, Wendell, Hancock and Hewes, though their greatest concentration was in other lines, would never have gone as far as they did but for the lowly cod. 'Twas said of Thomas Boylston that he was the richest man in Massachusetts, and that his estate amounted to something over £80,-000. Charles Apthorp was not far behind him with an estate of £50,000. Thomas Amory, who distilled his own rum and built his own ships, amassed a fortune of £20,000, not counting a brewery, a wharf, a large home, and considerable holdings of land in the Carolinas and the Azores. As for the Hancocks, before anyone could begin to count their wealth they were accused of being smugglers. And possibly they were!

Smuggler or financier, however, trader or shipbuilder or rum distiller or landowner, it was fish that lay behind them all. Small wonder, then, that when prosperous Bostonians journeyed to London, English merchants turned jaundiced eyes upon them and jealously sneered, "Codfish Aristocrats!"

It would appear, judging from the struggle which presently was to come, that London could have used a few such aristocrats herself at that time.

CHAPTER VIII

An Obstacle Is Removed

WHILE the ethnic and religious forces which we have watched were combining to create in New England a new race of men—Yankees, as opposed to mere English colonials—certain economic factors were likewise combining with various spacious notions of the rights and dignity of man, apparently inherent in the air of the Western Continent, to bring forth a new nation. Boston, as the metropolis of the region, was the center and fountainhead from which it was to spring. By the same token it was likewise the focal point upon which the mother country centered her wrath when the colonists began to express their new convictions in somewhat radical ways.

That the Revolution came at all is not nearly so much to be wondered at as is the fact that it did not come sooner. From the very beginning England had taken a proprietary and jealous attitude toward colonial trade. It was the attitude of the dog in the manger. Unable to compete in the open market with colonial shipping, the Lords of Trade, at the instigation of British merchants and shipowners, leaned over backwards to reduce to a minimum the colonies' chances of prosperity. It is scarcely to be wondered at that this was resented in the colonies themselves. When we consider the principles of freedom—religious and economic—which had prompted the first settlers to migrate to these shores and upon which the entire existence of the colony was based—when we consider the kind of man it required to pick up from the comparative comfort and anciently established order of things at home and go out into the New World to make his way afresh—when we consider the spirit which set these men to building their own ships and sending out their own sea-borne trade, finding their own sources of profit and revenue in every corner of the world and building up a commerce which in vigor and pride and returns was second to none—it must be obvious that the ultimate result of British interference was inevitable.

The Navigation Act of 1650 was the first of a long series of attempts on the part of England to meddle with the commerce of the colonies. The whole series of Acts of Trade and Navigation, indeed, the Staples Act of 1663—which required that practically all articles of European manufacture must pass through Britain en route to the colonies—the fumblings of the Lords of Trade and Plantations, the establishment of royal customs and the appointment of Randolph as collector, the Molasses Act of 1733; all of these were prime examples of the British tendency toward interference. They were blows of the British flint of stubbornness upon the colonial steel of determination, and they struck out sparks that fell upon the dry tinder of mutual resentment. Any one of them might well have been the one to blaze into the flame of rebellion. That none of them did so prior to the latter half of the eighteenth century may be attributed to the dampening influence of the French presence on the northern and western frontier. England, almost constantly at war with France during that period, had sore need of colonial help in coping with her enemy. The colonies, only too well aware of the French threat, for their part felt the need of British assistance to hold the French in check. In consequence, so long as the threat remained, neither side was quite willing to goad the other beyond the limits of endurance. For her part England forbore to enforce too strictly all the terms and measures of her restrictive acts, while the colonists on the other hand made a mild show of obedience to the mother country's wishes.

Boston took her part in the French wars which marked the period. Though she was never the scene of action herself, she was almost inevitably the fitting-out point from which the expeditions against the French were launched; the spot to which news of victory or disaster was first dispatched and made public for later dissemination among the colonies, up and down the seaboard or in the interior.

From the very outset the French and British colonists eyed one another with mistrust. In the earliest years of the colony French and English pinnaces and shallops fell upon one another at intervals up and down the coast of Maine and off Nova Scotia. And when, in 1632, Dixey Bull eluded the expeditions sent out in pursuit of him, it was said that he had "gone over to the enemy"—by which was meant that he had joined the French. Clashes with the French in the disputed eastern territories were inevitable and constant in the first seventy years of the colony's existence. Numerous expeditions went out from Boston against the French and their Indian allies, in Acadia, New Brunswick, and Maine. Port Royal and Pemaquid were almost constant objects of attack by one side or the other, and almost invariably the English expeditions had their starting point in Boston.

The French retaliated by loosing their Indian allies upon the frontiers. Boston never felt the brunt of these, for never, after the first five or ten years, were the redskins themselves a threat to the town. But it was from Boston that vengeance was invariably launched. And upon several occasions it seemed likely that the French were about to retaliate upon Boston themselves.

An expedition led by Sir William Phips against Port Royal in 1688 was an outstanding success and stirred proposals in Canada for a retaliatory movement against Boston. The French attack never got beyond the talking stage, but sufficient rumors of it reached Boston to arouse a flurry of excitement and to result in a general patching up of the batteries and repair of the works, looking toward the town's defense. Two years later Phips headed another expedition, this time against Quebec, and for a brief space Boston's streets echoed and re-echoed to the thump of the recruiting officer's drum and the tramp of marching feet, while the harbor was dotted with vessels gathered from all parts of the coast to take part in the affair. In all, thirty-two ships sailed in August from the anchorage at Nantasket, where the fleet had rendezvoused. Including sailors, the expedition numbered some twenty-four hundred and carried provisions for four months. But their ammunition was insufficient, and they carried no pilot for the St. Lawrence. After losing several of his vessels in the lower reaches of the river, Phips finally brought his fleet before Quebec and managed to fire a few guns against the cliffs. But accurate gunnery from the batteries above soon played hob with the ships, and in the end Phips was forced to withdraw without having accomplished anything.

In spite of this failure a second expedition against Quebec was undertaken in 1693. Oddly enough, the first Boston knew of the undertaking was the sudden appearance of a vast fleet, under Sir Francis Wheeler, who sailed into the harbor one fine bright summer day and nonchalantly announced the project.

The method of announcing the affair in itself would ordinarily have been enough to cause a fatal delay. But unfortunately Wheeler had been ordered first to reduce Martinique, in the West Indies, then to rendezvous at Boston for recruits and provisions, and thence proceed to Quebec. Before the reduction of Martinique could be effected a fatal epidemic swept the fleet, with the result that by the time Wheeler reached Boston three thousand of his original five thousand men had died. As a result this expedition went no further.

In 1696, and again in 1704, there was a flurry of panic in Boston town when it was feared that a French fleet was preparing to attack. But nothing came of it beyond a strengthening of the city's defenses and another angry outswarming of the English bees against the French of Acadia. In 1710 Port Royal was once and for all reduced, and the following year saw the arrival in Boston of the greatest fleet that the English had yet sent against the French in America.

Judge Samuel Sewall was presiding at some court proceedings on the 8th of June when, as he wrote later, "the drums put us to silence," and there "was an alarm at the Castle." The drums and the alarm, it turned out, heralded the approach of the van of Admiral Sir Hovenden Walker's mighty fleet, comprising fifteen ships of war and forty transports, bringing to Boston five regiments of Marlborough's veterans to take part in the reduction of the French citadel on the St. Lawrence. A few days later the rest of the fleet arrived in the midst of great excitement, for this was by far the greatest aggregation of vessels that Boston had yet seen. The troops were landed and paraded on Noddle's Island, and the sick were set ashore farther down the harbor, where a hospital was set up for their care. The soldiers and the sailors from the fleet flooded the town for almost two months and doubtless added much raucous revelry to the customary sounds of her streets.

Unfortunately, however, Boston was little better prepared for this expedition than she had been for that of 1693. There had been no warning, and it proved all but impossible to raise men and provisions for such a force upon such short notice. After a good deal of bickering and acrimony, in the course of which the admiral and his officers came to some rather uncomplimentary conclusions concerning the cupidity of Massachusetts men, and the Bostonians had a taste of official British arrogance, the fleet got under way toward the end of July.

Great things were expected of this expedition, but the story of what it accomplished is an old one. Arrived in the St. Lawrence in August, the ships encountered thick fogs. The admiral disregarded the advice of his pilots, with the result that eight of his transports piled up on the rocks in the gloom, with the loss of nearly nine hundred of his men. A council of war, called to contemplate the damage, flung up hands in despair and voted to return to England, which was forthwith done without striking a blow—not even stopping to reduce the French outposts on Newfoundland, as the admiral's orders required.

More successful was Boston's own project—the capture of Louisbourg, in 1745. There is some difference of opinion as to the originator of the scheme to reduce the huge French fortress at the tip of Cape Breton Island, but there can be no difference of opinion as to the moving spirit behind it. It was Governor Shirley of Massachusetts who took up the cudgels for the scheme and drove it through to completion in the face of considerable opposition.

No royal troops took part in this affair. Perhaps that was why it was so successful. It was a business engineered and executed from the start by provincials, and though it took some argument to set it on foot, once started it was carried out with remarkable singleness of purpose. Most of the troops gathered in Boston, save for a few who went directly from New Hampshire and Maine, and it was the first time that New Englanders had opportunity to see an army of their own encamped in anything like such force. That fact was of much greater significance than was generally realized at the time.

But Bostonians were not looking for significance that day. The troops poured into and through the town and out on board the ships, and on the 24th of March the fleet sailed—ninety trans-ports escorted by a handful of provincial cruisers—in a fine showing of wide white wings, from Nantasket Roads.

Wiseacres shook their heads and predicted disaster. It was impossible, they said, that raw militia, ill-armed and ill-equipped, could attack and whip the seasoned veterans of the King of France, safely sheltered behind the thick stone walls of the Gibraltar of America. Failure, they predicted, was inevi-table. But like all prophets they proved fallible. Admiral War-ren came from the south with his squadron to help blockade the French in their fort, and on the 16th of June the impregnable fortress fell.

The news reached Boston early in the morning of July 3, and at once such a clamor of bells and shouting arose as tumbled every citizen from his bed. Illuminations, bonfires, fireworks, and services of thanksgiving were promptly set on foot in a celebration such as the town had never before seen.

The fall of Louisbourg was a feather in New Englanders' caps and an accomplishment of which they could be justly proud. But its real result was something far more subtle and far-reaching than that. Like a youthful giant suddenly made to realize his own strength, New Englanders were all at once brought face to face with their own hidden and hitherto un-suspected power. It was a dark day for Britain, though nobody realized that yet, and even the British naval officers of Admiral Warren's squadron, in the warm flush of success, were saying kind and generous things about the valor and military abilities of the colonists.

But the wars were not yet over. A proposed gigantic expedi-tion for the following summer came to naught, owing mainly to the dilatory policy of the home government, and in the fall —this was 1746—came the dread word that a great French fleet and army were on their way to retake Louisbourg, reconquer

Acadia, burn Boston, and lay waste the coast. The report was half true. A great fleet had been dispatched under the Duc d'Anville, with rather vague orders to recapture Louisbourg if possible and do such damage upon the coast as might be. But the military end of the expedition was not nearly so great as report had it.

It was enough, however, to alarm the people of Boston. As soon as the report was received there was a great flurry of preparation. A call was sent out for militia to hasten to the defense of the city, and for days men poured in from the back country until close to eight thousand were encamped upon the Common and the surrounding hills. If this were not enough, the neighboring province of Connecticut promised to send an additional six thousand on the day the French appeared off Boston Harbor. Meantime the defenses of the batteries and Castle William in the harbor were strengthened. Additional batteries were erected on the islands at the harbor mouth, and some of the channels were closed off by booms.

Bostonians might have spared themselves the trouble. Misfortune dogged the footsteps of the French throughout the undertaking. D'Anville sailed from Brest in May, but immediately put in at La Rochelle for some reason. It was not until near the end of June that he set out from there and headed westward with what was estimated at nearly half of the entire French Fleet. Disaster almost immediately overtook him. The first part of the voyage was stormy, and a good deal of damage was wrought to sails, spars, and rigging. This was followed, off the Azores, by a period of flat calm, which was broken by a violent thunderstorm in which several ships were struck by lightning, several men killed, and at least one serious explosion occurred. Next pestilence broke out in the fleet and decimated both the crews and the regiments on board the transports. It was September before they approached Nova Scotia, and no sooner were they come there than a terrific storm arose and scattered the ships willy-nilly, sending some aground upon the treacherous sands of Cape Sable, breaking up others as they floated in the water, and driving still others as far south as the West Indies. With the shattered remnants D'Anville crept into Chibucto, where he looked upon the havoc with a heavy heart and died—some say of apoplexy. Others hint that he took poison. D'Estournel, his successor, threw himself upon his sword in his despair, and La Jonquiere, who succeeded to the command, decided that in their now straitened circumstances an attack upon Annapolis, in the Bay of Fundy, was as much as they could hope to accomplish.

Even this feeble effort, however, was destined to failure, for before the attack could be made still another tempest arose, scattering the fleet beyond all hope of recall, and there was nothing left for those that remained but to limp home as best they could to France, where they arrived well on in December.

So ended the last, and most serious, French threat to Boston.

But there were other repercussions yet to be felt from the French wars. In the very next year—1747—there was a dangerous clash between the Bostonians and Commodore Knowles over the matter of impressment. The commodore, who had been named governor of Cape Breton, had come to anchor in the harbor with his squadron. The British naval service in those days was harsh in the extreme, and it is scarcely to be wondered at that some men of the squadron, now come near shore for the first time since shipping on, took advantage of the opportunity to desert. It is hardly likely that these men would linger long in the vicinity; nevertheless Knowles sent several press gangs ashore at night and in the early morning, with orders, if they were unable to find the deserters, to seize such able seamen as they could find. As a result not only were a good many seamen pressed from vessels cleared and outward bound, but the wharves and waterfront were also swept, and a number of ship's carpenters, shipwrights, apprentices, and longshoremen were taken.

This was something new to Bostonians. Or if it was not altogether new it was the first time it had been done on such a scale and in such a spirit. They resented it vigorously, and before the day was half over, a mob had been raised and armed with "a few rusty swords, pitchmops, cat-sticks and clubs" and set out in search of vengeance. Such officers of the fleet as were encountered were seized upon, roughly handled, and forced to give their parole not to return to their ships until the matter was settled. The mob then marched to the governor's house, where they milled about for some time in a threatening manner. They were diverted from breaking in upon His Excellency by the appearance of a sheriff who attempted to disperse them. Him they seized and marched to the stocks.

This lightened their temper somewhat, and they dispersed to go home to dinner. In the afternoon they did not gather again. But in the evening they reassembled and, after stoning the Town House, where the General Court was in session, they turned away to the waterfront, where it was rumored a barge was coming in from one of the ships. The barge in question escaped them, and instead they seized upon a boat belonging to a Scotch vessel by mistake. This they dragged up the hill and burned. The governor then gave orders for the militia to be turned out, but the town by now was in such a tumult that the drummers were interfered with and the governor began to think it would be safest for him if he withdrew to the Castle. Hearing this, a number of solid citizens banded together and assured the governor of their protection. Their stand brought some order out of the chaos, and the military was finally organized and the mob— by now tired of their sport anyway—dispersed.

In all this time Knowles had made not the slightest move to indicate that he was even aware of the tempest his orders had stirred up. In the morning the governor wrote to him, setting forth what had happened. Thereupon Knowles flew into a rage, not at his own officers for the highhanded way in which they had carried out his orders, but rather at the people of Boston for having the spirit to resent them. Unless, he vowed, those officers of his who were kept ashore on parole were immediately released, he would fetch up his ships from the lower harbor and bombard the town. To lend weight to this pronouncement he had the ships' batteries unmasked and the vessels warped into position for firing upon the town.

The threat, however, was not carried out. Cooler heads prevailed upon the commodore to withhold his fire. The mob, which had reassembled for another day's sport, was gradually dispersed and order was restored. In the end the impressed men were returned to shore and the officers were released. Commodore Knowles sailed the following day, but he left a good deal of hard feeling for His Majesty's forces in his wake.

The War of the Austrian Succession—or King George's War, as it was known in America—came to an end in 1748 following the treaty of Aix-la-Chapelle, under the terms of which Louisbourg was returned to the French—a move scarcely calculated to rouse enthusiasm in the hearts of the people of New England. One more war remained to be fought before the continent was to be cleared of the French, and English and Americans were left free to turn on one another. This was the Seven Years' War—or, as our forefathers knew it, "the Old French War." More bitterly contested than any that had gone before, fought with a sounder eye to strategy and tactics, and spread more generally across the length and breadth of the continent, this war was more than a struggle between Englishmen and French. It was also a training ground for Americans.

For the first time great numbers of British regular troops fought, side by side with provincial levies, upon American soil.

The regulars did not think much of the provincials and did not hesitate to say so. But then, to judge from all accounts, neither did the provincials think much of the regulars. But they were not above learning from them—which could not be as easily said for the regulars. It was in this war that such men as Washington, Putnam, Schuyler, Gates, Thomas, Heath, Stark, Morgan, and a host of others active in the Revolution received their first military experience. They had a taste of powder and a taste of command, and, moreover, they learned that British redcoats were not invincible. Indeed they discovered that they could sometimes prevail where the redcoats could not, and in that discovery a long step was taken toward the ultimate and inevitable break.

In this war Boston took small part, beyond sending her privateers out to prey upon the French, with considerable resulting glory to herself and profit to her sons. She served, too, as a port of embarkation and debarkation for several of the various armies which Britain sent to the colonies' support, thus gaining a considerable experience with the ways of British regulars—experience that left her, frankly, unimpressed.

The Old French War ended in 1763. For Boston it was over before that. The final fall of Quebec, in 1759, marked the end of hostilities as far as Boston was concerned. From that day, save for a brief flurry over the raising of troops for the Havannah Expedition, the minds and energies of Boston men were directed rather toward the pursuits of peace than of war.

One event, however, which occurred about this time was fraught with significance for Boston. On the morning of October 25, 1760, King George II died. "He was suddenly seized, at his palace at Kensington, by a violent disorder, when he fell speechless and, notwithstanding every medical aid, almost immediately expired, in the seventy-seventh year of his age, and

An Obstacle Is Removed

the thirty-fourth of his reign." On the following day, about noon, his grandson, George, the son of Frederick Lewis, the Prince of Wales, was proclaimed George III, King of Great Britain, France, and Ireland, Defender of the Faith, etc., etc. The news did not reach Boston until Christmas Day, exactly two months later. When it did arrive the new king was proclaimed from the balcony of the Town House. Cannon were fired solemnly at all the forts. A torchlight procession moved through the streets, and a sumptuous banquet was served at Faneuil Hall. A week later, on the first of January, a day of mourning was proclaimed for the old king. Bells were tolled throughout the city, and services were read.

To one who looks back upon it, over the span of recorded time, there is something almost grimly ironic about that juxtaposition of ceremonies. For surely Boston never had a more implacable enemy than George III—or a more complaisant monarch than his grandfather. In celebrating the accession of the new king and then a week later bestirring themselves to mourn the passing of the old, it is almost as if the Bostonians had belatedly come to the realization that their lot had not been bettered by the change.

CHAPTER IX

Thunderheads

GEORGE III has been called both stodgy and insane. He may have been both in his later years—which is the period of most of his portraits. But he was certainly neither at the time of his accession to the throne, or even during the period of the American Revolution. On the contrary, he was distressingly sharp, bitterly stubborn, and untiringly active in his efforts to restore to the Crown those ancient rights and privileges which had been so neglected by his forebears of the House of Hanover.

The trend of political thought for a century had been away from the absolutism of the Crown and in the direction of a greater expression of will on the part of the people. At least this was so in England and her dominions. It was a new concept in Cromwell's day. But by the time of the third George it had been accepted as the general rule. The first two Georges, strangers in a strange land, not fully comprehending what was taking place or understanding to what extent their ancient prerogatives were being curtailed, were content to sit by and let nature take its course—to let the politicians divide the power among themselves and the people.

By the time George III came to the throne, however, the

House of Hanover had become acclimatized to the English environment. George III saw what was happening to the power of the Crown, and he came to a settled determination to put a stop to it. What, he may well have asked himself, was the good of being king in name only? If he was to be king at all he would be king in the old sense, with all the power and prerogatives of ancient times centered in his hands. The time was come for a showdown, win, lose, or draw, and George III was not one to give in easily. If it hadn't been for the men of Boston . . . Small wonder that he hated them!

The time was ripe for the showdown indeed. What could be more auspicious for the change than a change of rulers? Moreover the political situation was made to order for the purpose. Never had English politics been more corrupt. Never had the two great parties been so sadly lacking in leadership. To be sure, there was Pitt, but even he had his enemies and could be gotten rid of. Once that was done and the two parties were leaderless, the king could set about molding his own party, which he could manipulate to his own purposes. This he set out to do. Even at the age of twenty-two, George III was no mean politician.

Playing directly into his hands was a situation which called for firm action. The French were whipped at last—but at what incredible cost! England held the world in the palm of her hand. She was supreme in India, in America, in Europe. But the nation lay gasping under a mountain of debt. Taxes must be raised to meet the cost of victory. Troops must be stationed in the outposts of empire to make sure that what had been so hardly won should not be lost again, and someone must support them. The revenue laws must be strictly enforced, for there was much needed gold slipping between the fingers of His Majesty's customs officials. Every means must be taken to squeeze out every possible farthing to pay for the war and the peace that followed. And in this necessity, so evident to all men, might there not be a hidden instrument useful in restoring the power of the Crown?

George saw it and he used it, and had he had only England and a Parliament brought to heel through politics to oppose him, he might well have won. But there were factors that he overlooked; factors lying hull down beyond the horizon, three thousand miles beyond the sea, whose power and force he underrated. Parliament's ineffectuality did not blind the men of Boston, for they were not represented there anyway. Besides, they were too well accustomed to the free way by now. So they fought—fought not only as Americans but as Englishmen as well—for those rights which they had come, in the course of a century and a quarter, to regard as inherently theirs as Englishmen. Every schoolboy knows the result.

The Boston of the 1760s was a far cry from the village of Sir Edmund Andros's day. Toward the mid-forties the town had reached the ultimate of its possible expansion. Into the bulbous little peninsula had been crowded some twenty thousand souls, and there was not room for more unless some of the hills were cut down and thrown into the bay, or unless the houses were built higher. As yet neither of these expedients had been resorted to.

Trade was flourishing—at least in the first part of the decade. But shipbuilding had fallen off considerably. There was a reasonably flourishing press. Several merchants had established substantial fortunes. Silversmiths, like Paul Revere, were turning out to their order wares of considerable taste and distinction, not to mention originality. Copley was painting their portraits. The life that flowed through her streets was as cosmopolitan as any in the world. Her taverns and coffeehouses were on a par with those of London, and her salons gave not one whit in elegance to any. In short, having passed through the hurly-burly of her youth and attained her growth, Boston was now about to settle down to a rich maturity. In all the colonies she had but two rivals commercially—New York and Philadelphia. Culturally there was only Philadelphia.

The fall of Quebec and the approaching, but evident, end of the French war brought a wave of prosperity to Boston Port such as it had never known before. Even the golden age of the thirties and forties paled to insignificance beside this brief surge. Boston privateers brought in rich prizes, and Boston letter-of-marque men, besides fetching in lucrative captives, traded with the far corners of the world, bringing rich cargoes to the crowded wharves and jetties and bulging warehouses of Saint Botolph's town. But it was a false boom—a snare and a delusion, for already, though they were blissfully unaware of it, the Damoclean sword of regulation was hung suspended by the thinnest of hairs above the heads of the blissful Boston merchants.

The accession of George III marked the snapping of that hair. Though it apparently fell with the first touch of a feather, it was, nevertheless, to sink deep before it was brought to a stop. For many a day Bostonians were ignorant of the identity of their arch-enemy. George III was popular, and Parliament was blamed for all their ills. When the lenient customs officials of George II's day were relieved and their place taken by a group of Shylocks who called to their aid the courts of admiralty —in which no man had the benefit of jury—and the writs of assistance—by which they were empowered to break into any man's house without so much as by your leave—it was the Parliament which, in the gospel according to the Bostonians, was to blame. When the Stamp Act was imposed it was the King's ministers, not the King, who were responsible. "Taxation," they cried, "without representation is tyranny!" And so it was. But whose? Ah, that was what they were to find out—in due time.

The thing was that the Crown, the King's ministers and the Parliament were all pretty well agreed. Britain had come through a great war; a most expensive war. And it was the attitude of all Englishmen that the colonies should bear their share of the cost of the war. Especially was this so when one, particularly if he were an Englishman, stopped to consider that in driving out the French the British had saved the colonies' hides. Of course the point that was overlooked in Britain was that the colonies themselves had contributed a good share of blood and treasure to that end, and they were not so solidly convinced that they might not have been able to accomplish the job themselves, by the time it was done. In England—and it is to be feared that the Army fostered the notion—it was believed that it was all done by redcoats. According to the home government, England had contributed troops and treasure; it was up to the colonies to pay at least a part of the cost.

Viewed across the perspective of a hundred and eighty years, it was not an unreasonable point of view. But at the moment it seemed hardly fair to the colonists. They protested.

Protest, however, was of slight avail. London had made up its mind, and whether that mind spoke with the voice of Parliament or the Crown or the King's ministers, it was all one. Sir Harry Frankland, the collector of the port, who had so conveniently looked the other way on occasion, was recalled, and his place was filled by Charles Paxton—most astoundingly incorruptible in a most corrupt age.

Paxton was active. He had a notion of his duty, and he was diligent in the doing of it. He haled evaders of the customs—they were not called smugglers yet—into court. But judge and jury were sympathetic to the defendants and returned verdicts which nullified the collector's efforts. Paxton appealed for the establishment of courts of admiralty, which eliminated the jury nuisance and threw the responsibility upon the shoulders of judges appointed by the Crown. It worked well—when offenders could be brought to book. In particularly difficult or troublesome cases it was even possible to arrange for the trial to be held in England, where the defendant, for lack of witnesses, might not have a leg to stand on. The only trouble was in fetching men into court. Evidence disappeared—oftentimes not so mysteriously as might be expected. The Crown officers bent upon the execution of their duty found their ways obstructed by mobs which got in their way until the suspicious cargoes were removed from the vessels or warehouses in question, sometimes even by the simple expedient of being locked up below deck while the offending goods were removed, and no man would bear witness against the culprits.

Once the goods were ashore, were they wines from Spain and the Canaries or salt from the Indies, it required a search warrant to invade the warehouse in which it was suspected that they were hidden. But it took time to swear out these warrants, and in the meantime the suspected goods could be moved. It became a game of hide-and-seek, and the collector's patience grew lean. He called upon the authorities at home for the power to issue writs of assistance, empowering him to call in the aid of the Navy to break into any man's home, warehouse, or vessel, in which he might suspect the contraband cargo had been hidden, without warning.

Whatever the means by which the goods were brought into the country it is scarcely remarkable that such measures met with a storm of protest. The practice of evasion of the King's laws of revenue was widespread, and there was not a merchant in Boston, indeed there was scarcely a merchant in the colonies, whose shelves did not hold some smuggled goods. This was not his fault. Richard Roe, the tavernkeeper, might have twelve pipes of Canary which he had purchased in good faith from John Doe, which he, in turn, had purchased without question from Joe Glow, who had imported them. Now, if Joe Glow had followed the usual custom of the day and slipped the wine in under the noses of the authorities, the goods were contraband and under the law might be seized from Richard Roe, for whom there was no redress.

Stephen Sewall, who was then chief justice of the colony, was a liberal man, and he entertained grave doubts as to the legality and constitutionality of the writs. Consequently he ordered that the subject should be brought before the court in Boston. Before the court could meet, however, in February 1761, Judge Sewall died, and Thomas Hutchinson, the lieutenant governor, was appointed to act as his successor.

Now Thomas Hutchinson was a different sort from Judge Sewall. He was by way of being a colonial aristocrat, a self-styled friend to what he was pleased to call the "commonality" —so long as the commonality kept its place, which was quite definitely subservient to that of Thomas Hutchinson. He was a "King's friend" and already held several offices by royal appointment, such as lieutenant governor, judge of probate, and councillor. In addition, several other members of his family held similar offices, largely, it was suspected, through his influence. There had been a time when he was extremely popular, but his popularity had waned, and his appointment as successor to Judge Sewall was extremely unpopular.

Opposed to Mr. Hutchinson in the hearing on the writs of assistance was a brilliant young lawyer, and one who might well be called Father of the Revolution—James Otis. Otis knew what he was up against. He knew that he had not a chance to win. The letter if not the spirit of the law was against him. And the power and the inclination to use it all lay upon the other side.

Nevertheless he argued long and brilliantly. In the words of John Adams:

He displayed so comprehensive a knowledge upon the subject, showed not only the illegality of the Writ, and its insidious and mischievous tendency, but he laid open the views and designs of Great Britain in taxing us; of destroying our Charters and assuming the powers of our Government, legislative, executive and judicial; external and internal, civil and ecclesiastical, temporal and spiritual; and all this was performed with such a profusion of learning, such convincing argument and such a torrent of sublime eloquence, that a great crowd of spectators and auditors went away electrified.

In a sense Mr. Otis lost his case. Yet in a broader sense he won it. The writs were upheld, but the people were, for the first time, aroused to the dangers inherent in the situation. They protested in no uncertain terms, and that year the celebration of Guy Fawkes Day, which was a traditional day of rivalry between the north and south ends of the town, was more riotous than ever.

Such men as Jonathan Mayhew, James Otis, Oxenbridge Thacher, Benjamin Pratt, Thomas Cushing, Sam Adams, and John Hancock were quick to perceive the effect and gauge the temper of the people.

In passing, it might be well here to pause and remark that of late it has become the fashion to sneer at Sam Adams as a demagogue, a rabble rouser; and to speak contemptuously of John Hancock as a mere smuggler. In the strictest sense of the words, the charges may be true. Adams may have stooped to demagoguery in the furtherance of his ideals. In the eyes of the law Hancock may have been a smuggler. If so, he had plenty of good company, so widespread was the practice. But that is neither here nor there. The point that remains, when all other arguments are exhausted, is the fact that, rabble rouser and smuggler though they may have been, the results which they achieved have well justified any means which they may have used. I think there is no one who would maintain that the United States would be better off today as a dominion of Great Britain. Without such men as Adams and Hancock—men who had a dream of liberty and the courage to fight for it with every means at their disposal—there might well have been no United States today.

Those who held the power might well have seen the handwriting on the wall in the reaction of the people to the writs of assistance. It is axiomatic, however, that those who have too long held power eventually forget how to read. That there was much to be said in favor of the colonists' stand against the writs was ignored in London. As Otis and Adams and their colleagues foresaw, the clamor and resistance was only resented, and more stringent measures were adopted, as if, by rubbing salt upon a wound, the sting of it might be lessened.

The year 1764 opened in an aura of gloom. The war was ended, and with its end the boom bubble burst. A severe smallpox epidemic broke out, and trade and shipbuilding came almost to a standstill. This, in combination with seizures under the hated writs, sent many of Boston's foremost merchants upon the rocks of bankruptcy. At Cambridge, in January, a good part of Harvard College caught fire and burned to the ground. On top of all this the rumors of new taxes to be laid, of more stringent regulation of shipping, of the assignment of still more revenue cutters to the New England coast, were doubtless even more irritating than they might otherwise have been. The crowning blow came in May, when vessels arriving from England brought word that, while the duty on molasses and syrup was to be reduced to threepence, other articles of import were to be taxed more heavily by means of a proposed stamp tax.

By way of retaliation a series of boycotts were agreed upon. Under the non-importation agreements many Boston merchants banded together to block the importation of British goods; other inhabitants of the town signed non-consumption agreements by which they banned the use of such articles as might be brought in. These agreements are well remembered in our history books. But less well known is a parallel agreement by which many of the inhabitants of the town bound themselves to eat no lamb for a period of a year. This was intended to increase the sheep flocks in the country and thereby to encourage the manufacture of woolen goods which hitherto had been imported from England in large quantities.

This move to encourage manufacturing in New England might, on the surface, seem a side issue. Actually it played an important part in what was to follow, for thereby certain British manufacturers, alarmed at the prospective loss of so lucrative a trade, were induced to add their protests to the clamor already besetting Parliament, with the result that further laws were passed with the object of controlling and prohibiting the manufacture of certain goods in New England. This further evidence of an inclination on the part of the mother country to dictate the means whereby a man might make a living for himself in the colonies did much to alarm many upon whom the restrictions already laid upon seagoing trade had had no immediate effect. The restrictions on manufactures were henceforward to be regarded in much the same light as the restrictions already placed upon trade.

It was not until March 1765, however, that the Stamp Act was actually passed, and although rumors of it were swift to cross the ocean, the official word did not arrive until some time later. Not until July was news received in Boston that a large quantity of stamp paper had been shipped from England, and it was not until August 5 that the *Massachusetts Gazette and News Letter* published a list of persons appointed to distribute the stamps in the various colonies. Chief among these, so far as Boston was concerned, was Andrew Oliver, who was Thomas Hutchinson's brother-in-law.

Possibly one of the greatest sources of irritation in connection with the stamp tax was the impossibility of evasion. The revenue laws might be got around by any number of different means. Cargoes might be landed at obscure points on the coasts. Inspectors might be bribed. Ships might be unlawfully unloaded and the goods spirited away to secret hiding places. But the Stamp Act appeared to be foolproof. In any business in which a written instrument was required or, indeed, which had to do with words set upon paper, nothing could be done legally unless the paper in question bore the hated stamp. Newspapers could not be issued. Courts could not act. Subpoenas and legal processes were invalid. No vessel could go to sea. No person could move from one house to another. No one could be married. No debts could be collected. Even a corpse could not be buried. And for each stamp a certain amount of money had to be paid into the treasury of Great Britain.

How the news of the act was received is well known. In general it met with a storm of protest throughout the colonies, but in Boston the protest was particularly violent.

In 1765 there stood at the junction of Essex and Newbury streets (now Essex and Washington), in the area then known as Hanover Square, a tremendous elm known as "the Great Tree." In this tree, early on the morning of Wednesday, August 14, were found hanging two effigies, one of which was labeled to represent "The Stamp Officer," while the other was a huge jack boot, out of the top of which peeped the head and horns of what was obviously intended to be the devil. This was evidently intended for a crude pun upon the name of Lord Bute, who had been primarily responsible for the hated stamp tax. What followed is described in an account, published in the Boston *News Letter*, eight days later:

Thunderheads

The report of these images soon spread through the Town, brought a vast number of spectators, and had such an effect on them, that they were immediately inspired with a spirit of patriotism, which diffused itself through the whole concourse. So much were they affected with a sense of liberty, that scarcely any could attend to the task of day labor, but all seemed on the wing for freedom. About dusk the images were taken down, and placed on a bier, supported in procession by six men, followed by a great concourse of people, some of the highest reputation, and in the greatest order, and echoing forth "Liberty and Property! No stamps!" &c. Having passed through the Town-house, they proceeded with their pageantry down King-street, and, it is said, intended for the north part of the town. But orders being given, they turned their course through Kilby-street, where an edifice had lately been erected, which was supposed to be designed for a Stamp office. Here they halted, and went to work to demolish that building, which they soon effected and without receiving any hurt, except one of the spectators, who happened to be rather too nigh when the brick wall fell. This being finished, many of them loaded themselves with wooden trophies, and proceeded, bearing the two effigies to the top of Fort Hill, where a fire was soon kindled, in which one of them was burnt; we can't learn whether they committed the other to the flames, or, if they did, whether it did not survive the conflagration; being it is said, like the salamander, conversant in that element.

The populace after this went to work on the barn, fence, garden, and dwelling-house of the gentleman [Andrew Oliver] against whom their resentment levelled, and which was contiguous to said hill. And here, entering the house, they bravely showed their loyalty, courage, and zeal, to defend the rights and liberties of Englishmen. Here, it is said by some good men that were present, they established their Society by the name of the Union Club. Their business being finished, they retired and proceeded to the Province house, which was about 11 o'clock, gave three huzzas, and all went quietly home.

The next day the Honorable Gentleman who had been appointed to the duty of Distributor of the Stamps when they should arrive, supposing himself to be object of their derision, informed the principal gentlemen of the Town that, as it appeared to be so disagreeable to the people, he should request the liberty of being excused from that office; and in the evening the populace reassembled, erected a pyramid, intending a second bonfire; but upon the hearing of the resignation, they desisted and repaired to the gentleman's gate, gave three cheers and took their departure without damage.

Boston: Cradle of Liberty

Having heard it propagated that an Honorable Gentleman [Lieutenant Governor Hutchinson] at the North part of the Town, had been accessory in laying on the Stamp duties &c., they repaired to his house, where, upon being informed, by some gentlemen of integrity and reputation, that he had not only spoke but wrote to the contrary, they retired, and, having patrolled the streets, returned to their respective habitations, as quietly as they had done the night before.

It is evident from this, and it was obviously intended that it should be, that the leanings of the writer, and of the journal for which he wrote, were in favor of the mob, for it would seem that a good deal more damage was done than was reported. "They pulled the Garden Fence of Mr. Oliver," wrote a contemporary in his journal, "entered his House, drank some of his Wine, and, broke some windows. They would not have entered his House had it not been for some irratating Language from those within." The supposed stamp office was completely demolished and a number of pates were cracked. The immediate causes of the uproar, it appears, were, first the arrival of Mr. Jared Ingersoll, who had been appointed stamp officer for Connecticut, and his reception by Mr. Oliver, which was apparently extremely cordial; and, second, the news of the Virginia resolutions against the stamp tax, which had but just arrived and which encouraged the people of Boston to resistance.

Results were naturally promptly forthcoming. The authorities could scarcely afford to overlook so flagrant a flouting of law and order. On the day following the riot, Governor Bernard issued a proclamation offering one hundred pounds reward for the conviction of anyone concerned in the disturbance. It is not recorded that anyone came forward with information. Nor was there prosecution. And it does not appear that anyone claimed the reward.

Meantime, on the very day of the governor's proclamation, the mob again assembled and moved once more upon Mr. Oliver's house. This brought Oliver to "a sudden resolution to resign his office before another night, and he immediately signified by a writing under his hand, to one of his friends, that he would send letters by a ship then ready to sail for London, which should contain such a resignation, and he desired that the town might be made acquainted with it, and with the strong assurances that he had given, that he would never act in that capacity." The mob, hearing this, moved to Fort Hill and built a great bonfire in honor of the event.

This, however, was apparently too tame for the majority, and having danced about the fire and broached a number of kegs of rum, they then decided to move upon the house of the lieutenant governor, who, it was rumored, favored the act and had encouraged it by letters to the Ministry.

Who made the proposal is unknown. The fact remains that the mob appeared before the lieutenant governor's door and called upon him to come out upon the balcony and declare that he had not written in favor of the act. This he would not do, however, and all argument with the mob appeared to be of no avail until someone among them, more levelheaded than the rest, declared that, just before nightfall, he had seen the governor in his carriage on his way to his country house to lodge for the night. This information seemed to take the heart out of things, and after smashing the windows with stones the mob then dispersed.

Thus did the Liberty Tree first appear upon the stage of history. From that day forward it was the focal point for the Liberty Boys of Boston, and from beneath its spreading branches many a fiery speaker harangued the mob and sent them forth to do their work.

The more sober of Boston's merchants scarcely approved these actions even though they understood them. It was universally hoped that this would be an end to the matter. But the mob, having had a taste of fun, was out again within a fortnight. Exactly what it was that brought them out is not clear, but they appear to have been under the leadership of one "Captain" Mackintosh. From the best accounts it appears that, about twilight on August 26, a small bonfire was kindled in King Street by some boys. One of the fire wards saw it and watched it grow with considerable apprehension, and when it reached, at length, a point which he considered dangerous to the surrounding buildings, he attempted to interfere and put it out. By this time, however, a crowd had gathered, and it seems the officer's attempts to stop the fun were resented, and, "after several whispers from a person unknown, warning him of danger, he received a blow and such tokens of insults and outrage as obliged him to desist and take his departure."

From all accounts the day had been one of considerable heat, and why anyone should have chosen to build a bonfire is one of the mysteries of all time. However, that is what occurred. What followed is perhaps best described in the words of a contemporary account:

Soon after this, daylight being scarce in, the fire gradually decaying, a peculiar whoop and whistle was observed to be sounded from various quarters, which instantaneously drew together a great number of disguised ruffians, armed with clubs, staves, etc. No sooner were they assembled than an attack was made on the dwelling house of William Story, Esquire, opposite the north side of the court house; the lower part of which, being his office as Deputy Register of the Court of Vice Admiralty, was in a few moments laid open. The public files of that court, Mr. Story's private papers, books of accounts, etc. were exposed to ravage and destruction, and improved as fuel to revive the expiring flames of the bonfire. Little more than half an hour sufficed them here.

Boisterous and intrepid, from the first object of their rage, they rushed onward, increasing still in numbers and in fury, to the new and elegantly finished building of Benjamin Hallowell, Jr. Esq. Comptroller of the Customs in Hanover Street, where, after tearing down the fences, breaking the windows, etc., they at length entered the house, and, in the most savage and destructive manner, broke and abused the furniture, chairs, tables, desks, glasses, china, and, in short, everything they could lay their hands on; at the same time purloining his money, and dispersing his private books and papers, until, by the effect of wine and the other stores of his cellar they ripened in ebriety and madness, and became fit for the next more desolating and barbarous operation.

That "next more desolating and barbarous operation," as it turned out, was an attack on the house of Lieutenant Governor Hutchinson. Mr. Hutchinson himself describes for us what happened there:

The Lieutenant Governor had a very short notice of the approach of the mob. He directed his children and the rest of his family to leave the house immediately, determining to keep possession himself. His eldest daughter, after going a little way from the house, returned, and refused to quit it unless her father would do the like. This caused him to depart from his resolution a few minutes before the mob entered. They continued their possession until daylight; destroyed, carried away, or cast into the street, everything that was in the house; demolished every part of it, except the walls, as far as lay in their power and had begun to break away the brick work.

The damage was estimated at about twenty-five hundred pounds sterling, without any regard to a great collection of public as well as private papers, in the possession and custody of the Lieutenant Governor.

The town was the whole night under the awe of this mob; many of the Magistrates, with the Field Officers of the militia, standing by as spectators; and nobody daring to oppose or contradict.

The Governor was at the Castle, and knew nothing of what had happened until the next morning. He then went to Town and caused a Council to be summoned. Before they could meet, the inhabitants of Boston assembled in Faneuil Hall; and in as full a meeting as had been known; by an unanimous vote, declared an utter detestation of the extraordinary and violent proceedings of a number of persons unknown, against some of the inhabitants of the Town the preceding night; and desired the Selectmen and Magistrates of the Town to use their utmost endeavors to suppress the like disorders for the future; the freeholders and other inhabitants being ready to do everything in their power to assist them. It could not be doubted that many of those who were immediate actors in, as well as those who had been abettors of, those violent proceedings, were present at this unanimous vote.

The governor's resentment is readily understandable. Still it was hardly just in him to accuse the leaders of the Liberty Party, however much he may have suspected them, of having participated actively in the affair. The evidence in general is to the contrary. All right-thinking Bostonians were equally outraged by the event, and even Sam Adams expressed his opinion of it in no uncertain terms. While there is little question that he was involved in the riots of August 14, it seems clear that he had no hand in that of the 26th. Nevertheless, when Mackintosh was subsequently arrested as a ringleader of the affair, it was Sam Adams who got him off by hinting that unless the man was released there was likely to be further violence. Doubtless Adams saw a useful tool in this mob leader. Certainly he had his own intentions regarding him, and these purposes became apparent on the following Guy Fawkes Day, when the rioting customary to that anniversary, which everyone particularly feared that year of all years, failed to materialize. Instead Mackintosh, one of the leaders of the South End gang, appeared arm in arm with the leader of the North End, and the two factions which hitherto had taken such delight in breaking one another's heads sat down together to a peaceful feast and celebration which signified their joining together henceforward, in the interest of the Liberty Party. Sam Adams had begun by organizing the mob.

A month later, on December 17, Andrew Oliver, who, rumor had it, was dickering again for the post of stamp officer, was forcibly required to appear before the Sons of Liberty under the Liberty Tree, where, in the presence of Justice Dana and several thousand spectators, he gave his solemn oath never to attempt to carry out that office.

CHAPTER X

First Blood

THE action of the mob, violent and brutal though it was, was no more than an external manifestation of the general feeling in the city. It has become fashionable in recent years to belittle the movement which led to the Revolution; to deny that it was popular. There are those who would have us believe that the whole business was manufactured out of thin air by a little knot of wild-eyed radicals, headed by that arch rabble rouser, Sam Adams; that the people of Boston and of the colonies in general were a docile, sheeplike lot, who were generally pretty well content with things as they were and who would not have dreamed of resistance if the thought had not been planted in their minds by a few evil leaders who sought change for their own benefit.

The ultimate result, of course, is the best and final answer to that. That, at least, is conclusive and admits of no denial. But there are other propositions that deserve to be stated. Admittedly it is dangerous to take too literally all the stories of our Parson Weems and Jared Sparks. Our history as it has been fed to our children has not always been altogether fair to the other side. Still, that is no reason why we should forthwith accept as gospel all that the other side's historians have written about us.

Conceivably they, too, had their counterparts of Sparks and Weems. It would certainly be naïve to assume that they did not.

Much of the history of Boston during this period comes to us from the pens of Tory writers. An outstanding example is Hutchinson himself, who is unquestionably the foremost authority on the city of that day. He was honest, undoubtedly. He tried to give an honest account. But he was a Tory. He was unpopular and he knew it. He would be scarcely human if he did not color his story with his own point of view.

There were Tories in Boston then and later—a good many of them. Being mainly of the moneyed class—the local aristocracy —they looked with suspicion on anything that tended toward what they called "leveling." Being also, because of their wealth, more generally educated than their opponents, they were, for their numbers, rather more vocal. But as all conservatives who oppose themselves to progress inevitably are, they were in the minority nevertheless. Had they not been, the behavior of the less articulate mob would hardly have been possible.

Not all men of substance and intelligence, background, and education, however, were Tories. Indeed, even in that upper bracket of society there was division, as is amply borne out by the merchants' journals of the day, by the records of the colonial assemblies, and by innumerable old letters still in existence. In the main these people were merchants who must have foreseen that continued resistance must bring retaliation. Yet they persisted in their efforts for freedom as they conceived it.

These undoubtedly deplored the violence of the mob. Yet most recognized it as a necessary evil. The ills of state, like boils, cannot be successfully treated without first being brought to a head. To put it metaphorically in the medical terms of the day, the body politic must be bled before the patient's fevers could be cured. It was the mob which must do the cupping. Meantime those more sober, thoughtful, and responsible citizens who recognized the full significance of the situation were engaged in matters, less spectacular, but of more far-reaching importance.

The Stamp Act did more to unite the American colonies in opposition to Great Britain than any other act which up to that time had been passed. Hitherto the jealousy of the colonies for one another had been proverbial. Each had its own political, economic, and social problems, and each was inclined to look with suspicion upon its neighbors. Frequently what affected one did not affect another. The Acts of Trade and Navigation, for instance, which had rested with such weight upon the seaport centers, were not felt by the settlers of the hinterland, by the Indian traders of Pennsylvania, or the rice planters of the Carolinas. Nor did the regulations concerning the settlement of the territories beyond the mountains seem oppressive to the people of Boston, whom they did not concern. But the Stamp Act affected all. From Maine to Georgia there was not a person who was not touched by it, and in their common woe they drew together to act in concert.

On October 7, 1765, delegates from all the colonies met at New York to protest the Stamp Act. This "Stamp Act Congress," as it was called, sat until the 25th of October, and after some deliberation passed resolutions declaring their loyalty to the King and respect for Parliament, but at the same time setting forth, in reasonable language, the demands of the Americans to the right of trial by jury—as opposed to the late extension of Admiralty jurisdiction—and the right of freedom from taxation except through their own colonial assemblies. They likewise made an address to the King, a memorial to the House of Lords, and a petition to the House of Commons, asking relief from their present burdens.

Other measures were taken locally. In cities and towns throughout the colonies Liberty Poles were erected, stamps, where obtainable, were solemnly burnt, unpopular ministers and officials were burnt or hung in effigy, and collectors were forced to resign their offices. The Massachusetts Assembly unanimously adopted a series of fourteen resolves prepared by Sam Adams asserting the inherent and inalienable rights of the people. By the time the stamps began to arrive in any quantity the people were solidly prepared to nullify the Act by refusing to buy or use them. In Boston church bells tolled as for a funeral, and minute guns were fired from the batteries. Vessels in the harbor carried their flags at half-mast. "Liberty, Property and no Stamps!" was everywhere the watchword.

The determination of the people to resist had immediate and drastic results. Courts were closed. Marriages ceased. Ships were unable to come to dock to unload their cargoes. Commerce was paralyzed. All through the ugly winter that followed, it was a tug of war between the governor and the people, with the Assembly protesting that the courts must be reopened, and His Excellency replying by pointing out smugly that, since the courts could do no business without the stamps, the people had brought this state of affairs upon themselves.

Matters appeared to be deadlocked until late spring, when vessels from England brought word that the act was likely to be repealed. This triumphant outcome for the colonies was the result neither of the violence of the mob nor of the congresses and petitions of the more formal-minded. Nor was it fundamentally carried through by the friends of the colonies in Parliament. What actually forced the measure was the refusal of the American merchants to buy British goods. The threat of bankruptcy which this boycott brought upon many British merchants roused such an uproar among them that they, too, bombarded Parliament with petitions and demands for repeal, and it was ultimately their weight which tipped the balance.

News of the actual repeal of the act reached Boston in the brigantine *Harrison*, Captain Shubael Coffin, on the 16th of May

1766, and resulted in wild demonstrations of joy. The Liberty Tree was decked with lanterns. Church bells rang wildly. Cannon in the batteries of the Castle and the Fort fired salutes throughout the night. A great pyramid was erected on the Common by the Sons of Liberty, and a huge display of fireworks was given. There was a wild round of toasting and banqueting and feasting and dancing in the streets. Governor Bernard and Lieutenant Governor Hutchinson viewed the proceedings in sober silence and later withdrew to the Province House, where, together with other Crown officers and Tory sympathizers, they drank His Majesty's health and "many other loyal toasts."

But there was a catch! In their delight at the repeal of the Stamp Act the colonists overlooked the Declaratory Act, which had been passed at the same time. This set forth, in no uncertain terms, the power of the King and Parliament to "make laws and statutes with sufficient force and validity to bind the colonies in all cases whatsoever."

This was a plain statement of the British intent to subordinate the colonies. At the same time a change in the trade laws, imposing light duties on both British as well as foreign molasses—a move which changed a law for the regulation of trade into one for the raising of revenue—also passed unnoticed. Blinded by delight, the colonists were apparently unable to see the forest for the trees. A wave of grateful loyalty swept the colonies, which, had the King and his friends but the wit to see it, might well have been turned to their advantage and that of the Empire.

For a brief period matters were comparatively quiet in Boston. The great cause of friction had been removed, and, in the main, the merchants were intent upon recouping their battered fortunes—an undertaking not of the easiest, because of tightened customs regulations. However, they manfully did their best and smuggled wherever possible. Once again Boston ships sailed the seven seas and the harbor teemed with activity. To be sure, there were minor clashes and irritations which served to keep the spark of rebellion alive.

Captain Daniel Malcolm was a merchant who lived in Fleet Street. He was suspected—probably justly—by Charles Paxton, by this time marshal of the Court of Admiralty in Boston, of having illegally imported some wine, supposed to be stored in his cellar. Paxton, in pursuance of his duty, appeared one day before Malcolm's door with a writ of assistance and a sheriff and demanded to be admitted to search the house. Malcolm refused to let them in, and Paxton and the sheriff were either not sufficiently sure of their legal ground or feared the possible consequences if they proceeded to break down the doors. They chose to stand outside and argue, and presently they attracted a large crowd which appeared by no means friendly to them. Feeling themselves endangered, Paxton and the sheriff withdrew and complained later to the governor that Malcolm had used insulting manners and threatening gestures to them. Whether this was true or not, the incident is eloquent of the ways in which, upon the one side, the authorities endeavored to assert themselves, while on the other the citizens of Boston still resisted.

But even though these echoes of older storms had not yet fully died away, the rumbling of other thunders were already beginning to be heard in London, and this time it was to be a tempest that was to shake the colonies more drastically than any that had hitherto preceded it. Charles Townshend, Chancellor of the Exchequer, and by far the most powerful member of the Ministry, was no friend to the colonies. He had supported Grenville on the Stamp Act. He snorted at any distinction between internal and external taxation. He insisted that the American colonies must be made to share Britain's financial burden, as well as carrying their own, and he stated his policy in so many words:

First Blood

I would govern the Americans as subjects of Great Britain; I would restrain their trade and manufactures as subordinate to the mother country. These, our children, must not make themselves our allies in time of war and our rivals in time of peace. . . .

I am still a firm advocate for the Stamp Act, for its principle, and for the duty itself, only the heats which prevailed made it an improper time to press it. I laugh at the absurd distinction between internal and external taxes. If we have a right to impose the one, we have a right to impose the other; the distinction is ridiculous in the opinion of everybody except the Americans.

As it happened, in this case it was the opinion of the Americans that mattered, but that was a point which escaped the Honorable Chancellor.

In the face of such a declaration of policy, any acts which Townshend sponsored were bound to be viewed with suspicion by the colonists. The two which bore his name were no exceptions, and indeed there was good cause for mistrust. The first provided for more effectual execution of the Laws of Trade and for the appointment of commissioners for that purpose. The second placed duties on glass, paper, colors, and tea, and, to end all argument, specifically legalized the writs of assistance. The revenue raised under the acts was to be used "for defraying the charge of Administration of Justice, and the support of the Civil Government in such Provinces where it shall be found necessary; and towards further defraying the expenses of defending and protecting and securing the said dominions."

On the face of it this seemed little more than a repetition of laws already in existence. But there was this difference: the Townshend Acts had teeth in them. They were provided with clauses for the setting up of the machinery of enforcement and its maintenance, and they might be so construed as to permit the establishment and maintenance of a British army upon American soil. The acts passed on the 29th of June 1767 and were to go into effect the following November.

Word reached the colonies during the summer, and one and all immediately cried out in protest. Bostonians regarded the acts as primarily directed against them, as indeed they were, and considered them a direct challenge to be instantly taken up. "The die is thrown!" they cried out. "The Rubicon is passed! . . . We will form an immediate and universal combination to eat nothing, drink nothing, wear nothing, imported from Great Britain. . . . Our strength consists in Union; let us above all be of one heart and one mind; let us call on our sister colonies to join with us in asserting our rights."

A petition was presented to the governor to summon the legislature. This was refused. Thereupon a town meeting was called on October 28, and the people voted neither to import nor to use articles of British manufacture. All of these matters were brought before the Massachusetts Assembly in January 1768, when they met, and a protest was drawn up addressed to the members of the cabinet and to the province agent in London, as well as a new petition to the King and a circular letter to the sister colonies. All of these were drafted by Sam Adams.

All of these activities were well received by the other colonies, but the letter to the King was regarded as insulting and presumptuous in London, while the circular letter was held to be seditious. On top of this the Board of Commissioners were pusillanimously frightened into sending a memorial to England expressing apprehension for their personal safety and complaining of the license and outspokenness of the American press; protesting the non-importation league and the New England town meeting; and calling for help in enforcing the revenue laws. There was, they asserted, not a ship of war in the province nor a company of soldiers nearer than New York.

With this plaintive closing note they confirmed a point that Governor Bernard had long been striving to make. He and Lieutenant Governor Hutchinson now availed themselves once more

It was from this point that General Washington applied the final pressure which, on Saint Patrick's Day, 1776, drove Howe and his redcoats from Boston.

The commission of a volunteer defender of Boston's South Battery. Note the ship in the stocks in the shipyard close under the battery's guns.

Paul Revere's famous engraving of "the Bloody Massacre of 1770" was strictly for propaganda purposes and had little relation to the actual facts.

of the opportunity to hint that the recalcitrant people of Boston town might be less refractory if there were a regiment or two of the King's troops quartered among them to keep them in line.

"Incidents" now began to come thick and fast. Whether as a result of these complaints or as a matter of routine, the frigate *Romney*, fifty guns, Captain Connell, was assigned to the Boston station from Halifax. En route from Nova Scotia, Captain Connell halted and boarded several Boston vessels, from which he impressed a number of seamen to round out his crew. This did not go down at all well with the Bostonians, who had on previous occasions expressed themselves in no uncertain terms on the question of impressment. By the time the *Romney* hove into port, such was the spirit of tension in the town that any spark might have touched off serious riots. As soon as the *Romney* cast anchor, a deputation waited upon Captain Connell to protest his action. The captain, however, must have been possessed of talents rare in the British naval officer of his day, for he greeted them with such a spirit of conciliation that they returned to shore without accomplishing the object of their visit. The affair passed off without violence.

The matter was by no means settled, however, for there was still resentment among the waterfront people, who were most liable to impressment, and the merchants of the town were still convinced that the *Romney* had been sent for by the commissioners to compel submission to the revenue laws.

It was only a few days after this that the sloop *Liberty*, belonging to John Hancock, laden with wine from Madeira, arrived in port. Those in the know instantly sat up and took notice, for it was obvious that here was a challenge, inadvertent though it might be, to the authorities. Under the combined circumstances, for them to ignore it would constitute a damning confession of weakness.

The authorities were well aware of this also. Not long after the sloop's arrival, and as she was lying at Hancock's wharf, she was boarded by the Tidewaiter, Thomas Kirk. As a Crown officer there could be no doubt of Kirk's intent.

He was followed on board immediately by Captain John Marshall, who commanded Hancock's ship, the *London Packet*, and who had seen him go aboard the sloop, and by five or six others. These, by hook or crook, inveigled Kirk into the cabin below, slammed the hatch shut upon him and locked him in, keeping him there in confinement some three hours or more. In the meantime all the wine was removed from the hold and taken elsewhere and hidden, and no declaration was made of it at the Custom House or the Navy Office. On the following morning Nathaniel Barnard, the master of the sloop, entered four or five pipes of wine at the Custom House and made oath that that was all he had brought into port.

This was too strong for the official stomach. It was decided that the sloop must be seized upon the charge of false entry. Between six and seven o'clock in the evening Joseph Harrison, the collector of the port, and Benjamin Hallowell, the comptroller, proceeded to Hancock's wharf. Mr. Harrison was nervous lest the seizure of the vessel at a time when the waterfront people were just leaving their work might cause some disturbance. But Mr. Hallowell was insistent and the seizure was made. Harrison then proposed to let the vessel lie at the wharf for the night, arguing that, since she now carried the broad arrow, the mark of the King's property, she would be safe there. Hallowell, however, was not so sanguine. He held that it would be safer to move the sloop out where she could lie under the guns of the *Romney*. Accordingly signals were made to the frigate to send boats to the wharf.

By this time a large crowd had gathered. They watched solemnly the approach of the frigate's boats, and, when it was realized what was proposed, some among them cried out in protest that she would be safe where she was and that no officer had the right to move her. In spite of this, when the boats' crews from the *Romney* arrived they did not even stop to cast off, but hastily cut the sloop's moorings and retreated with the vessel to the shelter of the warship's batteries.

Hallowell and Harrison and their assistants made the grave mistake of not accompanying the sloop to her berth of safety. The mob, by now, had grown to considerable proportions, and it was evident that Harrison's earlier apprehensions were not without foundation. A good many of the newcomers, not understanding what had happened, supposed that here was a fresh matter having to do with impressment and, pressing in from behind, thrust those in front forward to the attack. Whether these misinformed persons ever learned the real cause of the disturbance is uncertain. The fact remains that they were in a mood for violence in any case, and they set upon the officers with such fury that they barely escaped with their lives.

Having settled that matter to their satisfaction, the crowd now looked around for new objectives for their wrath. The nearest of these proved to be the house of Mr. Williams, the inspector general, where they hurled stones through the windows, smashed benches, and did other damage. Hallowell's house, not far distant, suffered similar damage. Next they laid hands upon the collector's boat, dragged it ashore and through the streets to the Common, where they smashed it in fragments and burned it.

Now, if it had not already been decided to send troops to Boston, these acts, coupled with the defiant attitude of the town meeting which was called immediately after, must certainly have settled the question. In July orders reached General Gage in New York to remove one or two of the regiments then stationed at Halifax to Boston, and shortly afterward orders were given for two more regiments to embark from Ireland. In August, Governor Bernard returned to England, leaving Hutchinson as acting governor.

The troops from Halifax arrived in Nantasket Roads on the 28th of September. These, the Fourteenth and Twenty-ninth regiments, numbered about a thousand men, all told, and came in six ships of war. They were followed closely by a portion of the Fifty-ninth Regiment and a company of artillery. An old almanac of the day reports:

On Thursday, the 29th, the boats from the fleet came up and sounded the channel all around the town. On Friday the ships of war came up, and anchored off the town, extending from the North Battery to South of the Long Wharf; their cannons loaded and tompkins out, as if intended for a formal siege.

On Saturday, October 1, the troops were landed at the Long Wharf, and for the first time since the Old French War the silent streets of Boston echoed to the growling mutter of drums and the tramp of marching redcoats.

The dispatch of troops to Boston was beyond question the Ministry's prime blunder. Without that move some method of reconciliation might have been worked out. But the threat of coercion was more than Bostonians could peaceably swallow. It was an insult, and the fact that the regiments were to be quartered in the town rather than at the Fort and at the Castle only added fuel to the public indignation. Nor did the attitude of the soldiers themselves tend to ameliorate matters. They came not in the friendly spirit of troops sent to garrison a post for its protection, but rather with the swaggering arrogance of conquerors. They made no secret of their purpose, which was to put the damned, bloody, rebellious, cod-eating Bostoners in their proper place.

Under such circumstances clashes were inevitable. Organized armed resistance was, of course, out of the question. No one in the colonies was as yet prepared for that. But there were other ways of showing public resentment. Soldiers could be snubbed and jostled and insulted; pelted with filth as they marched; beaten up when there were not too many of them to handle. And in retaliation the soldiers could pick on many an innocent bystander simply because he happened to be a Bostonian and so a legitimate object of their resentment. In short, the people of Boston went out of their way to make trouble for the red-coats, and they in turn came more than halfway to meet them. And there were other equally potent forces at work at the same time. The Sons of Liberty, foreseeing the inevitable future, were busily organizing and preparing for open resistance. The Massachusetts Assembly was recalcitrantly quarreling with the governor and demanding the withdrawal of the troops, while the other colonies looked on with a sympathetic eye.

All in all, the wonder is not that an explosion eventually oc-curred. Rather it is a matter for amazement that such a situation could exist for nearly a year and a half before such a climax could be reached. That there were incidents in that time goes without saying. A respectable physician was assaulted by an officer. A tradesman passing under the rails of the Common, on his way home, was bayoneted in the back by a sentry. A mer-chant was struck down in the street by an officer who went im-mediately into a coffeehouse near by. When several gentlemen followed him to protest, they were roughly handled by the offi-cer's comrades. One, Captain Wilson, was accused of inciting the slaves of the town to rise against their masters, assuring them that if they did so the soldiers would support them.

But there is not space here to recount all of the minor clashes that led up to the inevitable final outburst. It is enough to say here that both sides were spoiling for a fight and each was watch-ing for a favorable opportunity. That opportunity appeared to come, at last, on a snowy night in early March, 1770.

The sequence of events which led to this final outburst began on the 2d of March, when a soldier of one of the regiments in barracks at Water and Atkinson streets presented himself at Gray's ropewalk in search of employment whereby he might be enabled to augment somewhat his meager pay. Now the ropemakers of Boston were hard men; as hard as the Irishmen of the regiments, upon whom they looked with such scorn, and they dearly loved a fight. When the soldier appeared at the walk, the owner was not present, and one of the workmen, Sam Gray by name, asked him what he wanted. The soldier replied that he wanted work.

"Will ye work?" demanded Gray scornfully, eying the soldier belligerently.

"Aye," the redcoat replied, sourly no doubt.

"Then ye may go clean my shithouse," Sam Gray told him, and the fight was on.

That remark was to cost Sam Gray his life, but not yet awhile. The soldier had the worst of that encounter, for he was greatly outnumbered, but after his mauling he made his way back to the barracks and presently returned with several of his comrades armed with clubs, bludgeons, and swords, intent on vengeance.

The ropemakers, nothing loath, fell to with sticks, ropes' ends, and tar pots, and a pitched battle ensued which was only stopped by the combined efforts of officers, constables, and citizens, and that only when the soldiers appeared to be getting the worst of it.

Nothing further happened that day, though one might say it almost did. In the afternoon some thirty or forty soldiers set out in a body for the ropewalk, but it happened that they were met by the owner, a Tory, who finally persuaded them not to carry out their purpose of revenge. The next day, late in the afternoon, three grenadiers, well armed, appeared at Archibald M'Niel's ropewalk and, finding only three men there, attempted to draw them out with insulting language. The accounts of this affair are sketchy, but it appears that reinforcements for the ropemakers came up, and once again the soldiers were put to flight.

The 4th, being Sunday, was comparatively quiet, but both sides were making preparations for the greater clash to come. In barracks and on the streets the soldiers were putting their arms, clubs, cutlasses, and bayonets in readiness and swearing sulphurous and bloody oaths against their tormentors. What the Sons of Liberty were doing remains to this day a matter for conjecture.

On Monday, March 5, 1770, it snowed in Boston. Anyone familiar with Boston's weather can picture that day. Probably it was wet, and without wind, since no record tells us that the snow drifted. It was a good fall—one that had probably been going on since nightfall Sunday—for there seems to have been about a foot of it. Toward evening, however, the snow, as they say in Boston, let up. The afternoon sun broke through the clouds, and for a time it was warm enough to set the snow to melting around the eaves of the houses and little runnels to trickling in the gutters. As night came on, it turned cold again. Icicles formed upon the eaves. A crust lay over the snow. Ice formed in the gutters and on the paths that men had trod as they passed back and forth about their business. The footing became treacherous and slippery. As darkness fell, a thin moon rose, casting its light into shadowy streets and, by its reflection on the snow, giving the scene an effect of peculiar eerie brilliance.

There was tension in the town. Soldiers had been heard to say that there were "them in Boston as would eat their suppers Monday night would never eat another." On the other hand, Sam Adams had hinted to friends in towns around about that

Boston might well need their help that night. As evening came on and the townsfolk were released from their labors and the soldiers from their duty, bands of each took to roaming the streets. The soldiers swaggered, jostled the citizens, threatened them with cutlasses and cudgels, with bayonets and musket butts. The citizens were not meek. They responded with jeers and taunts, and they, too, carried cudgels. They got in the soldiers' way as much as possible. They pelted sentries with snowballs and brickbats and insulting language. But this was nothing new. They had been doing it for so long that it had become almost habit with them. It is scarcely surprising that the redcoats hated them.

What happened then? Who started it? Who can now tell? The accounts are so many, so varied, and so conflicting that it is next to impossible to sift the true from the false. As nearly as can be determined, there appear to have been three separate and almost simultaneous disturbances, which produced an alarm that many mistook for fire, and which tumbled Bostonians out of their beds ready for anything—ready for anything, that is, except what happened.

The first spark seems to have been struck about eight o'clock, when four young men were making their way down Corn Hill, then known as Brattle Street, in the direction of Boylston's Alley and the Murray Barracks, in which the Fourteenth Regiment was quartered. As they were passing through the alley they either met with or were overtaken by—the testimony is conflicting on the point—a sentry armed with a cutlass. With this sentry was a "mean-looking Irishman" who had in his hand a stout cudgel. It appears that someone of the group told the soldier to put up his cutlass, as it was not proper for him to have it out at that hour of the night.

In what terms this suggestion was made is not revealed, but doubtless they were not complimentary. At any rate one word

First Blood

led to another. Two of the young men attempted to pass the
sentry without answering his challenge, and thereupon a fight
began. One of the young men was knocked down, and another
had his clothes slashed and was given a slight wound on the arm.
In response to this, one struck the soldier with a stick which he
had in his hand, and thereupon the Irishman ran to the barracks
to bring out the soldiers, and in a few moments the street was in
an uproar. Several soldiers poured out armed with fire tongs and
shovels and fell upon the young men. These, calling loudly for
reinforcements, soon fetched other townspeople to the scene.
Several on both sides were severely battered, and presently the
soldiers withdrew to their barracks, only to reappear a moment
later with arms in their hands, and the people, who had gathered
about the barracks gate, scattered.

About this time Samuel Atwood, a sailor of Wellfleet, who
was aboard a vessel then lying at the Town Dock, hearing sounds
of uproar in the town above, hurried ashore to see what was
afoot. He passed by Faneuil Hall, making note of no disturbance there, and up through Dock Square and took the direction
of Brattle Street and Boylston's Alley. There, according to the
deposition which he later made, he found the soldiers and inhabitants engaged in the narrow passages around Murray Barracks. The latter, being mostly boys, unarmed, dispersed, on
which ten or twelve soldiers, armed with drawn cutlasses, clubs,
and bayonets, bolted out of the alley into the square and met
Atwood, who called out to them, asking if they intended to
murder the people.

"Yes, by God! Root and branch!" they replied. And one
cried out: "Here is one of them!"

The soldiers then set upon Atwood, knocked him down, and
battered him with clubs. He scrambled to his feet and, turning,
tried to run off, upon which he received a blow from a cutlass
which laid open his shoulder to the bone. He stumbled a few

steps and met two officers, whom he asked, "Gentlemen, in God's name, what is the matter?"

"You will see by and by," they replied, and then went on up toward the barracks, where Atwood presently heard the shout, "Turn out the guard!"

Meantime the soldiers who had set upon him had poured on down into Dock Square, yelling, "Where are the Yankee boogers? Where are the cowards?"

Boston's night of horror was by now fairly under way.

While this was going on, the crowd above Murray Barracks, which had dispersed upon the appearance of the armed soldiers, evidently reassembled in even greater numbers, the moment the soldiers began to return to their quarters, and bombarded them with stones, sticks, snowballs, and epithets, with the result that in as little time as it takes to tell it there was a full-fledged brawl being waged in the shadows of the dim, moonlit street. Beyond the fact that it must have been a bitter battle and a scene of utmost confusion, it is impossible to know exactly what took place here. On the one hand we have the testimony of witnesses who say that they saw soldiers coming out of the barracks yard armed with cutlasses and bayonets, rushing through Boylston's Alley into Corn Hill; that some officers came out of the messroom and attempted rather halfheartedly to persuade the soldiers to return, and that other officers came out into the barracks yard and urged the soldiers on; that at least one soldier was presenting his piece to fire upon a fleeing citizen when he was prevented from doing so by an officer who knocked up his musket. On the other hand we have the testimony of an officer who maintains that the people were pelting the soldiers with snowballs and the soldiers were defending themselves at the entrance to the barracks yard; that the soldiers had no cutlasses or arms other than a fire shovel; that the soldiers were amenable to his orders and withdrew to their barracks when he commanded them to do so, while the mob milling about the gates "abused the men very much indeed in bad language so that the men must have been enraged. . . . I never heard such abuse in all my life from one man to another." You pay your money and you take your choice.

While all this was going on, an officer making his way through King Street was followed by a boy, a barber's apprentice, who kept calling out to him to pay his master's bill. There seems to be some difference of opinion as to whether Captain Goldfinch had paid for his hairdressing or not. The "greasy barber's boy" said not. Captain Goldfinch's testimony stated that he had the receipt for the bill in his pocket at the time. At any rate the captain ignored the urchin and continued on his way. The taunts and insults which the boy hurled at the captain, however, were evidently too much for Private Montgomery, who was doing sentry duty at the Custom House. Montgomery, coming down from his post, stopped the boy and told him to show his face. To this the lad replied that he was not ashamed of his face, whereupon Montgomery lost his temper and struck him a glancing blow on the side of his head—some say with his musket, others with his open hand—and the boy went off crying loudly that he had been killed. There were some witnesses to this, and they began to crowd around Montgomery in a threatening manner, whereupon he retreated, first to his sentry box, and then up the steps of the Custom House.

Meanwhile Captain Goldfinch, noting only that he was rid of his tormentor, pressed on toward Murray Barracks. As he approached that scene from one side, Ensign Mall approached from the other with a file of soldiers in formation, just coming off duty. Mall, finding the way to the barracks, down the dark, narrow alley through which he had to pass, choked by the mob, lost his head and ordered his men to clear a path through with their bayonets. This was as much invitation as the soldiers needed, and they fell to with a will, quickly driving a way through to the barracks. No one, fortunately, was killed in this rush, but there were bloody bayonets in the detachment when Captain Goldfinch appeared in the barracks yard and ordered the men back to their quarters. Some went. Others apparently did not.

Captain Goldfinch, according to the testimony of witnesses, stood for some time in conversation with other officers at the messroom door.

While all of this was going on, there was a third crowd which had gathered somewhat mysteriously—for there appears to have been no reason for them to have been there—in the vicinity of Faneuil Hall. It has been suggested that Sam Adams was responsible for this crowd; that they were the organized nucleus who were to goad the soldiers into just such action as followed. Whatever the truth of this, one thing is certain—that there were about two hundred of them gathered there for no apparent purpose. Whether it was one of these, or whether it was one of the crowd engaged near Murray Barracks, or whether it was someone else deliberately set on to it—someone, at about this time, entered the Old Brick Meeting House and began to ring the bell.

Now the ringing of bells in Boston at that time, suddenly and in the night without warning, meant either an alarm or fire. The people of Boston turned out in their nightshirts, or wearing whatever clothes were handiest, some with fire buckets, some with arms, prepared for what might be afoot. At the same instant the crowd at Faneuil Hall was being harangued by a "tall gentleman in a red cloak and a white wig."

What this tall stranger had to say to the crowd is not recorded, nor, despite a good deal of conjecture, has anyone been able to identify him. It is sufficient to say that a number of witnesses were agreed as to his existence. It is said that he spoke to the mob for four or five minutes, until the sounds of the disturbance in Dock Square above began to come down to them. This evidently diverted the attention of the crowd, and the tall gentleman in the red cloak and white wig disappeared, most conveniently. The crowd moved off in the direction of Dock Square and joined in the fighting there. At the same time the cry, "Town Born turn out! Town Born turn out!" began to be heard in all parts of the city.

Upon the appearance of reinforcements to the civilians about Dock Square and Murray Barracks, the soldiers apparently withdrew once more and slammed the gate behind them. At the same time the bells began to ring and the "greasy barber's boy" came blubbering down Exchange Alley from King Street. One eye after another turned toward him, and presently the mob, now joined, surged off up the alley in the direction of the guardhouse, in King Street near the Custom House. Above the uproar a good many ominous threats and shouts could be heard:

"To the main guard!"

"Kill the bloody bastards!"

"Drive out the lobsterbacks!"

Private Montgomery, on the Custom House steps, was nearly numb with cold. All evening long he had endured the insults of the mob and had defended himself as best he could against the stones and snowballs and sticks and chunks of ice they had hurled at him. Now, all of a sudden, the crowd, bursting out of Royal Exchange Lane, swirled all about him. A ragged little brat leveled a dirty finger at him, bawling, "There he is! That's the one that knocked me down!" The crowd surged forward.

"Kill him!" someone shouted.

"Knock him down!"

"Tar and feather the son of a bitch!"

Montgomery retreated up the steps of the Custom House and, having thus placed himself in plain view, was promptly showered with snowballs, chunks of ice, filth, and sticks of wood. In desperation and self-defense he loaded his musket. The crowd whooped.

"The bloody bastard's goin' to shoot!" a boy shouted.

"If you fire you'll swing for it," Henry Knox, rotund Boston bookseller and later general in the Revolutionary American army warned. What he was doing there has yet to be explained.

"If th' bloody boogers come near me I'll blow their bleedin' brains out!" Montgomery replied.

"Fire and be damned, ye bloody rascal!" someone yelled.

They pushed forward. Montgomery leveled his piece.

"Shoot! Shoot if ye dare, and be damned!" he was told.

The crowd had him well sized up.

Instead of shooting he raised his voice and yelled: "Main guard! Turn out the main guard!"

The officer of the day, on duty at the main guardhouse, was Captain Preston, a man of good reputation and generally held to be cool and discreet. His superior officers considered his judgment good. But his judgment was at fault here. Instead of holding his scant forces in check and waiting the arrival of reinforcements to disperse the mob without the necessity of violence, he took a file of seven men and drove across the square to Montgomery's support.

Perhaps the urgency of Montgomery's voice led him to believe that there was nothing else to do; that it was a case of go to the man's assistance now and make do with such forces as he had at his command, or see him butchered before his eyes. It was only with considerable difficulty and at the cost of a great deal of insult and buffeting that the soldiers were able to make their way to the Custom House steps. There they fell in line and were joined by the sentry. Several of them fell to loading their pieces.

The sight of the soldiers appeared to rouse the mob to a greater pitch of fury than ever. They booed and hallooed and shouted catcalls and insults, and battered them with anything that lay handiest for throwing. Henry Knox pushed through to Captain Preston's side.

"In God's name, Captain," he begged, "take your men back! The people are angry, and there will be bloodshed. If you fire upon them your life must answer for it."

"I am sensible of that," Captain Preston told him soberly.

"No bloody fear," someone in the crowd shouted. "The guns ain't loaded."

Knox looked inquiringly at the captain.

"They are loaded," Preston told him, "with powder and ball."

"Do you mean to fire upon the people?" Knox demanded.

"By no means!" the captain assured him. But Knox noted that he appeared uncertain as he said it.

By this time the crowd had grown to alarming proportions. A number of people were trying to persuade them to go home. But they would not. They pressed in upon the soldiers, and Montgomery was knocked down. There was a scuffle between him and a huge mulatto, Crispus Attucks, for possession of his musket. When the two men scrambled to their feet the mob was pressed close against the soldiers. The noise was now so great that it was all but impossible to make out words in any connected order. But some shouts rose above the others.

"Kill the bloody rats!"

"Fire! Fire if you dare!"

"Damn you! Why don't you fire?"

One voice rose above the confusion in an order: "Present!"

There was an instant's deathly silence at the word; then a hoot of derision from the crowd—a shower of snowballs. At the same instant a second voice gave the command. Even hostile witnesses agreed later that it was not Captain Preston who spoke.

"Fire!"

[183]

Boston: Cradle of Liberty

A musket cracked. Crispus Attucks, the great mulatto, who was now leaning upon a piece of cordwood which he had been carrying about as a club, pitched forward in the snow. Two other shots followed in quick succession. Sam Gray, he who had offered insulting employment to the soldier at the ropewalk three short days since, fell dead. So did James Caldwell, a sailor. Four or five shots followed these first three, and a number of other men went down; among them seventeen-year-old Samuel Maverick and stouthearted Patrick Carr.

The mob, frightened now, and seeing that the soldiers meant business, broke and fled, scrambling up side streets and alleys, leaving behind them, scattered in the snow, hats, coats, weapons, and eleven twisted bodies. Nonchalantly one of the soldiers stepped forward and drove his bayonet through Sam Gray's lifeless head, scattering his brains, a dark and tangled smear upon the white snow in the moonlight.

CHAPTER XI

Sons of Liberty

THE Boston Massacre, as the riot of March 5 was called, had a long reach. Blame for the event has been laid to both parties, but as yet no one has been able to show conclusively which was more at fault. All that is evident is that there was fault on both sides. What is important, however, is not who began it, or even the "massacre" itself, but rather its effect.

Passing over its lesser echoes—the public indignation which it aroused, the stormy town meetings, the demands of the assembly, the attitude of the governor and the military, and the effect upon the surrounding countryside and the other colonies—which would take too much space here to detail, the effect was twofold. The immediate, and lesser, result was the prompt removal of the troops from the town to quarters in Castle William in the harbor.

It must have been apparent to the authorities that if further bloodshed were to be avoided, such a move was necessary. Indeed, for a few hours, when the townsfolk had rallied after that first shock of surprise, and when the troops had been turned out under arms in support of the guard, it had been touch and go whether the situation might not develop into a general uprising. It was Governor Hutchinson who saved the day at that point by dispersing the mob with the promise of an immediate inquiry into the affair and with an order confining the troops to their quarters. Yet when the time came for such steps to be taken the authorities characteristically attempted to temporize by offering removal of only one of the regiments. The temper of the towns-people was shown in their immediate and unequivocal ultimatum: "Both regiments or none!" At the same time it was flatly stated, by delegates from the town meeting, that unless all the troops were immediately withdrawn no assurance could be given that there would be no further violence.

It would hardly seem that such hints would be necessary. All the following day people from the country round about, armed with all manner of crude weapons, had flocked into the town, and their numbers by nightfall have been estimated at anywhere from twelve thousand to sixty thousand. Nor was there any mistaking their sentiment. The troops were removed. By night on the 7th the only soldiers left in the city were officers and the eight men of Captain Preston's detachment who were held prisoners in the stone jail.

This was the effect most evident to most of the people of Boston. Certainly it was the effect that was looked upon at the time as the one good result of an ill wind. But it was the second effect which went deeper and had more far reaching consequences. It is axiomatic that revolutionary movements are benefited by a martyr or two. Hitherto the Liberty Party in the colonies had no one to whom they could point as the innocent victim of royal tyranny. Now, however, they had not one but five of these killed, as well as a number of others, living, who could proudly display scars received on the occasion.

We may be wonderfully sure that Sam Adams and his friends made full use of this weapon so gratuitously placed in their hands by the King's own men. By print and by handbill, by whisper and by word of mouth, the story of the redcoats' brutal behavior and unprovoked attack upon the innocent citizens of Boston town was carried from one end of the colonies to the other. And if in the telling of it the facts were distorted and magnified a little here and there, it was all in a good cause. It was propaganda at its most effective. It was to be many a long day and not until a long and bloody war had been fought that the incident was to be forgotten. It was longer still before the great mass of myths and distortions that grew up around it were to be a little bit dispelled and Americans in general were allowed a glimpse of the truth.

There is a curious twist to the business, too; one of those gestures of destiny by which that power which has the ordering of the lives of men demonstrates his contempt for the efforts of man to control his fate. On the very day on which King George's men were turning their muskets upon their tormentors and shooting down the men who were later to be held up as martyrs in the cause of liberty, the Townshend Acts, those hated acts which had caused all the trouble, were repealed in London —repealed, that is, except for a tax of threepence a pound on tea, a mere token, designed more to assert the right of Parliament to tax the colonies as they pleased rather than for the revenue. One may be permitted to wonder whether, had this fact been known in Boston, it might have made a difference in the way things fell out.

It is interesting to note, too, in passing, the fate of Captain Preston and his men. They lay in jail until October, when they were brought to trial and acquitted. But what is significant to us is that when the question of their defense arose there was not a single Tory lawyer in the city who would dare take the case. It almost seemed for a time that they would have to go undefended, until Josiah Quincy volunteered to take the case if John Adams would join him.

The Crown had no more outspoken enemies, the Liberty

Party no stancher supporters than these two. Yet in undertaking the defense of the "bloody butchers of King Street" they risked their reputations, their practice, their very lives in the interest of justice and in order that men accused might not want counsel. That stands to their credit, as it stands to the credit of the party for which they stood that they were permitted to do so and to win their case upon its merits. The history of other cases of the time shows that, had the situations been reversed, the same notions of justice would by no means have held.

Now much of this may seem irrelevant and little concerned with the story of Boston's port, yet actually that is not the case. It must be remembered that all of this had its roots in the repressive measures aimed at the curtailment of Boston's hitherto flourishing, seagoing trade. It was that which had first stirred resentment. It was that which, in the long run, embellished with other issues, was to lead further still.

After the removal of the soldiers from their midst the burghers of Boston settled down with something like a sigh of relief. As much as most of the town's merchants, who were, after all, the group which held the ruling power, wanted was a chance to send their ships to sea again and make a fair profit thereby, and now that matters seemed fairly settled it looked as though their opportunity had come. At least there seemed nothing in the way of trying. The redcoats were gone out of the city, even though they still remained on an island in the harbor. The tax which had produced the non-importation agreements, so disastrous alike both at home and abroad, had been repealed—all except that infinitesimal item on tea. Stocks were low and goods were in such demand as the oldest among them had never before known. If a man could not turn a penny in such a market, was the general feeling, he had none but himself to blame.

Once more, then, Boston's ships spread their wings upon the sea, and once again cargoes from the four corners of the earth landed on Boston's wharves and filled Boston's warehouses to the point of bursting. True, customs regulations were tightened and enforced as never before. Customs officials grew still more zealous, and Navy and Coast Guard activity increased. But Boston's merchants had learned something of give-and-take. For the most they had been well convinced that half a loaf is better than none. They met these burdens philosophically, and if smuggling declined, at least trade was up, and after the events of the sixties this seemed as much as anyone could ask. In general, time and increased prosperity obscured such abstract matters as principle, and for a time Boston seemed likely to settle back into something like her old way of life.

There was much lost ground to be regained. In the decade of dispute just past, with its non-importation agreements, its clashes with royal authority, and subsequent depression, Boston's foreign trade had fallen behind that of Philadelphia and New York. Trade with England and Ireland continued good, as was that with the West Indies, though here, too, Boston fell behind some other ports in the value of her exports. In the coastal trade she still held top place, supplying many of her neighbors with rum, shoes, and food products. Boston's merchants made a hasty mental survey of the situation and then set about the business of winning back much of their lost position.

It was not all plain sailing. Customs officials, as has been said, were more strict than ever and consequently more troublesome, and the rights of those who looked upon smuggling as a God-given privilege were apt to be disregarded. Then there was the attitude of the Royal Navy toward merchant seamen and shipping. It was not one to foster harmony and mutual understanding, and since a King's ship prowled night and day, up and down, before Boston's doorstep, stopping and examining, with supreme arrogance, all who would go out or come in, the old wound was never given time to close and heal altogether.

Boston: Cradle of Liberty

Such minor irritations as these served to keep alive a spark of resentment here and there, but in general the main issue—the question of whether or not the King and Parliament had the right to tax the colonies without by your leave—was well-nigh forgotten. Dutch tea was smuggled in, landed in cove and inlet or disguised as other goods amid legitimate cargoes, much as rum was to be run into the same ports a century and a half later. It was cheap and it was popular. But English tea, tax and all, was but little more costly. Liberty Boys and suchlike fanatics might lift their saucers in the coffeehouses and persuade themselves that it was Dutch tea that they were drinking. Among Whig housewives the insistence was upon Dutch tea. But the truth was that few actually knew whence came the beverage they tasted, and fewer still actually cared.

Such a situation could scarcely have been pleasing to Sam Adams and the Liberty Party, who saw all the work of years going for naught. The attitude of the majority of Bostonians, who suddenly developed a greater interest in business than in such abstract questions as rights and liberty, must have been a bitter pill indeed, and may well have been the making of many a cynic. The simple truth was that the merchants, now that they were no longer pinched where it hurt, were only behaving with simple human illogic. The problem was no longer pressing, therefore it was not worth thinking about. The more pressing matter of day-to-day living loomed larger. If others were hurt—well, that was their hard luck. They ought to be able to look out for themselves. It is often difficult to look sympathetically upon other people's troubles when we ourselves are doing comfortably enough. Adams and his followers did what they could to counteract the tendency with pamphlets and warnings. But on the whole it was a losing battle they fought. The situation seemed to be healing of its own accord, and the King and his ministers would have been well advised to let things lie as they were.

Fortunately for all those who believed in liberty, however, this was exactly what the King and his ministers seemed congenitally unable to do. They were their own worst enemies. Time and again they had shown it; even with colony agents at their elbows to guide them, it was impossible for them to understand the temper and the feeling of the Americans. Time and again they had blundered in their colonial policy. Given a little more time, they could be counted upon to blunder again.

Three years passed. It must have been an interminable three years to Sam Adams. But the end was now in sight.

In 1773 the East India Company, that powerful combination which held such a ruthless strangle hold upon the British Far Eastern trade, finding itself in difficulties, and having on hand a surplus of tea, appealed to the government for aid. In response the government granted the company a monopoly on all tea exported to the colonies, and the company thereupon decided to sell its tea directly through its own agents, thus eliminating the independent merchants, who had hitherto acted as middlemen. So far as the general public was concerned, the arrangement was rather advantageous than otherwise, for, under it, the price of tea was so reduced as even to undersell the smuggled Dutch product. Doubtless this was in the minds of the government and the company officials when the move was decided upon. Perhaps they thought they were doing the colonists a favor. But there was a fly in the ointment, and the Americans were quick to perceive it.

It was a small fly; a mere infant of a fly. But there was no telling how large it might grow. Here was injustice done, and injustice that hurt where it was most likely to be felt—in the pocket. In the twinkling of an eye a source of income had been turned off without so much as by your leave. Parliament said,

"Here is tea. No man may sell it but those the company shall designate." To be sure, tea was not a large source of revenue to many—English tea, that is. All could forego its sale and handling without great harm done to any. But if Parliament had the right to grant such a monopoly in tea, why could the same not be done with other articles—with glass, with woolens and linens and all manner of manufactured goods—until there was nothing left for the independent merchant to trade in? Was it, perhaps, the beginning of a trend; an indication of what might be expected in the future?

But that was not all. These three years past Sam Adams had been protesting mightily against the tax on tea. It was small. He admitted as much. But to pay it, he insisted, was tantamount to admission of Parliament's right to levy such tax. And if Parliament had the right to tax tea, why had it not the right to tax other articles as well? And was there any check upon the amount of the tax?

The tendency had been to hear him with tolerant amusement. But now, overnight, the picture changed. Adams became a prophet with honor in his own country, and the merchants found themselves thrust suddenly and squarely once more back into the camp of the Liberty Boys.

No small influence in producing this result was the fact that without exception the merchants appointed by the East India Company to act as agents for the tea were notorious Tories. Perhaps the most prominent among them were the sons of Governor Hutchinson, whose unfailing arrogance had tended to make them, if anything, more unpopular than their father. This, in itself, was an ominous portent which could not pass unnoticed. With one voice merchant and consumer alike, from Maine to Georgia, cried out in protest. Committees were formed. Resolves were passed. Housewives throughout the colonies banned tea from their tables. In Charleston, South Carolina, the tea which the company sent out was landed but not distributed. In New York, Philadelphia, Portsmouth the tea ships were returned unloaded. But Boston had her own way of dealing with such problems.

As might have been expected from her commercial character, Boston was by far the most outspoken in her protest, and when the identity of the tea commissioners became known public indignation knew no bounds. The Liberty Boys lost no time in meeting, and delegates were sent to the commissioners to suggest that they might do well to resign their offices. The feeling of tension and excitement ran high. But it ran higher still when Bostonians awoke on the morning of November 3 to find the town plastered with handbills:

To the Freemen of this and the neighboring towns:
GENTLEMEN:
   You are desired to meet at Liberty Tree this day at 12 o'clock noon; then and there to hear the persons, to whom the tea shipped by the East India Company is consigned, make a public resignation of their office as Consignees, upon oath; and also swear that they will reship any teas that may be consigned to them by said Company, by the first vessel sailing for London.
Boston, Nov. 3, 1773.

O.C., *Secretary*.

Show us the man that dare take down this.

At eleven o'clock bells all over town began to ring, and criers went through the streets summoning the people to Liberty Tree. Crowds began to move in that direction, at first by handfuls and then in a general movement. Shopkeepers and merchants, fearing that this might be the beginning of new disorders, such as had occurred in former years, put up their shutters and locked their doors for the day and thereafter joined the crowds. At Hanover Square the Liberty Tree was decorated with a large flag, and already the leaders of the Liberty Party were up on

[193]

their barrel tops haranguing the mob. By noon some five hundred had gathered about the great elm, and more were constantly pouring into the square. Tories were conspicuous by their absence. At half past twelve the consignees had not appeared. This was better than the leaders of the Liberty Party had hoped for. A hasty consultation was held among them, and presently the matter was put to a vote of all present: Should delegates be sent to summon the commissioners to appear?

The roar of approbation was deafening. Without delay the committee was appointed and went off to Clark's Warehouse, on the wharves, where the consignees had gathered. Some of the crowd followed. The rest waited at the tree, listening to the speeches.

One may readily imagine the scene at the wharf. The day is bright and chilled with sharp winds beating across the bay. Out in the harbor lie the King's ships; black hulls with broad yellow bands about them, yellow spars gleaming in the sunlight, Union Jacks snapping at the gaff, and gun ports frowning. Other ships lie alongside the wharves, shadowing them with networks of spars and cordage, or lie bow on to the quay, their long bowsprits thrusting out over the heads of the passing committeemen and the crowds that tag along behind, while the figureheads stare down woodenly at them as they pass. None of the tea ships have yet arrived.

At Clark's Wharf stands the long warehouse, with the leaded windows of its counting room across the front and its stout door midships. Here are the tea commissioners gathered together for mutual support, for they are well aware of what is afoot and know for a certainty that singly they have no strength. Oliver and Thomas Hutchinson are there; merchants and sons of the governor. Richard Clark is there, too, with his son and Benjamin Faneuil, Jr., and Josiah Winslow; the stoutest Tories in the town; proud, haughty, arrogant in their ruffles and laces, their silk knee breeches and velvet coats and powdered wigs. They are all there, waiting, drumming on the desks with impatient fingers, pacing to and fro, up and down the long room, pausing now and then to stare out through the diamond-shaped small panes of the windows that front along the wharf to see if anyone is yet coming. All about them is the smell of trade, the tang of spices and pitch and cordage mingling with the musty odors of grain and raw sugar and molasses, the sweet smell of West Indian fruits, and perhaps a hint of the rankness of raw hides, the whole overlaid with the salt breath of the sea, driven in by the wind from across the bay and gurgling amid the piles beneath their feet.

What they are waiting for comes soon enough. The delegation from the mass meeting comes striding, filled with a sense of the great weight resting upon them, grouped together, half reluctant to begin, yet determined that nothing shall stop them in this, their duty. Behind them the crowd halts at the edge of the wharf and stares after them, silent, solemn. The delegates halt before the warehouse door, and one of them—is it John Hancock?—raises his silver-headed stick and thunders upon it. There is a moment's pause. The door swings open. Whoever opens, we may be sure it is neither of the Hutchinsons. The delegates disappear within.

It is a long time before the delegates come out, and when they do they are grimmer and more silent than ever. Together they march up the planked wharf and thrust into the crowd, shouldering their way. Their pace does not slacken. They answer no questions. Stern-faced, determined, they go to make their reports.

At the Liberty Tree the leaders and the vast crowd are awaiting them. As they push their way through, a shout goes up. Under the tree they pause, and the leaders crowd around them.

"Where are the commissioners?"

"They will not come."

"Will they give up their commissions?"

"They refuse."

A growl goes up from those nearest, as they hear, and word flies through the crowd. There are those present who favor going now to the wharf and giving the commissioners a dose of tar and feathers, but more sober heads prevail, and by mid-afternoon the crowd is peaceably dispersed with the promise of a general town meeting to be held two days hence.

That meeting was held, and John Hancock was chosen moderator. At this meeting the people of Boston officially adopted the Philadelphia Resolves; denied the right of Parliament to tax America, specifically condemned the tax on tea, declared everyone who supported that tax or encouraged its imposition by buying the tea an enemy to his country, and requested the agents of the East India Company to resign. Once more a special delegation was appointed to wait upon the commissioners, and once more the commissioners refused to surrender their appointment. At this there were some calls for violence. Some spoke of taking up arms, and the idea was generally applauded. But in the end the meeting only voted that the commissioners' response had been "daringly affrontive," and adjourned.

On Wednesday, the 17th, there came a vessel into port, bringing word that the tea ships had sailed and might be expected daily. At once another town meeting was called, and once again the consignees were requested to resign their commissions. Once again they refused, and upon that refusal the meeting uttered no opinion and passed no vote, but immediately broke up.

To those who knew the ways of New England this abrupt ending of a town meeting was more sinister than any vote of censure or condemnation. To the commissioners it was the handwriting on the wall. They saw and read in it that henceforward they would be left to the tender mercies of the Liberty

Boys and the Committee of Safety, and accordingly, quietly and discreetly, they one by one picked up and quietly sought refuge in the Castle.

It was on Sunday, November 28, that the ship *Dartmouth*, Captain Hall, after a passage of sixty days, reached Boston with 114 chests of tea. The better the day the better the deed had not, even then, become the accepted theory of most Bostonians. It was customary to keep the Sabbath strictly, and strictly in those days meant something far different from what it does today. Men went to church then whether they wished or not. If they did not they were fined. It was illegal to travel or play games or to stroll, beyond what was necessary. There was no recreation of any kind, and anything that even remotely smacked of business was strictly taboo. Only taverns and alehouses remained open, and these did so only that those who went to church might warm themselves there before and after.

But here was a situation which called for immediate action. Sabbath or no Sabbath, the selectmen and the Committee of Correspondence met to take action against the entry of the tea. Since the commissioners had fled to the Castle there was no means of reaching them. Francis Rotch, a Quaker and the owner of the *Dartmouth*, however, was available, and from him was obtained—by what means is perhaps best not considered—a promise that the ship would not be entered at the Custom House until Tuesday. The next morning the town was again plastered with placards—sure proof that someone besides the selectmen and the committeemen had been at work that Lord's Day.

FRIENDS! BRETHREN! GENTLEMEN!
That worst of plagues, the detested TEA, shipped for this port by the East India Company has now arrived in this harbor. The hour of destruction, or manly opposition to the machinations of tyranny, stares you in the face. Every friend to his country, to himself and posterity, is now called upon to meet at Faneuil Hall at nine o'clock THIS DAY (at which time the bells will ring), to make a united and successful

resistance to this last, worst, and most destructive measure of Administration.

The turnout for this meeting was so huge that it was necessary to adjourn to the Old South Meeting House, which alone was large enough to hold the crowd. Sam Adams then started matters rolling by moving that the tea be sent back whence it came and that no duty be paid upon it. This met with shouts of applause. But Dr. Young rose to hazard the opinion that the only way to get rid of the obnoxious stuff was to throw it overboard.

It was now midday, and the meeting was adjourned to the afternoon. When it had reassembled, Mr. Rotch rose to protest the proceeding. This centered attention upon him, and it was immediately voted that if Rotch undertook to enter the tea he would do so at his own peril. At the same time Captain Hall was cautioned not to allow any of his cargo to be landed. To make assurance doubly sure, the Captain was ordered to bring his ship alongside Griffin's Wharf, where an armed guard of twenty-five determined citizens were stationed aboard to see that nothing was touched. Then, in order that time might be allowed to consult with the consignees, the meeting was adjourned to the following morning.

Next day those who had been delegated to consult with the consignees reported that those gentlemen stated that it was not in their power to return the tea, though they were ready to store it until they could receive instructions from England.

It was at this point, and before any action could be taken, that the sheriff of Suffolk County appeared with a proclamation from the governor, charging the people with violating the good and wholesome laws of the province, and "warning, exhorting, and requiring them, and each of them there unlawfully assembled, forthwith to disperse." Here the governor had the law upon his side, for this was no legally summoned town meeting. But the proclamation was greeted with jeers, boos, and hisses.

The sheriff was hustled out to report to his master, and the meeting proceeded in a tumult. John Singleton Copley volunteered to go to the Castle and reason with the commissioners—one of whom was his father-in-law. He was given two hours in which to do so, but at the end of that time he returned with a reply which was voted "not in the least degree satisfactory." In the afternoon Rotch and Hall yielded to pressure and agreed that the tea should return without touching land or paying duty. A similar promise was extracted from the owners of two other tea ships which were hourly expected, and after passing a vote of censure upon such merchants as had "even inadvertently" imported tea while subject to duty, the meeting broke up.

Matters appeared to rest at this point for the time being. Presently the other two ships, the *Beaver* and the *Eleanor*, arrived, and by order of the committee were brought alongside the *Dartmouth* in order that one guard might do for all.

Now it was the law that the ships could not be cleared from Boston without first unloading their cargo consigned to that port. Since the tea was a part of that cargo, it was evident that until it was landed there could be no legal clearance. By the same laws the ships could not re-enter a British port until they had discharged their Boston lading. Obviously, since both sides were adamant, an impasse had been reached. But there was another ingredient in the dish that added spice: if in twenty days from their arrival the ships had not been cleared, they would be liable to seizure. This put a time limit upon the matter and made it imperative for the Sons of Liberty, if they were to act at all, to act promptly.

On December 11 Rotch was again summoned before the committee and asked why he had not kept his agreement to send back the ships. He replied that it was not in his power to do so, upon which he was unequivocally informed that the people of Boston and the neighboring towns absolutely required it. In the meantime, however, Governor Hutchinson had stubbornly taken steps to prevent any such move without his permit. No vessel was allowed to put to sea. The guns at the Castle were shotted and laid to cover the channel, while Admiral Montagu, in command of the warships in the harbor, had sent two frigates to blockade the passages leading from port.

Still the committee did not despair of settling the matter by peaceful means. On the 14th Rotch was again summoned before a mass meeting at the Old South and was ordered in no uncertain terms to apply for a clearance. This the harassed Quaker did, being by now only too anxious to be shut of the whole affair. But the collector refused to give his answer until the next day, whereupon the meeting was adjourned until the 16th, which was the last day of the twenty before confiscation of the vessel should be legal.

On Wednesday, the 15th, Rotch was once more escorted to the Custom House, where a clearance for the *Dartmouth* was again "unequivocally and finally" refused unless the tea was discharged or a permit was secured from the governor. There seemed nothing more to be done.

Thursday, the 16th of December 1773, was a raw and dreary day, with leaden skies that wept on Boston. But the weather did not keep people home. They crowded in from all the outlying towns, and by ten o'clock in the morning there were two thousand packed into the Old South and spilling out into the surrounding streets.

Mr. Rotch was called upon and reported that a clearance had been refused. He was thereupon directed, as a last resort, to apply to the governor for a passport which would permit his ship to pass the Castle. Apparently Hutchinson had anticipated some such move, for, it appeared, he had gone out to his country estate in Milton, and it would take some considerable time for Rotch to get there and back. Accordingly the meeting was adjourned until three o'clock in the afternoon. By that time it was estimated that there were seven thousand people in and around the Old South—by far and away the largest crowd that had ever assembled at a Boston meeting.

By three—by four—even by five o'clock Rotch had not returned. In the meantime the crowd was regaled with speeches—always a good way to hold a Boston crowd spellbound. Sam Adams spoke, and Dr. Young, and even the hitherto sedate John Rowe. "Who knows," said he, "how tea will mingle with salt water?"

It was a question which met with huge applause.

Josiah Quincy spoke from the east gallery.

"Shouts and Hosannas will not terminate the trials of this day," he said, "nor popular resolves, harangues, and acclamations vanquish our foes. We must be grossly ignorant of the value of the prize for which we contend, of the power combined against us, of the inveterate malice and insatiable revenge which actuate our enemies, public and private, abroad and in our bosom, if we hope that we shall end this controversy without the sharpest conflicts. Let us consider the issue before we advance to those measures which must bring on the most trying and terrible struggle this country ever saw."

Down on the floor old Harrison Gray rose and warned the "young gentleman in the gallery" against the use of such impetuous language.

"If the old gentleman on the floor intends by his warning to the 'young gentleman in the gallery' to utter only a friendly voice in the spirit of paternal advice," replied Quincy passionately, "I thank him. If his object is to terrify and intimidate, I despise him. Personally perhaps I have less concern than anyone present in the crisis approaching. The seeds of dissolution are thickly planted in my constitution. . . . I feel how short is the day allotted to me. . . . I see the clouds now rise thick and fast upon our horizon, the thunder roll, and the lightning play, and to that God who rides the whirlwind and directs the storm I commit my country."

"The hand is to the plow," said someone else. "There must be no looking back."

It was voted by all present that the tea should not be landed. What was more, it was voted to use no tea at all.

It was a fine meeting.

Darkness fell. The rain stopped. Candles were lighted, and about six o'clock Rotch returned from Milton and reported that although he had waited upon the governor he had been unable to obtain a pass. Hutchinson had refused, saying that the vessel was not properly cleared.

He had scarcely finished speaking when Sam Adams mounted to the pulpit and faced the crowd below.

"This meeting," he said, "can do nothing more to save the country."

The words were evidently a signal, for there was instantly a whoop from the doorway and a chorus of Indian yells from the gallery. Forty or fifty men suddenly appeared near the outer door, each wrapped in a blanket, each with his face blackened, and each with a small ax or "tomahawk" in hand.

Did they come from the street? Or had they been waiting in the gallery? What matter? They were there. They were ready. They led the rush for the doors and windows, greeting each other hilariously as they went with shouts and whoops and mock Indian language.

"How!"

"Ugh!"

"Me know you!"

Somewhere the shout went up:

"To Griffin's Wharf!"

And it was echoed.

"Boston Harbor a teapot tonight!"

Down through the darkened streets they sped, these fifty men told off to do the work. In their wake came others; a good hundred others who smelled excitement in the wind and were bound they would have a hand in it.

It was as well those others came, for there was work to be done that night; work aplenty for all who would participate. The ships lay black along the wharf. The guards had disappeared, and there was no watchman—or if there was one, no one knows what became of him. At least he was not harmed. At the ships' sides the party was divided into three groups, and one told off for each vessel. Up they swarmed and over the side and scattered on silent feet across the decks. Within the space of a few moments the hatches were off and cases of tea were being tumbled out on deck. "Tomahawks" rose and fell by the light of the lanterns, and the way they flashed was indication enough that they were of no Indian manufacture. Sounds of splitting wood, boisterous laughter, Mohawk whoops, and then loud splashes carried all along the waterfront and out into the harbor. Almost within cables' length lay His Majesty's ships of war. They showed no light and they made no sound. If they were aware of what was afoot they gave no indication of it, for they made no move to interfere with this most orderly of Boston's mobs. One by one the tea chests were hoisted upon the bulwarks, turned bottom up, and their contents emptied into the harbor.

It was hard work, for there were 348 of the chests to be emptied. Moreover it was the kind of work to which many of those present were not accustomed. There were William Molineaux —something of a dandy—and Dr. Young, and John Hancock and Sam Adams. Paul Revere was there. So were Dr. Warren, John Scollay, Thomas Wyeth. "I never worked harder in my life," one of them remembered afterward. "Although it was late evening when we began we had discharged the whole three cargoes by dawn of day."

There were plenty of witnesses to the business. Thousands crowded to the wharf and by the bright light of the moon, which had followed the rain and the clearing clouds, watched the tea cascading over the sides of the ships into the harbor. It is even said that Admiral Montagu himself, who happened to be spending the night at the home of a Tory friend near the head of Griffin's Wharf, watched all that occurred from an upstairs chamber window. If he did he kept discreetly silent and made no effort to interfere.

A few there were who tried to fill their pockets with the precious tea and carry it home. But as much as possible this was prevented, and it is probably true that little of the stuff found its way into Boston teapots. The following morning the harbor was afloat with choice Bohea and other lesser grades of India tea, and there was a fringe of it all about the shore line at the high-water mark, where the tide had left it, from the Charles mouth clear around to the Dorchester shore. It has been estimated that eighteen thousand pounds sterling's worth of tea went into Boston's harbor that night.

CHAPTER XII

British Flint and Boston Steel

O UR story now enters a region of pitfalls for the unwary
chronicler. There is a good deal of justice in Boston's
claim to the title of "Cradle of American Liberty," Philadelphia,
Virginia, and other claimants to the contrary notwithstanding.
It was British restraint of the swift-growing colonial trade—
which centered first and mainly in Boston—that brought on the
first resistance on the part of the colonies to the authority of
the mother country; the first challenge of her right to do as she
pleased by them. It was this challenge which led the British
Parliament to further acts of repression and infringement that
went far beyond the mere bounds of trade restriction in an
effort to assert its authority, and, because it was against Boston
that these measures were primarily directed, it was Boston
which, in the main, rebelled. To be sure, she was supported by
her sister colonies, who by their own involvement were quick
to see the justice of her cause, but it was Boston which bore
the brunt of royal displeasure. In the ultimate end it was Boston which had the fundamental guts to fling down the gauntlet
to Parliament, the Ministry, and the Crown, and precipitate
the conflict which was by then inevitable.

The overwhelming sentiment of Parliament was expressed by a member of that body:

"The town of Boston," said he, "ought to be knocked about their ears and destroyed. *Delenda est Carthago*. You will never meet with proper obedience to the laws of this country until you have destroyed that nest of locusts."

Lord George Germain, advocating the abrogation of the charter of Massachusetts—which to Britons was synonymous with Boston—expressed the attitude of the Ministry:

"I wish," he said, "to see the council of that country on the same footing as that of the other colonies. Put an end to their town meetings. I would not have men of a mercantile cast every day collecting themselves together and debating about political matters. I would have them follow their occupations as merchants, and not consider themselves as ministers of that country. I would wish that all corporate powers might be given to certain people in every town, in the same manner that corporations are formed here. Their juries require regulation. I would wish to bring the constitution of America as similar to our own as possible; to see the council of that country as similar to a House of Lords in this; to see chancery suits determined by a court of chancery. At present their assembly is a downright clog; their council thwart and oppose the security and welfare of that government. You have no government, no governor; the whole are the proceedings of a tumultuous and riotous rabble, who ought, if they had the least prudence, to follow their mercantile employment and not trouble themselves with politics and government, which they don't understand. Some gentlemen say: 'Oh, don't break their charter; don't take away rights granted them by the predecessors of the Crown.' Whoever wishes to preserve such charters, I wish him no worse than to govern such subjects. By a manly perseverance, things may be restored from anarchy and confusion to peace, quietude, and obedience."

The King's feelings were expressed in his reply to petitions from Massachusetts, announcing that he "considered his authority to make laws in Parliament of sufficient force and validity to bind his subjects in America in all cases whatsoever, as essential to the dignity of the Crown, and a right appertaining to the state which it was his duty to preserve entire and inviolate." "All men," he said, "now feel that the fatal compliance of 1766 has increased the pretensions of the Americans to absolute independence." And he condemned the address of Massachusetts as the product of "falsehood and malevolence."

Since it was the town of Boston, acting on behalf of all, albeit in the judgment of her own citizens, which had incurred this wrath, it was upon Boston—and through her upon all—that punitive measures were inflicted. Hence the story of Boston, and her part in the precipitation of the American rebellion, is the story of America during that period.

In Boston the reaction to the Tea Party was one of satisfaction. There was some consternation, to be sure, among the timid, for there was not a man, woman, or child in the town but was aware of the inevitable results of the deed. But in the main people were jubilant. Almost before the sun rose the Boston Committee of Safety had drawn up a formal report of the affair and had sent Paul Revere with it to New York and Philadelphia. "We do console ourselves," said John Scollay, selectman, who had a hand in the business, "that we have acted constitutionally." To refer to the act as constitutional might have been a bit far-fetched, but the statement is eloquent of the popular state of mind. "This is the most magnificent movement of all," wrote John Adams in his diary. "There is a dignity, a majesty, a sublimity, in this last effort of the Patriots that I greatly admire."

In passing, it is interesting to note that a fourth tea ship was wrecked on the back of Cape Cod en route to Boston. The Boston committee promptly sent the following message to the Cape: "The people of the Cape will, we hope, behave with propriety and as becomes men resolved to serve their country." A letter from Sam Adams, dated January 10, 1774, tells us all we know of the fate of the tea and casts a light upon the spirit of the times. He wrote:

> The tea which was cast on shore at the Cape has been brought up, and after much consultation landed at Castle William, the safe asylum for our inveterate enemies. . . . It is said that the "Indians" this way, if they had suspected the Marshpee tribe would have been so sick at the knee, would have marched on snowshoes to have done the business for them.

The tea, it seems, was rescued by a lighter, sent out by merchant Clarke, one of the consignees, before the Sons of Liberty on the Cape could be brought to do anything about it.

In the other colonies approval of Boston's action was unanimous. But in England the indignation which it aroused was instantaneous and violent, as the opinions of Parliament, the Ministry, and the Crown, quoted above, show. The question which the news instantly aroused was not whether or not Boston should be punished, but rather how. In due time, and after considerable debate, Parliament passed, one by one and by impressive majorities, the five Intolerable Acts.

Intolerable was certainly the name for four of the acts. The first, the Boston Port bill, called for the absolute closure of the Port of Boston. Until the people of that town had reimbursed the East India Company, and until they otherwise signified that henceforth they would show the proper attitude of deference and submission to the wishes of the Crown and Parliament, no goods whatever might leave or enter the port. No ships could

Old Faneuil Hall was the heart of Boston's Revolution—

-but the Green Dragon was the scene of secret meetings which furnished the heart's blood.

The Boston Port Bill drew comment from all sections of the British press. This cartoon, showing the Bostonians in a cage on the Liberty Tree being fed with codfish, is a Tory jibe.

move, even within the harbor. The seat of government was to be moved to Salem, and Marblehead was to be constituted a port of entry in Boston's stead. Without question it was a blow aimed at Boston's pulsing heart, and it was to be carried into effect by joint operation of the Army and Navy.

The next three acts were known as the Regulating Acts and had for their purpose "regulating the government of the Province of Massachusetts Bay." They were scarcely less punitive than the Boston Port bill.

By the first, in direct contravention of her charter, the councilors, hitherto chosen by the legislature, were to be appointed by the governor under a writ of mandamus from the Crown. They were to be paid by the Crown and were to hold office at the King's pleasure. Superior judges were to hold office at the King's will and were to receive their salaries from him, while the inferior judges were to be appointed by the governor. Sheriffs, likewise, were to be appointed and removed by the royal governor, and juries were to be appointed by the sheriffs. Town meetings were to be abolished, except for the election of town officers or by special permit from the governor.

By the second act, magistrates, revenue officers, and soldiers charged with capital offenses were to be tried either in England or in Nova Scotia, rather than in the courts of the community where their crime was committed. The third act swept away all legal barriers to the quartering of troops upon the towns and laid the people, so to speak, under the burden of supporting their own jailers.

The fifth Intolerable Act was the Quebec Act. It applied to Canada and the recently acquired territories beyond the mountains. By its terms the free exercise of the Catholic religion was recognized in Canada, the old French law was restored in the courts of Quebec, and the limits of Canada were extended southward to the Ohio and westward to the Mississippi. This bill was resented in Boston as favoring the Papists of Canada at the expense of loyal Protestants. But it aroused particular anger in the lower colonies, notably Pennsylvania and Virginia, as interfering with the claims of their citizens to lands beyond the Alleghenies.

Governor Hutchinson, who should surely have been better acquainted with the spirit of his Boston neighbors, declared that these oppressive measures would soon bring the colonies to their senses. In May he was recalled to report to the King on the state of his province. General Gage was at that time military commander on the continent, although, at the moment, he was in England for a brief visit. Like Hutchinson he should have been familiar with the temper of the colonists, for he had fought beside them on the occasion of Braddock's defeat on the Monongahela. He had married an American wife, and he had had ample opportunity as commander at New York since before the Boston Massacre to observe them. This did not prevent him from boasting that with a mere four regiments he would quickly bring Massachusetts to heel. "I am willing to go back at a day's notice," he assured the King, "if coercive measures are adopted. They will be lions, while we are lambs; but, if we take the resolute part, they will undoubtedly prove very meek."

The King snapped up his offer with an alacrity that was significant. Gage and his four regiments were promptly sent out to rule in Hutchinson's stead. He arrived in Boston on the 17th of May, while Hutchinson sailed for England on the first of June—the very day on which the Boston Port bill went into effect.

That must have been a somber day in Boston. It is unfortunate that the descriptions we have of it are so meager. For a long time before—ever since the news arrived of Parliament's decision, on the 10th of May, in fact—the town had been in a hubbub of preparation. Merchants hastened to stock up with wares which after the 1st of June they would be unable to bring in. Shipowners were removing their vessels to safer ports. Shipyards were hurrying to finish the craft on their ways before the fatal day came to put a stop to their labors. Barges, whaleboats, ketches swarmed the harbor, bringing in provisions of food and firewood from the islands and the nearby towns, for in a few days, now, even such water-borne traffic would be prohibited.

On the 1st, however, all that was suddenly stilled. The wharves that fringed the harbor front, usually so swarming with life, so redolent of flavor, stood deserted and abandoned. Between Nantasket Roads and the Mystic mouth there was "not a topsail vessel to be seen—save ships of war and transports." Indeed, not so much as a skiff moved upon the surface of the harbor. Until this day not only had Boston depended upon her sea-borne trade for her livelihood, but she had also used water-borne means of securing the very necessities of existence. Almost entirely surrounded by water, nearly everything on which she depended—food, fuel, fodder for her livestock—had come to her by boat.

But today all that was ended. With a severity which even the framers of the bill had not contemplated, the new governor interpreted his orders literally. No ship was allowed to enter the blockaded port save those that came on His Majesty's business. No vessel might leave but it went on the errands of the governor and the Crown. All intercourse by water, even among the nearest islands or from pier to pier, was strictly forbidden. Not even the ferry to Charlestown was permitted to operate. A farmer could not row an ox in a scow across Dorchester Flat. A man could not put out a skiff to catch a mess of fish to fill his own and the bellies of his wife and children. In the shipyards not a hammer tapped. What was the use of building boats that no one would be able to use? The ropewalks all were idle. There was no sense in making rigging for ships that could not exist. Distillers looked at their slender stocks of molasses and shook their heads. What would become of them when that was gone? Where would they get more to carry on their business? Nor were they alone. Nearly every man in the town could ask himself the same question. That day the streets were deserted, silent. The bells alone tolled, breaking the deathly silence that settled over the harbor. Boston was in mourning, and well she might be, for her arteries had been slit and her life's blood was swiftly ebbing away.

Yet there was no regret. Boston stood firmly upon her rights and looked to time and her sister colonies to vindicate her.

She had not far to look. It is notoriously a dark cloud that has no silver lining, and it is a fine old saw that runs, "Adversity shows us our friends." Salem and Marblehead were in many respects rivals of Boston. They stood now to profit by her misfortunes. That they did not speaks volumes for the honor of their citizens. Both Salem and Marblehead threw open their wharves and warehouses to the free use of Boston's merchants, and their people offered freely to load and unload goods consigned to the stricken port. In no time at all long trains of carts and wagons—Lord North's Coasters, they were impudently called—crept in an endless stream, by the long land circuit, thirty miles around, between the beleaguered port and her magnanimous neighbors. It was a tedious business and expensive, but in this way some measure, at least, of Boston's trade was kept alive.

But not all of Marblehead's and Salem's assistance was by way of trade. The problem of food and fuel was soon acute in Boston. Her need was distressing and apparent, and but for the charity of her neighbors her situation must have been dire indeed. In this situation, too, Marblehead once again showed the stuff of which her people were made by generously donating a large shipment—by overland freight, of course—of dried cod-fish. Salem helped with other provisions, and its example was followed by other communities in the province, from one end to the other, with such prodigality that throughout the rest of that hot summer no one in Boston wanted for bread.

But it was not Massachusetts alone that rushed to Boston's aid. Other cities and provinces also sent material encouragement and assurance of support. Paunchy old Colonel Israel Putnam himself, on foot, drove a flock of sheep all the way from his home in Brooklyn, Connecticut. Portsmouth, New Hampshire, sent money and provisions. Philadelphia sent money. Baltimore, ever practical, sent bread and grain. Alexandria, Virginia, sent flour and money. Even London sent a donation of money. In South Carolina the lowland rice planters banded together to send a shipload of rice. Christopher Gadsden, in dispatching the vessel from Charleston, sent with it the message: "Don't pay for an ounce of the damned tea!"

In the meantime the storm clouds were piling higher and ever higher upon the horizon. Material support was not all the other colonies gave to Boston. Contrary to all the expectations of the King and ministry, the other provinces arrayed themselves solidly behind Massachusetts. Britain had shown her hand, and who knew where the next blow might fall? It had been one for all. Now it was all for one.

Word of the Boston Port bill had no sooner been received than proposals for a general congress of all the colonies were advanced in several quarters. The news reached Boston on May 10, and on the 12th, Committees of Safety from several Massachusetts towns came together at Faneuil Hall and adopted a circular letter, prepared by Sam Adams, which was sent to all the other colonies, asking their support. But even before this was received the New York committee had proposed a congress of all the colonies to decide upon a general course of action. Connecticut quickly fell in line with the suggestion, and the freemen of the town of Providence, Rhode Island, on their own proposed a similar congress. In Virginia members of the legislature, sitting in informal convention in Williamsburg, at the Raleigh Tavern, following the dissolution of that body by the governor, took up New York's proposal and invited Massachusetts, as the aggrieved party, to set the time and place for the meeting. In Massachusetts itself the towns, at the instance of the Committee of Safety, entered into a "solemn league and covenant" to suspend all trade with England and Ireland and forego the use of all British merchandise. The names of all those who refused to sign were to be published, while some even went so far as to cut off their trade with the West Indies.

In accord with his instructions General Gage convened the Assembly at Salem. Their first act upon coming together there was to protest the order for their removal. Their second, a gesture of open defiance, was to take up Virginia's proposal and appoint September the time and Philadelphia the place for the meeting of the Continental Congress.

This was not accomplished without opposition. Tory members attempted to block the move and went to Gage with word of what was afoot. He immediately drew up a writ dissolving the Assembly and dispatched it with his secretary to be read at once. That gentleman, however, upon his arrival found the doors locked against him, and since no one would let him in he had to be content with reading the writ aloud and with as much dignity as he could summon to the crowd assembled on the stairs. Before the doors were unlocked the Assembly had done its work and the measure had been approved.

Gage was furious at this turn of events, and in a spirit of vengeance he now issued a proclamation denouncing the combination not to buy British goods as "unwarrantable, hostile, and traitorous." Its subscribers he pronounced "open and declared enemies of the King and Parliament." And he "enjoined and commanded all magistrates and other officers . . . to apprehend and secure for trial all persons who might publish or sign, or invite others to sign, the covenant." This was all very well, but no one seemed to pay any attention.

Meantime Boston was once more in the hands of the military. The Fourth, Fifth, Thirty-eighth, and Forty-third regiments, with three companies of artillery and twenty-two pieces of cannon, were encamped on the Common. The Royal Welsh Fusiliers were posted on Fort Hill. Several companies of the Sixty-fourth were at Castle William, whither most of the powder and military stores had been brought from New York. The Fifty-ninth was stationed at Salem to keep a protective eye upon the new mandamus council, while the rest of the Sixty-fourth were at Danvers, acting as guard for the governor's residence, which had been established there what time the business of the province was being carried on at Salem.

These troops were better behaved than the last that had visited Boston; doubtless, in the main, because Gage was determined to give the Bostonians no reason to complain of the behavior of his men. He even went so far as to issue orders for the arrest of all military men found engaged in any disturbances, whether aggressors or not.

The people themselves were under no such restraint. Because of the blockade, with its consequent stoppage of business, there was a vast deal of idleness and unemployment, though the town fathers did their best to keep folk busy with civic projects, such as cleaning up the wharves, paving streets, repairing public buildings, and so forth. It was a situation productive of resentment, and it was not strange that that resentment should fasten itself upon the redcoats, as the visible symbol of that force which was so bent upon their destruction. Only the numbers of the troops and their obvious discipline—they drilled from morning till night upon the Common—prevented serious outbreaks.

No one was sure, however, that such outbreaks would not come. Earl Percy, in command while Gage was at Salem, wrote: "The people, by all accounts, are extremely violent and wrongheaded; so much so that I fear we shall be obliged to come to extremities." And another officer, complaining of an order of Gage's that no soldier in future should appear in the streets with his side arms, reveals the army's apprehensions: "Quaere," says he, "is this not encouraging the Inhabitants in their licentious and riotous disposition?"

Nor were a good many of Boston's patriots at all sure that all would be quiet for long along the Charles. Those who could —and who were willing to risk leaving homes and business behind them—were moving out into the country as quietly as might be. At the same time Tories, apprehensive of the rising tide of sentiment against them in the outlying districts, were moving in, to be nearer the protection of the troops.

Some of these were well enough off to furnish their own provisions. Others added to the already heavy burden of relief which the town was carrying. No doubt a good many benefited by the generosity of the South Carolina and Virginia and Maryland Whigs and ate the bread and meat and grain which patriots outside the town intended for patriots within—that is, of course, provided they were willing to work for what they got.

The three Regulating Acts were received in August, and it was immediately apparent that it would require more than legislation to accomplish the aims of the government. All over the province events occurred which set the acts at naught. Wrote Percy:

We have at last got the new acts and twenty-six of the new council have accepted and are sworn in; but for my own part, I doubt whether they will be more active than the old ones. Such a set of timid creatures

I never did see. Those of the new council that live at any distance from town have remained here ever since they took the oaths, and are, I am told, afraid to go home again. As for the opposite party they are arming and exercising all over the country.

And well might the new councilors be afraid to go home. The temper of the people was unmistakable. At Great Barrington the new magistrates were not permitted to hold court. At Worcester two thousand men marched in companies to the Common and there forced Timothy Paine to read aloud his written resignation from the council. Councilor Williams, of Hatfield, chose the wise course and refused to accept his commission, saying that to do so meant certain ruin. So did Worthington, of Springfield. The patriots moved to seize Murray, of Rutland, but he had escaped just before their arrival. They were met by Murray's younger brother, who said to them: "The consequences of your proceedings will be rebellion, confiscation, and death."

"No consequences," they are reported to have replied, "are so dreadful to a free people as that of being made slaves."

If the words are to be doubted, the gist is probably correct. Young Murray, at least, promptly sat down and wrote to his brother: "This is not the language of the common people only: Those that have heretofore sustained the fairest character are warmest in this matter; and, among the many friends you have heretofore had, I can scarcely mention any to you now."

Timothy Ruggles, of Hardwick, that old veteran of the French wars, esteemed the best military man in the province, and a confirmed Tory, went to Boston to take his oath as councilor. He received this message from a fellow townsman: "If you value your life, I advise you not to come home at present."

In Plymouth, George Watson went to meeting on the first Sunday after his appointment. As he took his place the rest of the congregation silently rose and left. It is only fair to Watson to report that he forthwith resigned. In Bridgewater a deacon who accepted found that when he read the psalm the congregation refused to sing.

In Boston there was a town meeting.

General Gage called the attention of the selectmen to the fact that the act forbade such meetings, except on the express permission of the governor.

"It is only an adjourned one," said the selectmen.

"By such means," Gage said, "you may keep your meeting alive these ten years."

The selectmen laughed in their sleeves but said nothing. Gage brought the matter before his new council.

"It is a matter for the Crown lawyers," they cried hastily, sidestepping the issue.

Gage sought their concurrence in removing a sheriff.

"Only the governor," the council replied, "has the power to remove sheriffs."

The council was not much help.

But New England found another way round the ruling which prohibited town meetings—just in case the council should suddenly develop a backbone. Earl Percy describes it well enough for our purposes. He wrote:

> Their method of eluding that part of the act which relates to the town-meetings is strongly characteristic of the people. They say that since the town-meetings are forbid by the act, they shall not hold them; but as they do not see any mention made of county meetings, they shall hold them for the future.

Of course county meetings were not specifically forbidden. Nobody had ever heard of a county meeting. It took a Bostonian to invent one—and thereby place the governor on the horns of a dilemma.

A number of these "county meetings" were held. But one of them was outstanding. In September the Suffolk County

Convention convened, first at Dedham and then at Milton, and adopted the famous "Suffolk Resolves." These declared that the sovereign who breaks his compact with his subjects forfeits their allegiance. They denounced as unconstitutional the late acts of Parliament and rejected all officers appointed under them. They ordered the tax collectors to make no payments to the royal treasurer. They advised the towns to make certain that the officers of the militia were chosen from among the friends of the people. They were favorable to a Provincial Congress and promised to abide by the decisions of the Continental Congress. They would, they said, act upon the defensive as long as reason and self-preservation demanded—"but no longer." They warned the governor that if anyone were arrested for political reasons they would seize every Crown officer in the province. They reorganized the Committees of Correspondence and set up a courier system by which messages might be carried to town officers. They stood for the American principles of social order as a basis of political action, and they called upon all Americans to refrain from rioting and attacks upon the person or property of any person whatsoever. It was of the utmost importance, they declared, to convince their "enemies that in a contest so important, in a cause so solemn, their conduct should be such as to merit the approbation of the wise, and the admiration of the brave and free of every age and of every country."

This was enough to turn the governor's hair gray. But it was not the top of Gage's worries. On the 1st of September he had sent out a detachment of 260 men to seize the store of arms and powder which the province had collected in an old mill near Winter Hill.

This collection of military stores was an extraordinary one. Since the earliest days it had been the custom for the province to maintain a deposit of such supplies of war with which to equip the militia in case of need. Its value had been shown in

Indian times and again during the French wars. Now Gage feared it might prove useful to the Massachusetts men once more.

There was some justification for his apprehension. The supplies were considered on deposit and were apportioned among the towns of the province according to population and the strength of their militia companies. Now, in the summer of 1774, the towns began, one by one, drawing out their share.

It is possible that Gage was unaware of this. But William Brattle, who held the rank of brigadier general in command of the province militia, and an outspoken if eccentric Tory, knew perfectly well what was going on. He wrote to Gage, suggesting among other things that it might be as well if the powder and arms were removed to a safer place. It was a sensible suggestion and quite a reasonable one, in the circumstances. But its results were far from anything that either Gage or Brattle had anticipated.

The whole affair was carried out with the utmost secrecy. The detachment embarked long before dawn, in boats, at the Long Wharf, landed at Charlestown, and marched directly to Winter Hill. The surprise was complete. They there seized 250 half barrels of powder and two field pieces and before noon were back in Boston with their booty.

The move, catching the patriots flat-footed, aroused great indignation, and the men of the nearby companies flocked, too late, to Charlestown and Cambridge to recapture, if they could, the precious powder. In the confusion of the moment the word was spread by word of mouth, far in advance of the couriers of the Committee of Correspondence, from town to town, county to county, province to province. As rumors will, it grew like a snowball as it went, until, by the time it reached Worcester, the report had it that the redcoats and the patriots had fought a pitched battle for the possession of the arms. By the time Israel Putnam, in Pomfret, Connecticut, heard it, not only had Gage seized the province's powder, but the warships in the harbor had fired upon the people, killing six at the first shot!

The response of the people to this false alarm was wonderful to see. In all the near parts of the province, north and south and even west as far as Holyoke and Springfield, men snatched up their guns and marched toward Boston. By nightfall it was estimated that twenty thousand were on the move in Massachusetts alone. "Old Put," in Connecticut, sent on the report to Norwich, New London, New Haven, and New York—whence it was sent on to Philadelphia—and issued a call for volunteers. Before he could march, however, came the true version of the affair together with assurances that no one had been injured and that, for the present, at least, no retaliation was to be sought.

"But for this counter intelligence," Putnam wrote to the committeemen at Boston, "we should have had forty thousand men, well equipped and ready to march this morning." "Old Put" undoubtedly exaggerated somewhat. Forty thousand men in arms gathered overnight would be a remarkable feat for that part of the country, even in these times, when the population is much thicker. One may be pardoned for doubting if there were forty thousand men capable of bearing arms in the province, eastward of the Connecticut River—from beyond which it would have been well-nigh impossible for many volunteers to come at such short notice, considering the means of transportation then available. Nevertheless the fact remains that the spontaneity of the movement and the numbers who responded —for even allowing for exaggeration they still outnumbered the British by an overwhelming majority—were enough to give Gage a severe case of the jitters. "The people are numerous, waked up to a fury, and not a Boston rabble, but the freeholders of the county," he wrote, reporting to the Ministry his reasons for not marching at once with his troops to meet the risen countrymen. "A check would be fatal, and the first stroke will decide a great deal. We should therefore be strong before anything decisive is urged."

He would have done well to remember his own words eight months hence.

In the meantime, however, he read the signs as ominous. Accordingly he fell to fortifying Roxbury Neck and sent home a vigorous appeal for reinforcements. His four regiments, it seemed, even with the three others he already had, were not going to be enough, after all.

But this was only the beginning of his troubles. The inhabitants of Massachusetts, like all men of occupied countries, found sabotage an effective weapon. Straw carts were overturned. Roads which foraging parties had to follow suddenly became well-nigh impassable. Boats carrying supplies and building materials to or from the islands sank mysteriously. Piles of the King's stores unloaded at the wharves somehow turned up in the harbor itself. In spite of the shortage of work no one could be found to help with the fortifications or to build the barracks that were so desperately needed against the coming winter.

Gage was forced to import labor. He appealed to the governors of the neighboring provinces, and John Wentworth, of New Hampshire, who had hitherto remained popular despite his known loyalism, played a scurvy trick upon his people in order that the general might be supplied. Wentworth hired an agent to hire men—carpenters—for unspecified work in Boston. At the last moment, however, it became known upon what the men were to work and the whole project fell through. The men refused to go, and Wentworth's popularity was never the same in his province again.

In the end Gage had to fetch his laborers from Nova Scotia, where they were not so particular about serving the King.

In the meantime Boston Harbor was closed tight as a drum. Not a vessel that was not in the King's service passed in or out.

In the fall Gage refused to convene the Assembly. It scarcely mattered. The leaders half suspected that that would be his game anyway. They accordingly met of their own accord, at Concord, and dubbed themselves the Provincial Congress. Gage had another name for them. He promptly issued a proclamation denouncing them as "an unlawful assembly whose proceedings tend to ensnare the inhabitants of the Province, and draw them into perjuries, riots, sedition, treason, and rebellion." The congress ignored him and proceeded to business.

The reinforcements which Gage had asked for were now beginning to arrive. By the end of the year he had eleven regiments in all and felt much more sure of himself. Meantime, with the first of the regiments came news of further punishment for the recalcitrant people of New England. Because of their refusal to co-operate with the King and Parliament, they were to be excluded from the fisheries on their own doorstep. This ruinous measure—ruinous, that is, for a people so dependent upon the products of the sea for their very food—could be, and was, interpreted to mean that no man could so much as put out in a dory in his own cove to fish with a hand line for his family's supper. Only a handful of proven Tories of Scituate and Marshfield were excepted from the provisions of this harsh ruling.

In addition to this came the word that henceforth it was to be unlawful to export arms or ammunition, powder or ball, to the colonies save for the use of the King's men. At once the colonies began collecting all such supplies they could against their day of need. In Rhode Island the Assembly in secret ordered the removal of the province's military stores from the fort at Newport to Providence, whence they were distributed and safely hidden. All over New England towns stirred themselves to gather what arms and powder they could, and all up and down the coast merchants moved to import additional supplies.

Now it was well known in Boston that the province of New Hampshire had stored a considerable quantity of arms and powder at Fort William and Mary, located at the entrance to Portsmouth Harbor. General Gage, now feeling himself sufficiently strong to make the attempt, decided that this supply should be seized before it, too, was spirited away and hidden. His plans were laid in strictest secrecy, but the patriots were not without their spies. The Boston committee was informed, and on December 13 Paul Revere rode posthaste to Portsmouth with word of what was afoot. On the following day a Portsmouth mob stormed the fort and removed the arms and powder to a safe hiding place, whence, at a later date, they were dispatched to the army assembled before Boston and put to excellent use at the Battle of Bunker Hill.

It was a good thing for all concerned that that winter of 1774–75 was the mildest "in memory of man." There was not much food in town, and hunger is more easily borne when it is warm. As for the military, they were pleased that the Charles never froze, for they were not at all sure that when the ice was strong enough to bear them the people of the surrounding country would not rush in to take the town. Inside Boston itself the people behaved with remarkable patience and fortitude.

But this did not necessarily mean that all was peace and harmony between the people and the troops. The events of the 5th of March are eloquent of the tension that existed.

On that day Boston commemorated the "massacre" of five years before. There was to be a mass meeting at the Old South—in itself an act of defiance—and Joseph Warren was to be the speaker for the occasion. Sam Adams was to preside.

The Old South opened its doors early, but not too early, for there was already a crowd gathered outside, and more flocked in behind them. By the time the meeting began, the place was packed. A number of British officers also attended, and when Sam Adams saw them, with that unerring instinct for showmanship which he always exhibited he greeted them courteously and seated them all near the speaker, even placing some on the platform and on the pulpit steps. Thus conspicuously displayed, they became vivid illustrations for the picture which Warren painted of the events of that memorable night. One doubts if they were embarrassed. But Warren was not yet done.

"Our streets," he continued, having finished with the picture of the past, "are again filled with armed men, our harbor is crowded with ships of war; but these cannot intimidate us; our liberty must be preserved; it is far dearer than life. Should America be brought into vassalage, Britain must lose her freedom; her liberty, as well as ours, will eventually be preserved by the virtue of America. The attempt of Parliament to raise a revenue from America and our denial of their right to do it have excited an almost universal inquiry into the rights of British subjects and of mankind. The mutilation of our charter has made every other colony jealous for its own. Even the sending of troops to put these acts in execution is not without advantages to us; the exactness and beauty of their discipline inspire our youth with ardor in the pursuit of military knowledge.

"Our country is in danger; our enemies are numerous and powerful; but we have many friends; and, determining to be free, heaven and earth will aid the resolution. You are to decide the important question, on which rests the happiness and liberty of millions yet unborn. Act worthy of yourselves.

"My fellow citizens, I know you will not want zeal or fortitude. You will maintain your rights or perish in the generous struggle. You will never decline the combat when freedom is the prize. An independence of Great Britain is not our aim, but if pacific measures are ineffectual, and it appears that the only way to safety is through fields of blood, I know you will undauntedly press forward, until tyranny is trodden underfoot."

Warren had some heckling from the officers, but on the whole things were quiet until the speaker had taken his seat and Sam Adams rose to move the appointment of "an orator for the ensuing year to commemorate the horrid massacre." At this point the officers in the audience began to hiss and boo and jeer. There was an angry stir all through the house, but Adams imperturbably called the meeting to order and the vote was taken. Soldiers and civilians came near to blows that night, but it was Sam Adams who averted them. Some six weeks later, when the time for blows arrived, Adams, though not an active participant, was at hand. This time, however, he made no move to prevent them.

In the course of the winter, Gage had sent out parties from Boston on a number of forays. One went to Marshfield to protect a company of loyalists that was forming there. It is said that as long as the redcoats were in town, all was well, but no sooner had the soldiers marched back to Boston than the loyalists dispersed and were never heard of again. This, however, is probably a rank libel on those Marshfield Tories hardy enough to stick as tightly to their convictions as the patriots clung to theirs, for after Concord and Lexington, and while Boston was ringed round with angry farmers, Gage found it necessary to send a detachment of the King's Own, under Captain Balfour, to the rescue of the Tories of Marshfield.

There was another expedition that winter to Jamaica Plain which did not amount to a great deal. But one more important attempt was made. This was the effort to seize certain arms and powder known to have been collected by the patriots at Salem. On Sunday, February 26, a detachment numbering some two hundred embarked at Castle William under the command of Colonel Leslie. This detachment landed near Marblehead, about three in the afternoon, while the people were in church.

No one in the church waited for the closing prayer. On the contrary, at first sight of the transports' boats moving in toward shore with their red-clad cargoes, the congregation rose and left as one man, and thereafter scattered to spread the alarm. The redcoats were out, and were on the road to Salem.

Leslie and his men landed and marched. They marched by the cove road and around into Salem itself. But the arms they sought were not there. Through their Tory informants the soldiers had pretty accurate information as to just where they were stored, however. Accordingly they marched on northward, along the road to Danvers, and stopped only at the North River, where they found the drawbridge up. Colonel Leslie, shouting across the river in a manner that must have hurt his sense of dignity severely, demanded to know why the progress of His Majesty's troops along a public highway was thus impeded. The only reply he got for his pains was that it was not a public highway, but the property of the town, which they might close at any moment they saw fit.

Leslie's men, then growing impatient, for it is cold standing on the North River in February, attempted to seize a couple of barges that were moored near by. Their owners responded promptly by scuttling the craft; not, however, before two or three of them, in the ensuing scuffle, were pricked by British bayonets—a circumstance which in later years was to give rise to Salem's claim of first blood of the Revolution.

Meantime the bells had been ringing and the drums beating, calling up the militiamen to the defense of their stores—which, incidentally, had long since been moved from their original hiding place to another. Colonel Leslie began to grow apprehensive lest the business ultimately grow to be something larger than he had bargained for, and at last he promised that if the draw were lowered to permit his men to pass he would not march them more than thirty yards beyond it.

Why this stipulation was made, or why the colonel felt it necessary to march his men across the bridge, only to turn them about and march them back again, is an unsolved mystery. No doubt it had some peculiar importance to the colonel's pride. Orientals are not the only ones who have felt it necessary, on occasion, to "save face."

At any rate the terms were all complied with. The bridge was lowered, Colonel Leslie and his men marched across, and then turned about and marched right back again. Nor did they stop thereafter until they reached the shore where their boats were drawn up.

The minute men of Salem and Marblehead and Beverly and Danvers escorted them every step of the way.

These picayune movements were all very well so long as it was winter and more ambitious projects could scarcely be expected of troops that, like bears and woodchucks, invariably took to winter quarters at the first flake of snow. But now that spring was approaching, Gage looked forward to more ambitious undertakings. By now he had some five to six thousand men under his command, and it was his secret feeling that the summer would bring matters to a head; that it was a case of move first or be moved against.

What he had in mind was an inland sweep in sufficient force to carry him to Worcester, there to seize the sizable cache of arms and powder which everyone knew the patriots had collected. To this end he sent out a number of spies to search out the lay of the land, to taste the temper of the people, and if possible to locate exactly the hiding place of the ammunition and the roads that led to it.

Most of these volunteer sleuths were officers and gentlemen, who got themselves up ludicrously in costumes to represent the bumpkins they believed the patriots to be. Most of them were so transparent that everyone who met them recognized them instantly for what they were. A few got through. All of them had interesting adventures to relate. But to a man they all agreed that to move on Worcester would be an undertaking of extremely doubtful consequences. One, a private who had perhaps better opportunities than any of the others to observe what went on, for his disguise was only once or twice suspected, went so far as to declare that if ten thousand regulars, with a full train of artillery, were to attempt it not one of them would come back to Boston alive.

That seemed to settle the question of a raid on Worcester. Even with his reinforcements Gage did not have enough men to contemplate such an undertaking; not even if he stripped Boston of its garrison, and that, of course, was unthinkable. There was, however, one other possibility.

In the course of the winter a considerable store of arms and ammunition had been gathered by the patriots at Concord, a scant seventeen miles outside of Boston. This had been done with the utmost secrecy, and only a few men knew of it in Boston. But somehow word of it was now carried to Gage. For a long time it was a mystery, how he came by the information. But now it seems certain that his informant was Dr. Benjamin Church, who, although high in the counsels and confidence of the patriots, was already playing in with the British. He, too, must have told Gage that Adams and Hancock had fled to Lexington to avoid arrest and were hiding at the Clark Parsonage there. Gage, at any rate, now decided to bowl over two birds with a single stone. He would send a strong force to seize Adams and Hancock at Lexington. They would then march overland and destroy the stores at Concord. If the cards were rightly played the game could be done and won, the rebels seized, the powder destroyed, and the troops back safe in Boston before anyone was the wiser.

The plans were laid in the utmost secrecy, sometime before the 14th of April. Apart from Gage himself, only two people were said to have known exactly what was to happen. These were Lord Percy, who was to command the reserve, and the general's wife, who was in her husband's confidence naturally. Even Colonel Smith, who was to have actual command of the raiding party, and Major Pitcairn, who was to be second-in-command, appear to have been ignorant of their objective until almost the final moment.

On the 14th the ship of war *Somerset* had been moved up out of the bay into the very mouth of the Charles, where anyone attempting to cross must pass directly beneath her guns. On the 15th the Grenadiers and light infantry were relieved of duty on the pretext of trying out some new maneuvers on the next day. At the same time a number of transports were warped up and anchored not far from the *Somerset*. Not until the afternoon of Tuesday, the 18th, did Gage issue his final orders to his officers and let his commanders know what their destinations were to be. Even then only a few learned all the details. Colonel Smith, with eight hundred men, was to embark in the transports' boats, already drawn up in the Back Bay, at the foot of the Common. They were to cross to Cambridge before dawn and immediately take up the march upon Lexington. In the meantime Lord Percy was to remain in Boston with the reserve, in readiness to march, at an instant's notice, by way of Roxbury Neck and the roundabout road through Cambridge, to the support of the advance if necessary.

Despite the secrecy, however, the news of the movement leaked out. By what means this was accomplished has been a better-guarded secret than how the British obtained their information. But doubtless the patriots also had their spies. There is a legend that says that Lord Percy himself, returning from Gage's headquarters in the Province House to his own quarters, passed near the point of embarkation. The boats were already drawn up on shore, and the soldiers were assembling. Civilians stood about in little knots watching by the light of lanterns. It was dark, and Percy was not recognized. As he approached one of the groups he heard someone say: "The troops have marched, but will miss their aim."

Percy stopped.

"What aim?" he asked.

"Why," said the man, not recognizing the man to whom he was speaking, "the cannon at Concord."

It must have given Percy quite a start to hear their destination spoken of with such assurance. He went at once to Gage and told him that the secret was out.

"We have been betrayed!" said Gage. "Only yourself and Mrs. Gage know our objective."

The implication is clear enough, and there may be some truth in it. After all, the general's lady was an American. However, it is worth noting that the story was chiefly circulated after the event by certain officers who had no love for their commander, and who were fond of saying that she betrayed his secrets.

However that may be, there is a better-substantiated story which runs that some of the officers, following the council at which the objective was revealed, discussed the expedition in the presence of an hostler as they tended to their mounts. The hostler is said to have reported the conversation to a stableboy, ostensibly loyal but actually in league with the patriots. The stableboy at once carried the news to Warren. But even he was told that he was the third to bring the tidings.

At any rate the word was out. Warren, warned betimes of what was afoot, summoned William Dawes and sent him away on horseback, over Roxbury Neck and around by back roads through Watertown, to Lexington to warn Adams and Hancock that the British were coming. British officers had already been sent out to cover the various roads in the event of just such a contingency, but there were none of them on the route that Dawes covered.

Having sent off Dawes, Warren next sent for Paul Revere, who had already, on several occasions, ridden express for the Committee of Safety. Revere himself described the occasion:

> About ten o'clock Dr. Warren sent in great haste for me, and begged that I would immediately set off for Lexington, where Messrs. Hancock and Adams were, and acquaint them of the movement, and that it was thought that they were the objects. When I got to Dr. Warren's house, I found that he had sent an express by land to Lexington—a Mr. William Dawes.

Revere had prepared for this moment. He had already arranged for the lanterns to be hung in the belfry of the Old North Church—not as a signal to him, for he was still in Boston at the moment they appeared, but rather as a signal to other watchers on the other side of the river that a movement of British troops was on foot. "One if by land and two if by sea." Longfellow drew heavily upon his poet's license here.

Nevertheless the lanterns were hung, and riders did speed "through every Middlesex village and farm," carrying the warning that the redcoats were out. Paul Revere rode, too.

The true version of that ride is scarcely less thrilling than the legendary one, especially that part of it which deals with Revere's escape from Boston.

Revere had a boat, hidden no doubt in one of the empty warehouses along the North Boston waterfront. He went home and dressed for the ride. Booted, but not spurred—he had forgotten the spurs, so the tale has it—he left the house and headed for the point at which he was to meet Joshua Bentley and

Thomas Richardson, who were to row him across. His dog followed him. Halfway to the rendezvous with his companions he remembered his spurs. Still according to the legend, he stopped and attached a note to his wife to the dog's collar and sent him back to the house. Soon the animal reappeared with the equine accelerators dangling beneath his chin. Revere went on, carefully avoiding the soldiers who swarmed all over the town, going and coming in preparation for the coming sortie.

At the appointed place he met Bentley and Richardson, and the three moved on toward the boat's hiding place. Now one of them thought that it might be a good notion to have some cloth wherewith to muffle the oars. Accordingly they stopped at the house of a young lady friend and whistled. The girl came to the window and put her head out. There was an exchange of whispers and the girl withdrew. A moment later a petticoat—still warm, so the story runs—floated down through the darkness into their waiting hands.

In the dark shadow of the wharf they tore the petticoat in shreds and wrapped the tholepins and gunnels so that the creak and rattle of the oars as they swung would be stilled. A moment later they pushed out into the darkened harbor.

The black bulk of the *Somerset*, a 64-gun ship of the line, rode in the ferryway, forcing them to make a wide circuit in the direction of Noddle's Island. The edge of the moon was beginning to show, and the tide ran strong. Beyond the man-of-war they could see the long black string of the soldiers' boats, already reaching out and moving up the river. As they passed the *Somerset*, even at such a distance they held their breaths. But no hail came, no shot or challenge, and presently Revere stepped ashore on the Charlestown side.

From there he went on alone, to Colonel Conant's stable, where he found a group waiting and John Larkin's good horse standing ready-saddled. Not many words passed between them.

Revere told the men what was up. As he swung up into the saddle someone spoke.

"Mind the patrols. They've been out thick as flies on the road since afternoon."

Revere touched his hat with his crop by way of acknowledgment and whirled his mount.

"Good luck!" someone called softly.

But his only reply was a shower of gravel and a rattle of hoofs in the dark. Paul Revere was away on his midnight ride.

CHAPTER XIII

Shots Heard round the World

> . . . The 18th of April, in seventy-five;
> Hardly a man is now alive
> Who remembers that famous day and year.

LONGFELLOW has commemorated that day for us in familiar, if somewhat inaccurate, lines. And Emerson has
done the same for the day that followed. But even without
these lyric reminders, these are two days which Americans will
scarcely forget.

Every schoolboy knows the story; how Revere warned
Adams and Hancock, and how the word passed on to Concord—Longfellow to the contrary notwithstanding, Revere
never actually reached Concord. He was captured by some
British officers on the road there and was released later only
when it became apparent that it would be impossible to carry
him to Boston. Every American knows how the British marched
to Lexington to find the minute men drawn up on the Common; how they fired—and marched on to Concord; and how, at
Concord, "by the rude bridge that arched the flood . . . the
embattled farmers stood, and fired the shot heard round the
world."

> You know the rest: in the books you have read,
> How the British regulars fired and fled,—
> How the farmers gave them ball for ball,
> From behind each fence and farmyard wall,

Boston: Cradle of Liberty

Chasing the redcoats down the lane,
Then crossing the fields to emerge again
Under the trees at the turn of the road,
And only pausing to fire and load.

In spite of its familiarity there is a strong temptation to retell the story; to clear away, perhaps, a few popular misconceptions, and to bring into the picture some of those lesser happenings, some of those little human touches, generally omitted in the cut-and-dried accounts. But this is a temptation to be resisted here. After all, the bulk of the action was in the main remote from the scene of our story, and the bare fact of its occurrence must be sufficient for our purposes. Our interest lies more in what was going on in Boston while the regulars were on the march; while the fighting was in progress; and while the redcoats fled.

This is quite a different matter in more ways than one. Where accounts of the doing of the troops, of the skirmishing and the retreat, are concerned, there is little difficulty in learning what happened. But of events in Boston on that day the records are distressingly sparse. Still, by piecing such as we have together, here and there, and by drawing a bit on our imaginations, we can put together a reasonable picture of what it must have been.

That there were some in Boston who knew the destination of the troops the night before, we already know. Dr. Warren knew it. The Committee of Safety knew it, therefore, for Warren would be prompt to pass on his information. The self-appointed Committee of Thirty, a sort of volunteer vigilance organization, of which Revere was a member, knew it. So did some of the townsfolk—or else they guessed—as the conversation overheard by Lord Percy on the Common shows. But the majority of the people were not aware of it. They could scarcely miss the unusual activity among the troops; the marching and counter-marching, the air of hurried preparation, that went on at an hour long after the soldiers were generally relieved of duty and lay snug in their quarters for the night. Anyone seeing it would have been dull indeed not to realize that some unusual movement was afoot; that a foray was being contemplated; and that the redcoats would strike somewhere on the morrow. But it is doubtful if many Bostonians had any real inkling of the true objective until the following morning. Most of them probably went to bed without the least notion that anything extraordinary was up.

It must have come as a surprise, then, to most of the townsfolk to awake the next morning to find Percy and his detachment drawn up on the Common, preparing to march to Smith's support.

Smith, it appeared, crossing the river between ten and midnight, had landed his men at Phipps's Farm, on the marshes of East Cambridge. The tide was high, and the men had had to wade up to their middles to reach dry land. Once there they were kept standing till past two o'clock—why, no one seems to know. At last they marched, however, through Cambridge, and then up through Menotomy (Anatomy, one of the British officers calls it), which was then the name for what is now Arlington. About here they met with two of the countrymen who had set out on Revere's signal from the North Church to rouse the countryside. Smith, of course, was unaware of their mission, but that mattered little now. The men had seen his column, and if the country was not already warned it soon would be. A little later came in one of those officers posted about the countryside, riding posthaste, to warn the colonel that the word was out. Hot on his heels came Major Mitchell—one of those officers who had intercepted Revere on the way from Lexington to Concord—to confirm the news in no uncertain terms. Almost as if in derision, at this moment an alarm gun sounded near by, to be echoed by another and another, and presently the bells began to add their clamor. Colonel Smith listened to the officers' reports and decided to be on the safe side —not that he anticipated any very spirited resistance from these yokels, but a stronger show of force than his little column could make might be called for. He sent back a courier to General Gage with word that the countryside was alarmed and gathering, and that reinforcements seemed indicated.

This was between three and four in the morning. Gage received the word before dawn and immediately sent word to Percy to muster his command in readiness to march at seven o'clock.

Now Percy's column consisted of infantry from the Fourth, the Twenty-third, and Forty-seventh regiments, a detail of light artillery, and a detachment of Royal Marines. In command of the marines was Major Pitcairn. But Pitcairn had already gone, as a volunteer, with Smith, and it was he who commanded the advance detachment which so neatly tipped the fat into the fire on Lexington Common.

Of course that had not yet happened. Still, one would think that Pitcairn's whereabouts would have been known to his superiors in Boston. Apparently, however, the fact that he had gone was forgotten, and the order to him to muster his marines with the rest of Percy's column lay several hours on his desk before anyone could seem to think why the marines did not show up.

Meantime Percy and the rest of the column, according to orders, mustered on the Common and waited. The missing marines did not come. Percy paraded his men, and the townsfolk turned out to stare. At Lexington the first shots of the Revolution had already been fired, but no one in Boston knew that yet.

The marines did not come and did not come. We can imagine

Lord Percy's impatience as he sat his horse, waiting and watching his men go through close-order drill. He sent messengers here and there, trying to rouse out the missing detachment. But no one seemed to know what was causing the delay. About this time Harison Gray Otis, then a schoolboy, was on his way to school. He has left us a description of the scene which gives us a hint as to the state of mind in Boston at the moment:

On the 19th April, 1775, I went to school for the last time. In the morning, about seven, Percy's brigade was drawn up, extending from Scollay's buildings, through Tremont Street, and nearly to the bottom of the Mall [the description was written long after the event], preparing to take up their march for Lexington. A corporal came up to me as I was going to school, and turned me off to pass down Court Street; which I did, and came up School Street to the schoolhouse. It may well be imagined that great agitation prevailed, the British line being drawn up a few yards only from the school-house door. As I entered the school, I heard the announcement of *"deponite libros"* [legend has it that schoolmaster Lovell said, "War's begun, and school's done; *deponite libros*." But there is no confirmation of this] and ran home for fear of the regulars.

It was two hours or more before someone remembered Major Pitcairn's whereabouts and the necessary orders were given to enable the marines to move out under their second-in-command. And so, at last, some time after nine in the morning, Percy's column got under way, flags flying, drums rolling, and the fifes, tradition has it, insolently piping out the strains of "Yankee Doodle."

Out along Treamount Street and into Orange, over the Neck and past the fortifications Gage had raised there with such difficulty, and into Roxbury they marched. It was a hot morning—hot with that breathless, humid stillness that sometimes comes in these parts in the early spring—and small boys and old men turned out along the route to jeer them on. There is a story that runs that in Roxbury Earl Percy spied a small boy who was jumping up and down, making faces, uttering shouts of derision and laughing as if to attract his attention. He sent for the boy and asked him what amused him.

"You go out," said the youngster, "to Yankee Doodle,* but you will dance by and by to Chevy Chase."

The "Ballad of Chevy Chase," which was popular about that time, referred to the death of an earlier "stout Erle Percy," so, whether the boy was aware of it or not, the allusion was quite apt. The tradition is that Percy was quite put out and that the incident plagued him all day long. One may be permitted to doubt this, however. Percy was a man of humor and some discernment, even if he was on the wrong side of the fence. It is hardly likely that in the seriousness of the moment he would allow himself to be unduly irked by the jibes of a schoolboy. On the contrary, it is more likely he would be amused at the erudition of the tyke.

The column did not halt. They pressed on along the road to Cambridge only to find, when they came to the bridge across the Charles—on the site of the present Larz Anderson Bridge— a little after noon, that the planks had been taken up.

Meantime back in Boston word of the skirmish at Lexington had reached Dr. Warren about eight in the morning—hours before Gage heard of it. He knew at once the significance of the news, as his own words show: "They have begun it." He let no grass grow under his feet. He passed the word to his fellow committeemen and then quietly slipped out of town, crossing the river to Charlestown by boat and thence pushing for-

*The tune they may have played. The song "Yankee Doodle," however, was not written until some time later, as the words indicate. It was set to the music of an old English song, "Lucy Locket," known in the time of Charles I, and familiar in New England in colonial times as "Lydia Fisher's Jig." It is said to have been the popular piece of band music among the troops at Castle William at the time, so it is scarcely extraordinary if they played it at this time. The youngster, however, could scarcely have referred to it, although he might have cited "Chevy Chase."

ward to meet the retreating British and take a hand in harassing them. How he managed to get over the river under the guns of the *Somerset* is a tale that has never been told. But it is a matter of record that he did it. Dr. Church also left Boston that day. Church was to return later to carry news of the rebel councils to Gage. But Warren had taken his last walk on Beacon Street and spent his last evening at the Green Dragon. He was not to return to Boston again.

Most of the members of the Boston committee also managed to leave that day.

It was as well for them that they did. As soon as Gage learned that the alarm had been given, the arrests began. How it became known that the first signal had come from the belfry of the Old North Church is not known. Perhaps someone on board the *Somerset* had noted that brief glimmer of light and, remembering it later, had put two and two together. However that may be, Newman, the sexton, although he made good his escape from the church without being seen after hanging the lanterns, was arrested the following morning and thrown into jail. Pulling, who also had a hand in the business—he accompanied Newman to the church—barely escaped by the skin of his teeth. It is said that he had to hide in a wine butt in his grandmother's cellar while a party of soldiers sent out after him ransacked the house. But the best birds had already flown. Warren was gone. So were Adams and Hancock. Dawes and Revere, as we have seen, had been caught near Lexington and then released, since it was impossible for their captors to bring them in and escape themselves.

It was nearly one o'clock in the afternoon before Gage learned of the skirmish at Lexington. The townsfolk must have heard of it at about the same time—or perhaps a little earlier. Gage must have realized the meaning of the news at once, as had Warren. Indeed it is likely that its significance escaped few.

Boston must have grown tense about that time. At any rate Gage issued orders for all troops not on duty to remain in quarters under arms, ready to move to any point at an instant's notice, yet at the same time out of the way of general mischief in the streets. It seems, too, that the general had some misapprehensions lest there be a general rising in the town and the barracks themselves be attacked.

This was probably not without foundation. One can imagine the excitement, the spirit of tension that must have lain over the city. All that was known in town was that fighting had taken place at Lexington; that a number of minute men had been killed; and that the British had then marched on to Concord. What followed that, what was taking place even then, was yet unknown on the peninsula. The questions uppermost in everyone's mind were: Had the provincials made a stand? If so, how had it turned out? And what was now happening out there beyond the Charles in the woody hills and dusty lanes? In the anxiety of the moment there would be restlessness, irritability, disquietude which might fulminate at the slightest provocation. It was too far yet from the scene of the fighting for any echo of firing to have reached the town. But the bells which brayed with brazen tongues on every side must have given some hint that the issue was not yet settled. It was for men's imaginations to supply the picture of what might be happening, and the temper of Bostonians toward anyone in a red coat may well have been short that day.

We may imagine, with no great strain upon our mental powers, that Boston was very still in the heat and sunshine of that April day, waiting . . . waiting . . .

In the meantime what was happening out there beyond earshot of Beacon Hill?

The removal of the planks from the bridge did not delay Percy's column long. The intentions of the selectmen of

Cambridge had been of the best in ordering them taken up, but with true Cantabrigian parsimony, rather than have them flung into the river or carted away, they had ordered them stacked neatly on the Cambridge side. It had been but the work of an hour or so for some of Percy's men to cross on the stringers and relay the planks sufficiently for most of the column to cross. Once on the other side, Percy marched directly to Cambridge Common. The train, with its heavy wagons, was left to follow as soon as the bridge might be made passable for it.

From the Common in Cambridge a number of roads radiated in various directions. Percy did not know which one to take. Nor would anyone tell him, though the redcoats thundered at a number of doors. It was only after considerable delay that a tutor of the college was routed out, one Isaac Smith, who later excused himself by saying that he could not tell a lie. He put the column on the road to Lexington and was later severely criticized for not having sent them to Lechmere Point and the marshes instead. But such deception was evidently not in his nature.

Percy pressed on rapidly from Cambridge in the direction of Lexington, for it was clearly evident by now that he was in hostile territory. Not until he reached Menotomy, however, did he learn that there had been serious fighting ahead. It was now sometime after one o'clock. He quickened his pace still more and arrived on the outskirts of Lexington just in time to meet the remnants of Smith's column fleeing, in ragged, exhausted disorder, before a fire that seemed to sprout from behind every tree and rock and bush behind and on both flanks.

Smith's withdrawal from Concord was no orderly retreat. For a mile or two his men had held their ranks, but as the provincials kept pouring in from towns round about, lining the fences, hiding in the thickets, flitting from tree to tree, to fire and run to a new vantage point and load and fire again, their pace quickened and became first a flight and then a panicky rout. All along the way they strewed equipment, too heavy to be borne longer—muskets, cartridge pouches, knapsacks. It has been said that Smith would have surrendered could he have found anyone in authority to whom to turn over his sword. But the provincials were not thinking in terms of military command that day. They were fighting, each one for himself, in the way their fathers—and a good many of themselves—had fought the French and Indians in days not so long gone by.

It happened that it was at a comparatively open, level spot that the fleeing column met the relief. Percy's ranks opened to receive them and formed a hollow square about them, while the exhausted men flung themselves upon the ground and lay panting, "with their tongues hanging out like dogs."

Percy had two field pieces with him, and so long as the redcoats remained where they were these held the provincials more or less at bay. But night was coming on. The afternoon shadows were already lengthening, and to delay too long would mean that retreat would be entirely cut off. As soon as the British began to move again, the provincials closed in once more and resumed their harrying tactics, reinforced now by thousands more of their fellow countrymen who had come up in the meantime.

It would be mere repetition to outline in detail the rest of that flight. Down through Menotomy and Cambridge the redcoats fled, with the patriots swarming behind like an inexorable wave. At Cambridge, Percy, by now in command since Colonel Smith had been wounded, bore off to the left, toward Charlestown, rather than attempt the long struggle through Roxbury and around by land to Boston. He feared further prolongation of that withering fire; feared, too, that the minute men from the south, who might not yet have arrived to join those of Lexington and Concord, would swing in athwart his path and perhaps cut him off. He did not know that by now the planks were up once more from the Cambridge–Brighton bridge, and this time the planks had been thrown in the river. Had he tried to take that route he would have found himself pocketed against the river, and his entire command would undoubtedly have been annihilated. As he went—from North Cambridge straight across through what is now Somerville, to Charlestown Neck—the way was shorter, he had Pickering's Essex Regiment on Winter Hill to protect his flank, and once across the Neck in Charlestown he would have a chance to protect his rear with a few men in case the provincials attempted to follow.

They did follow as far as the beginning of the Neck. The sun was down and dusk was falling. The flashes of the muskets as the troops retreated down Milk Row—now Washington Street, Somerville—were visible in Boston and told their own story to the watchers on the rooftops there. On the Neck the retreating soldiers met with crowds of refugees flocking out of Charlestown, fearful that their town was to become a battleground. The two groups passed each other, each fleeing toward its own. Once the redcoats were across the Neck the provincials, seeing the futility of further pursuit, drew off and threw up barricades against any possibility of escape on the land side.

But Percy had no thought of escape. He bivouacked his men on Bunker Hill and sent messengers with his report across the river to Gage. He expected to be reinforced where he lay, that Charlestown's peninsula at least might be held. But Gage had other ideas. His orders to Percy were to withdraw to Boston, and all through the night the boats plied back and forth, bringing off first the wounded and then the weary. It was approaching dawn before the last redcoat was safe again in Boston town. In a little more than twenty-four hours the British had discovered that the Americans would fight, and some had even learned that they were no mean opponents. American losses were forty-nine killed, thirty-four wounded, and five missing. The British loss, killed, wounded, and missing totaled 273.

What had started out to be a pleasant spring maneuver, scarcely expected to take the winter kinks out of the men's legs, had backfired sadly. Gage had almost literally set the countryside on fire, had started a long and bloody war, and had lost England a continent.

In a day in which the swiftest means of communication was by post horse, the speed with which the word that the long-expected day had at last arrived spread through the length and breadth of the colonies is little short of amazing. New York heard it almost before the last of Percy's men were ferried across the Charles. Philadelphia, that night. In another day it was in Virginia. Still another carried it to Charleston. And one more found it in the settlements below Savannah. Westward it spread to Kentucky and Tennessee; northward to Montreal and Quebec; eastward along the coast of Maine and New Brunswick and into Nova Scotia. And, everywhere it went, men sprang to arms.

In New England the word traveled even more swiftly, and the response was instantaneous. Before the blood was dry on the grass of Lexington Common the bells had waked the echoes in towns north and west and south, in New Hampshire, in Massachusetts, in Rhode Island and Connecticut, spreading the alarm that somewhere, somehow the time had come. Close behind their clangor came the messengers, relaying the word from village to village, town to town, mouth to mouth, into the back country, over the hills, up the rivers and along the brooks, into the deepest corners of the wilderness. Before the British had started their retreat from Concord the word had reached the Merrimack. By nightfall it had reached the mountains. The men of the villages between Worcester and Springfield and Holyoke and Greenfield were on the march east by sundown, and all night long Worcester was kept awake by the sound of their passing. Israel Putnam—Old Put—in Pomfret, Connecticut, was helping his hired men build a stone wall the next morning when the word came. He set out at once, pausing only to summon the men of his community and those immediately surrounding it. He reached Cambridge the next morning, still wearing the checked shirt in which he had been working on the wall. At the same time arrived the first contingent from New Hampshire under Dearborn and Cilley.

Everywhere the response was the same. All day on the 20th, the 21st, the 22d, the companies poured into the Continental camp. By the morning of the 23d there were sixteen thousand men in camp, and more were flocking in with every passing hour. There was talk of marching into Boston and driving the redcoats into the sea. But calmer heads prevailed.

Over in Boston, Gage watched the gathering of the clans with dire apprehension. He alone knew his own weakness. He had a scant five thousand men, obviously demoralized, as their attitude of bravado plainly showed. He was surrounded by a hostile population; faced by an army, disorganized it is true, but three times as large as his own and capable of inflicting heavy damage, as it had already proved. Some of the patriot commanders thought he would come out. Instead he sat down and hastily strengthened his defenses. Boston was besieged, and never again did Gage send out a soldier by land.

Perhaps it was as well for both sides that neither one moved. Gage might have made a sally and blasted the provincial camp. But he could not have chased them far before they would have fallen upon him as they had the smaller detachment at Concord and cut him to bits on his way home. Moreover to do so he would have had to denude Boston almost entirely of troops, and who could tell what the people of the town might be doing in his absence? On the other hand the Americans' organization was not yet such that they could feel confident of attacking strongly held defensive positions with any chance of success. Their numbers were uncertain. Many who turned out at the first alarm, as soon as they discovered that a pitched battle was not immediately in prospect, turned about and went home. There was no unity of command. The men of New Hampshire took their orders from Folsom and Stark, and no others. The men of Connecticut looked to Spenser and Putnam. Rhode Islanders placed their faith in Nathanael Greene. And the Massachusetts commander, General Ward, who had a sort of nominal command over all, had not the influence to weld them into a single force. Moreover, they were desperately short of arms, ammunition, and supplies. Had Gage but known it, General Thomas, who commanded at Roxbury, was forced to march his small handful of men round and round a hill, one side of which was in sight of the British lines, in order to give the enemy the impression that his strength was far greater than it was.

Even so it must have been an impressive sight to watchers on Beacon Hill and the rooftops of Boston to see the campfires of the provincials twinkling through the night in a solid line, from Winter Hill on the north to Dorchester on the south.

So the two armies lay and watched one another warily, over the broad expanse of the Back Bay and the slender thread of land at Roxbury. There was apprehension in the American camp lest the British come out, and anxiety in the British camp lest the Americans come in. Neither one, for the moment, cared to make the first move.

In the meantime, in spite of the siege, there was a good deal of movement in and out of Boston. Naturally those who sympathized with the patriots, and who could do so, wished to get out of a British stronghold which might at any moment be burned about their ears. At the same time, and by the same token, Tories from all about the surrounding country, seeing themselves more and more in danger from the aroused people, were making every effort to find shelter within the British lines.

The problem of supply within the city was soon critical. Private vessels were still forbidden to enter or leave the Port—even for the purpose of relieving the acute shortage of necessities which quickly developed out of a situation which, even before Lexington and Concord, had been none too good. Naturally the besiegers permitted no more than was absolutely necessary to sustain the lives of their own supporters within the town to pass through their lines, and when these were passed the provincials made as sure as possible that the supplies were destined for the right people.

Under these circumstances Gage was only too happy to simplify his problem by letting the Whigs leave the town. Every patriot who left Boston meant one less mouth to feed. Gage announced that permits to leave would be issued to all those who would turn over what arms they might possess and give their parole not to take up arms against the British once they were outside. A good many took advantage of the offer, and Gage's total haul was "1,778 firearms, 973 bayonets, 634 pistols, and 38 blunderbusses."

The system was hardly satisfactory, however. For every Whig who went out, at least one Tory came in, so the problem of food was hardly reduced. Before long, too, the Tory groups inside the city, who during the course of the siege came to have more and more influence on the commander, and who feared that once all the Whigs were evacuated the Americans would burn the town, brought pressure to bear upon the general to stop the issuance of passes and thus put a stop to further departures. In this way such Whigs as remained inside the city became, in a sense, hostages; and the provincials promptly retaliated by holding any Tories they could catch and by closing the lines. What was even more infuriating to the British was the

patriot claim that Gage, by his refusal to issue passes to Whigs
to leave the city, since a good many of those applying had already turned in their arms on the strength of his promise, had
himself violated his word, and, therefore, those who had already
left the town under parole were no longer bound and might
serve against the British if they wished. So the order actually
proved a boomerang in the end.

There were a good many patriots, however, who stayed in
Boston voluntarily. All that they had left in the world was there.
They had already seen what happened to the property of those
who left. Confiscation was the best that could be hoped for.
Looting and destruction by the redcoats was not unheard of.
But the most usual fate of such property was to fall into the
hands of the lawless mobs that prowled the streets, caring naught
for Whig or Tory so long as they found easy pickings. As a result a good many stayed on as the only means they had of protecting, to some extent, the little they still owned. Merchant
John Rowe was one of those reluctant to leave their "effects"
behind.

Life in Boston during that period was not easy for anyone,
unless it might be for the officers, who seemed to enjoy themselves hugely. For those patriots who remained, however, it
must have been trying indeed. With the great influx of Tories
into the city, the peninsula quickly became predominantly
loyalist in color—if not in general sentiment, for there was still
the bulk of the poorer population, which was overwhelmingly
Whig in feeling but, in the circumstances, quite inarticulate.
The Tories who came soon began to form themselves into companies and battalions in order that they might take their stand
alongside the King's troops when it came to fighting. In fact,
on the very day of Lexington and Concord, a number of them
met together and formed a corps, known as the Loyal American Associators, under the command of Timothy Ruggles.

Other corps formed during the course of the siege were the Loyal Irish Volunteers, the Royal North British Volunteers and the Royal Fencible Americans. These men were eager to serve in defense of their homes and their convictions. But neither Gage nor his successor, Howe, appeared to take them very seriously, and they were left the duties of patrol and guard throughout. They would not have been human if they had not kept a sharper watch on Tory than on patriots' property.

They are not recorded as having done anything else during the siege.

This is scarcely surprising, however—although it may have been to the eager volunteers. Under the circumstances Gage had no other use for them. Nor did Howe later. Quite naturally, for the present, both commanders preferred to put their faith in the regulars, whose action they could predict, for such tasks as were necessary. After all they were regulars themselves.

Such fighting as took place during this period was desultory. There is a pretty tradition that American snipers made life miserable for the British by picking off their officers whenever they showed themselves along the lines, knocking them off at extreme ranges and with an accuracy which amazed the redcoats. This is unlikely. In the first place, until the arrival of the Virginia and Pennsylvania riflemen in July, there was probably not a rifle in camp. The New England men were not familiar with that weapon. They were armed with smooth-bore muskets whose accuracy could not be depended upon even at short ranges. In the second place, powder was so scarce in the Continental camp that every ounce of it had to be hoarded against a more urgent need, such as a British sally. There was none to waste. Even after the riflemen came, the records rather indicate that not many officers were picked off on the British lines.

This does not mean, however, that there was no military activity whatever. In the American camp it took some time for the troops to settle down to the business of fortifying and entrenching their positions. Meantime there were some in positions of command who saw that unless the men were kept busy they would become preoccupied with their troubles and go home in droves. Putnam was one of these. He worked his men steadily, throwing up redoubts and earthworks along the river at Cambridge. He saw, too, that the men needed practice in fighting, or, if fighting was not to be had, some sort of warlike demonstration against the enemy, to maintain their martial spirit. This accounted, no doubt, for a curious foray which he led.

On the 13th of May, Putnam marched out at the head of some two thousand men, "to shoe themselves to the regulars," as one of the provincials recorded in his diary. They marched across Charlestown Neck, over Bunker's and Breed's hills in full view of the harbor, and thence descended into the now abandoned town. From there they marched back along the waterfront, halting for a few moments opposite where the *Somerset* still lay. There they indulged in a few defiant war whoops and thereafter marched back to camp along the causeway which connected Charlestown and Cambridge.

No shots were fired by either side, to the disappointment of many, both on board the *Somerset* and in the detachment. But the expedition apparently served its purpose. The Americans were the better for the drill, and the British were given additional evidence that the Americans meant business.

Away around on the other side of the town there were several alarms, the results of reports that the British intended to seize Dorchester. General Thomas, who commanded at Roxbury, as we have seen, being the nearest to that point, was charged with its defense, and he was kept constantly on the alert. None of these, however, bore fruit, and for the time being Dorchester remained, like Charlestown, a sort of no man's land, lying between but unoccupied by either force.

Shots Heard round the World

In the British camp Gage was not idle. Besides his fortifications on the Neck he erected batteries at various points about the peninsula, overlooking the harbor, the Charles and the Back Bay. Admiral Graves was responsible for a strong battery on Copp's Hill, facing Charlestown, from which position he could protect the *Somerset* and the other vessels lying at anchor off Charlestown which might otherwise be endangered by colonial batteries, which might be raised, on Breed's and Bunker's hills across the river. In addition to these efforts a number of floating batteries were constructed which could be moved about to protect otherwise weak spots. One of these was anchored in the Back Bay. And there was another in the Dorchester Flats, which worried poor General Thomas considerably.

But this is not the full story of the activities of the two forces which opposed one another through those early weeks of Boston's siege. In addition to strengthening his defenses, Gage deemed it wise to bring in the livestock which he had in pasture on the outlying islands of the harbor to nearer islands under the protection of the guns of the fleet. Such stock now was of vital importance to him, for it was his only source of fresh meat, and it was necessary to make it as secure as possible. But the one move made necessary another. In order to feed such a concentration of stock he had to have hay, and this, too, was available to him only on the harbor islands. Consequently it was necessary for him to send out, from time to time, expeditions under guard to cut the hay and bring it off. Naturally the provincials saw in these excursions opportunities to catch some of the redcoats off their base, and they took full advantage of this means of harrying the enemy.

One such occasion was a haying expedition which Gage sent to Grape Island, lying off the mouth of Weymouth Back River, and about midway between the towns of Weymouth and Hingham. As the British approached the island there was some uncertainty as to their exact destination, and the usual crop of alarms and rumor flew about the countryside. General Thomas was told that four sloops were landing troops at Weymouth, and he promptly dispatched three companies to oppose them, but these found, on arrival, that the soldiers had landed on the island instead and were busily cutting the hay and bringing it down to their boats. The tide was low, just at the turn, and since the vessels belonging to the townsfolk were high and dry there was nothing the provincials could do but wait until the tide returned enough to float them. In the meantime they lined the shore and helplessly watched and waited.

At the same time the alarm, spreading through the back country, not only brought reinforcements but also sent numbers of the inhabitants packing in fear lest this foray be the forerunner of the long-expected British attack. A letter from Abigail Adams to her husband described the state of Braintree, not far from Weymouth, on that day, and is eloquent of the general attitude around Boston during the early siege:

People, women, children, from the iron works, came flocking down this way; every woman and child driven off from below my father's; my father's family flying. [Uncle] in great distress, as you may well imagine, for my aunt had her bed thrown into a cart, into which she got herself, and ordered the boy to drive her to Bridgewater, which he did. The report was to them that three hundred had landed and were upon their march up into town. The alarm flew like lightning, and men from all parts came flocking down, till two thousand were collected. . . . [Uncle] is in a miserable state of health, and hardly able to go from his own house to my father's. Danger, you know, sometimes makes timid men bold. He stood that day very well, and generously attended, with drink, biscuits, flints, etc., five hundred men, without taking any pay. . . . Both your brothers were there; your younger brother with his company, who gained honor for their good order that day. He was one of the first to venture on board a schooner to land upon the island.

So the vessels did finally get off, as young Adams could testify. But when the British saw the Americans coming they withdrew at one end of the island as the provincials were jumping ashore at the other end. Some shots were exchanged, but no one appears to have been hurt. The British took some of the hay they had cut, but the rest, some eighty tons, the Americans burned.

The incident is cited as typical of the sort of activity that prevailed during this time about Boston.

Rather more exciting was the raid on Hog and Noddle's islands. These islands, the largest in the harbor at the time, lay north of the city, separated from Charlestown by the Mystic, and from Chelsea and Winthrop by Chelsea Creek. Noddle's Island, now much enlarged and extended, is now East Boston. Hog Island has since become Breed's and is the site of Suffolk Downs race track.

On these two islands the British had secured a large part of their supplies. Hog Island was pasture for a large number of sheep and cattle, while Noddle's, besides pasturing livestock, had been selected as a depot for naval stores. Against these two islands, on the 26th of May, the Americans made a surprise foray.

Some time after dark Colonel John Nixon marched with his regiment from Cambridge, "through Mistick, Moldin and to Chelsea," and thence across the creek at low water to Hog Island. There they set about driving off all the livestock they could find on the island. This took some time, and it was not until midday of the 27th that it was accomplished. Nixon then turned his attention to Noddle's Island, intending to do the same work there, and, if possible, destroy the British naval stores as well.

Now, however, the British became aware of what was happening, and Admiral Graves, becoming alarmed for his precious stores, sent the armed schooner *Diana* up Chelsea Creek to cut off the retreat of the provincials while a party of marines landed on the island to attack them in the front. Unable to reach the naval stores, the Americans retired before the marines in good order, driving off the sheep and burning the hay and slaughtering what stock they could not bring off. As they approached the creek between Hog and Noddle's islands, which they had to ford, they were enfiladed by the guns of the schooner, but apparently the range was too great for much damage. Amos Farnsworth, who went along on the expedition, has left a description of the event:

> Before we got from Noddle's Island to hog island we was fired upon by a Privatear Schooner But we Crost the river and about fifteen of us Squated Down in a Ditch on the mash and Stood our ground. And thare Came A Company of Regulars on the marsh on the other side of the river. And the Schooner: And we had a hot fiar untill the Regulars retreeted. But notwithstanding the bulets flue very thitch thare was not A Man of us kild. Suerly God has A faver towards us: . . . thanks be unto God that so little hurt was Done us when the Bauls Sung like Bees Round our heds.

The "retreet" of the regulars might have ended the affair, for the Americans then withdrew from Hog Island, but now the schooner seemed caught in a trap in her turn. Only the high tide had made it possible for her to run so far up the creek. Now the tide was running out, and if she was to escape she must move quickly. This she was unable to do, however, as the tide ran against her, and she was obliged to put out a kedge to warp through the passage between Noddle's Island and Chelsea. Admiral Graves, on learning of her predicament, sent ten or a dozen barges to help by towing and shortly afterward sent the armed sloop *Britannia*.

The admiral, however, was not the only one with eyes to see what was happening. The provincials were quick to take advantage of the situation. Putnam, with two field pieces and a thousand men, marched down to the Chelsea shore and took up a position where the *Diana* would have to pass close ashore, near the Winnesimmet ferry. Across the creek the British hastily set up a battery of three guns from the fleet and two twelve-pound-ers, which Gage sent, manned by marines, and even before the *Diana* came within range the two forces opened fire upon one another with no great effect.

As the schooner came sweeping past, close ashore, Putnam called upon her to surrender. A hail of shot was his response, whereupon the whole American line opened fire, and the British battery across the creek responded. At this critical juncture the *Diana* went aground in the dusk. For a few moments the barges tried to pull her off, but the fire from shore was too hot and they were forced to cast off. It is said that at this point Putnam led his men waist-deep into the water, in order to close the range as much as possible.

The fight continued in the darkness for some time, and the crew of the *Diana*, with the help of some of the barges, con-tinued their efforts to get the schooner off until the falling tide left her high and dry and she rolled over on her beam ends. Since she could no longer bring her guns to bear, her com-mander ordered her abandoned, and not long after his departure the provincials set her on fire. The British made one attempt to extinguish the flames, but they were driven back by heavy fire from the shore, and ultimately the little ship blew up and settled the matter.

This was the sharpest skirmish between the two parties since Concord and Lexington, and the Americans were jubilant. Their casualties were only a few slightly wounded, and on the British side the damage seems to have been almost equally insignificant —but the Americans were not aware of this. They were certain that they had inflicted heavy casualties on the enemy. The poor marksmanship displayed on both sides on this occasion is perhaps best explained by the darkness and the fact that most of the weapons were muskets used at long range. As for the artillery, Old Put himself is reported to have said that the fight would serve well to quiet his men's fear of cannon fire, for it would show them how little actual danger there was from their balls.

Following this attempt on the part of the Americans, Graves, alarmed for his stores, removed everything of use to him to Boston. In the course of the next two weeks the Americans revisited Noddle's Island several times in small parties, killing or driving off such livestock as remained, burning the rest of the hay, and destroying the buildings that were there in order that they might not give shelter to the enemy. The last of these forays was on the 10th of June, and thereafter the island lay abandoned, for both sides had other, more pressing matters to occupy their attention.

CHAPTER XIV

Bunker Hill

E VER since the 23d of April, Gage had been receiving driblets of reinforcements from abroad, a ship here and a ship
there, fetching now a company, now a battalion, now a handful
of officers or a detachment of marines. Toward the end of May,
however, the pace began to quicken, as the first transports of
what was known as "the first embarkation" began to arrive. On
the 25th of May, the day before the raid on Noddle's Island,
arrived the three new major generals, Howe, Clinton, and Burgoyne, who were to assist Gage in chastising the rebellious
Americans. With them came a great, white-winged covey of
convoys.

Boston Harbor was more active that day than it had been
for nearly a year—since the closing of the Port on June 1, 1774.
The great ships—great for their day—swept in line up the sparkling green waters of the harbor under their towering mountains
of snowy canvas, the scarlet-clad troops lining their decks in
rigid formation. All along the waterfront the wharves, the
quays, the warehouse roofs were black with the silent, watching
crowd. As the ships passed the Castle they puffed out white
smoke from their ports, followed, a long instant later, by the
rumbling thunder of the salutes. The Fort replied punctiliously.
The ships passed on proudly, turning the creaming aside to either

hand as they went. Past the flagship, where they saluted once again—fifteen guns this time, for the *Cerberus*, which carried the major generals, also carried Graves's promotion to Vice-Admiral of the White. At last they came about in line, off the Long Wharf, and for an instant their sails hung shivering in the breeze. In the next the ratlines were swarming with sailors, scurrying aloft to furl their canvas, and their cables were thundering in their hawse-pipes. Anchors splashed white as they fell into the harbor, and within an instant the water was aswarm with boats and barges, oars flashing, passing and repassing from ship to shore and ship to ship. It was quite some time, however, before the troops began to go on shore. There was no cheering from the onlookers when they did.

Estimates of the troops now at Gage's disposal run all the way from sixty-five hundred to ten thousand. The former figure is probably nearer the mark. Whatever the number, however, it was sufficient to make the governor feel that the time had now come to move. A council of war was held with the newly arrived generals and their staffs, and it was decided first to secure the strategic heights of Dorchester and Charlestown. Dorchester was to be attacked first. According to Burgoyne, Howe was to land his troops from transports at Dorchester Point, behind Castle Island. Clinton was to land in the center, between Dorchester Heights and Nook's Hill. Burgoyne himself was to cover the landings with a cannonade from the Neck. As soon as Dorchester was taken, the whole force was to move against the American positions at Roxbury, thus securing the entrance and exit to Boston. This whole movement was to be covered by artillery from the floating batteries anchored in the Back Bay and on Dorchester Flats, close to Roxbury Neck. Once Roxbury was taken, a force was to be left to garrison the post, and as many as could be spared were to turn about and move across the Charles to Charlestown. When the heights there were in the possession of the British the troops were to march upon Cambridge and either attack directly the main American camp or pass around it in an enveloping movement, as the nature of the countryside demanded.

The campaign as thus planned was expected to take several days, but no one doubted that it would be entirely successful. The first attack, on Dorchester, was to take place on the morning of Sunday, June 18, at daybreak, doubtless in the belief that the Americans would expect no move from the enemy on the Lord's Day.

One would think that, with the example of April 18 before him, General Gage would have taken extraordinary precautions to see that this time there was no leak by which news of the projected campaign could pass to the camp in Cambridge. He seems, however, to have made no special effort to keep the thing secret. In fact his carelessness in the matter almost seems to indicate that he despaired of hiding his movements from the Americans. Consequently there were so many reports of the proposed attack brought to the Committee of Safety in Cambridge that it is impossible to tell whence the first warning came. The New Hampshire Committee of Safety sent a warning of the plan on June 13, having heard of it from "a gentleman of undoubted veracity who left Boston last Friday, and who had frequent opportunity of conversing with the principal officers in General Gage's army." That same day the Massachusetts committee noted that they daily expected an attack. Thomas Hutchinson, writing on July 17, in London, mentions a gentleman recently arrived from Boston who claimed to have heard General Burgoyne, as well as inferior officers, speak of the plan. Hutchinson also speaks of letters, going out of Boston several days before the attack, mentioning it. There is even a romantic tale which relates that Dr. Warren rowed across the river to Boston June 15 or 16 and returned with the news. Whatever that may amount to, the Americans already knew of the proposal.

In the meantime Gage, serenely confident that his plans were undiscovered, made one last attempt at reconciliation. He issued, June 12, a proclamation—written by Burgoyne, who had a facile pen—offering pardon to all who had rebelled, excepting John Hancock and Samuel Adams, if they would lay down their arms. It was full of bombast and threat and between its lines expressed such complete contempt of the military efforts of the Americans that it defeated its own purpose. It was greeted with derision, and it is said that in response a committee of the Provincial Congress drew up a counterproclamation, which mockingly offered peace to all except Gage and Graves, Jonathan Sewall, Charles Paxton, Benjamin Hallowell, such mandamus councilors as had not resigned, and all "the natives of America, not belonging to the army or navy, who went out with the regular troops on the nineteenth of April last. . . ." But the proclamation was never issued.

No doubt much of Gage's—and his fellow generals'—apparent indifference to whether or not the Americans knew of their plan sprang from overconfidence. They were all, even up to the last moment, certain that it would be an easy matter; that the provincials could make but a feeble defense; and that the redcoats must, in the very nature of the event, sweep all before them. Had they been permitted to follow out the scheme as they had conceived it, had they been permitted to launch an attack against the poorly defended lines of Dorchester and Roxbury unmolested, no doubt it might all have been as easy as they pictured it. But even poor old General Ward was not such a dullard as to allow them that. A good way to forestall attack has always been to move first, and this was obviously the solution here. Accordingly on the 15th the Committee of Safety called for the "taking and keeping of Bunker Hill," in Charlestown, "by sufficient forces," and recommended that a council of war take such steps as seemed necessary for the securing of Dorchester, the state of whose defenses was unknown to the committee.

It was not until the following day that the council of war, presided over by Ward as commander in chief, met and decided to occupy Charlestown and to follow Thomas's advice to leave Dorchester alone for the time being. Had the British decided to ignore the Americans' activities of the Charlestown hills and followed their original plan of attacking Dorchester, Thomas's position would have been awkward to say the least, for he was in no position to defend that objective. He must have seen, however, that, once the Charlestown heights were occupied, they could scarcely afford to overlook it.

But it was not until late in the afternoon of the 16th that orders went down to the troops to prepare to move.

The story of the occupation and battle of Bunker—or more properly Breed's—Hill is one of blundering and stupidity on both sides that is more than redeemed by the heroism of the men who took part in the affair, and of the officers that led them. American history has no more glorious example of courage than that of the raw militiamen who stood that day in the face of the British charge. Nor can British history produce a finer tale of dogged, unbeatable valor than that of the men who attacked and attacked and attacked again in the face of that withering fire. By the same token it is difficult to find a parallel in the story of either nation for the confusion and disorganization that reigned in the American camp throughout the affair, or for the stupidity which led the British generals to order the attack as they did.

For the Americans there is some excuse. Theirs was a civilian army, hastily thrown together; still without adequate military organization; handicapped by lack of proper implements of war; without even a recognized scheme of leadership. For the British there is no such excuse. Their leaders were, presumably, the cream of a highly trained, experienced, veteran military organization. They were presumably past masters of military tactics and strategy. Yet they adopted a plan of attack which the most amateur of soldiers might well have rejected. And once they had adopted it they permitted procrastination and indecision to rob it of its possibilities of swift success, and bullheaded pride to prevent advantageous changes on the spot.

Colonel William Prescott, of Pepperell, was designated to command the detachment sent to occupy the Charlestown heights. With some eight hundred men, his own, Frye's and Bridge's regiments, he mustered on Cambridge Common on the evening of June 16. After a brief prayer by President Langdon, of Harvard, they moved out through the dusk to Inman's farm. There they were joined by Captain Knowlton, of Putnam's Connecticut troops, with two hundred more men. As they proceeded toward Charlestown Neck they were further joined by Colonel Gridley, the engineer, the wagons and the entrenching tools—and General Israel Putnam. Pushing on across the Neck in the silent darkness, they came at length to the foot of Bunker Hill. Here Prescott detached Captain Nutting, of his own regiment, to patrol along the shore and, with the rest of the detail, proceeded to climb the hill.

Every schoolboy knows that "the Battle of Bunker Hill" is a misnomer; that the battle actually took place on Breed's Hill, and therefore should be so named. The fact remains, however, that the battle was called "Bunker Hill," even in contemporary accounts written by men who should have been able to distinguish the difference, and for this there is good reason, despite all the controversy which has arisen.

The peninsula of Charlestown has—or had—two principal summits. The higher of these, Bunker's Hill, stood to the north, close against the Neck, and commanded the Charles mouth, the

The climax of the Battle of Bunker Hill, as Trumbull pictured it.

BOSTON

CHARLES TOWN

This rather fanciful view of the burning of Charlestown might be entitled America's first amphibious operation. Crossing the Charles and discharging on the Charlestown shore are Howe's troops

Mystic, and the deep cove of Willis's Creek and the Charles on the Cambridge side. In front of this, toward Boston, and separated from it by a slight depression, was the lower, more rounded summit of Breed's Hill. Off to the left of Breed's Hill, and a little behind it as one faces south, was a bit of swampy ground fanning around behind Breed's and in front of Bunker's and descending to the shore in Willis's Cove. Beyond this, to the east, a stone-and-rail fence ran down from the Mystic road, across the open pasture land, to a low bluff overlooking a narrow strip of beach and the Mystic River. Around on the opposite side of Breed's Hill from this fence, on the western corner of the peninsula, between the hill and the shore, huddled the village of Charlestown.

Now Prescott's orders from Ward, as suggested by the Massachusetts committee, called for the fortification of Bunker Hill. This fact is definite, and it is undoubtedly from it that the confusion as to nomenclature has arisen. It is doubtful if Ward was aware, until the fight was over, that the scene of battle was not Bunker Hill, but instead was Breed's Hill. At any rate there is nothing in the record to show that he was informed of that fact.

But what neither Ward nor Prescott had counted upon was Israel Putnam. Old Put was a general now, but the occupation of Charlestown was properly none of his affair. At least there are no orders extant to indicate that he had been sent there. Apparently he went out sniffing for action and accepted command as his right as senior officer. The fact in itself is eloquent of the state of disorganization prevailing in the American camp.

At any rate Old Put appeared on the scene, and it appears to be on his recommendation, nay, even on his insistence, in the face of the orders and inclinations of both Prescott and Gridley, that Breed's Hill was selected for the fortification instead of Bunker's. Old Put was no tactician, for all his general rank. He was a fighter, and a fight was what he wanted. Breed's Hill did not command all the waterways around the peninsula, as did Bunker's, nor was it anywhere near so suited to defense. But it was nearer to Boston and the Charles, and from it shells could be thrown across the river, into the batteries on Copp's Hill and into the ships anchored in the river. Beyond question this fact blinded the old campaigner to the weaknesses of the position. At any rate he had his way, and that is how the coming of dawn found the Americans on Breed's Hill instead of the point to which they had been ordered.

Gridley, yielding to Putnam's insistence, laid out a redoubt some eight rods square with a projecting angle on the Charlestown side, and about midnight the men took picks and shovels and went to work.

The night was dark, yet Prescott was afraid the sounds of digging would carry across the water to the sentries on the batteries across the river and the watch on board the warships, so near were they. Several times he and his officers went down to the waterfront to listen and make sure the British silence was not covering a trap for them. But each time he was reassured by the serene "all's well" of the guards across the river. Over in Boston, Clinton thought he saw the men at work on the hill and reported the fact to Gage and Howe, who laughed it off. The sentries, too, it appears, heard the Americans at work and thought little of it, for Howe later wrote: "As a Specimen of our knowledge of Service, the Centrys on the Boston side had heard the Rebels at work all night, without making any other report of it, except mentioning it in Conversation in the Morning."

So confident were the British of their success!

The dawn, however, brought surprise to both sides. To Prescott it revealed the awkwardness of his position, which in the darkness he had probably fancied secure. From the redoubt the flanks of the hill swelled gently downward, their own bulge hiding their full sweep from view above. An attacking party landing at Morton's Point, though visible at landing, could either flank the position on either hand or march around it entirely without coming in range. On his right the houses of Charlestown afforded some protection, for, as they were abandoned, they could be used by covering snipers, His left, however, was entirely open down to the Mystic, except for the slight interval of swampy ground that cut in between the summit of Breed's Hill and the rail fence. To remedy this as far as possible, Prescott now set some of his men to building a breastwork which extended the eastern angle of the redoubt some twenty rods across the summit and down toward the Mystic as far as the edge of the marsh.

Over on the other side of the river the day came to reveal to the startled eyes of the sentries what work the Americans had been accomplishing in the hours of darkness. Where the setting sun had looked on nothing more than open pasture, roughly divided in sections by ragged stone-and-rail fences, the morning saw the fresh-turned earth of the redoubt and breastwork, the flashing shovels of the Americans, and a swarming hive of rebels on the hilltop. Who gave the first alarm is not known, but the *Lively* was the first to open fire, followed by the other ships in the river. By the time the four generals were fully awake and out of their nightshirts the batteries on Copp's Hill had taken up the thunder and were spouting their angry destruction across the stream.

The generals met hastily, not even pausing for breakfast or to have their wigs powdered. For once they were shaken out of their lethargy, as they consulted together on what to do. As the Committee of Safety foresaw, they took the bait—hook, line, and sinker. There was no longer any thought of an attack on Dorchester. Had they made it they must have embarrassed the Americans sorely. But for the time being that plan was abandoned. The Americans had moved first, and though their threat held a huge element of bluff, it was enough to frighten the British generals out of their wits. From that moment they were on the defensive. Nor did they ever again, throughout the siege of Boston, resume the offensive, for even in spite of its costly success the Battle of Bunker Hill was a defensive action.

Being all agreed that the rebels must be dislodged from Charlestown, the generals now turned their attention to how it was to be done. One would think that, being what they were, a glance at the map would have been sufficient. Willis's Cove, in that day, swept in between Cambridge and Charlestown, taking a deep bite out of the land northward. On the other side of the Charlestown peninsula the Mystic River gouged a deep scallop out of the shore, just opposite the head of Willis's Cove. The neck of land thus formed between them was barely thirty yards wide, and in times of high water so low as to be entirely submerged. Down Willis's Cove, a hundred yards or so, was a barrier of rock and pilings, known as the mill dam. Over its top was a narrow footway, just barely wide enough for two men to walk abreast. These were the only land approaches to the position which the Americans now held.

On the south, from Willis's Cove, shallow water and the mill dam made it impossible for large vessels to approach the Neck. A shallow-draft vessel, however, such as the transport *Symmetry*, which mounted eighteen nine-pounders—more than all the guns which the Americans eventually mustered on the heights—could be warped in close to the dam and from there could fire across the Neck. Floating batteries could accomplish the same purpose. At the same time other floating batteries and light warships could move up the Mystic and shell the Neck from there. Such an enfilade could have made Charlestown Neck and the causeway over the mill dam impassable and thus would have isolated the American troops on the peninsula.

But that move alone could not bring victory to the British. Having placed their sea-borne artillery so as to cut off the American defenders, it would be necessary to land troops to force their surrender. This could best be done either in Willis's Cove, near the Charlestown end of the mill dam, or from the Mystic, near the Neck. In either case the Americans, whose positions were fortified only in the direction of Boston, would be taken from the rear and forced into the open. Trapped on the peninsula, there would be no alternative but to surrender.

Oddly enough neither of these obvious moves was adopted, though it is not quite fair to say that they were entirely ignored. The *Symmetry* and the *Glasgow* did take station in the Charles, at the mouth of Willis's Creek Cove, and from there raked the Neck with their heavy guns, while two floating batteries in barges warped in close to the dam and added their weight of metal to the bombardment. But no move was made—at least until the battle was well under way—to make any use of the possibility of close approach from the Mystic.

Similarly Sir Henry Clinton proposed that he be permitted to land near the Neck and seize the approaches to the peninsula, while General Howe landed in front of the rebel position. These landings accomplished, Clinton was to attack from the rear and dislodge the patriots, who could then be cut to pieces at leisure. But Gage is said to have objected to this plan since it would place his attacking force between two divisions of the enemy, namely, the main camp at Cambridge and the patriots on Breed's Hill. What he apparently overlooked was that the war-ships could easily prevent the Americans in Cambridge from coming to the aid of those on the peninsula, while those on the hill would themselves be placed in the very position which Gage dreaded.

Howe, who was to command the movement, supported Gage. It was still early in the morning. The redoubt was still unfinished and the breastwork was hardly begun. From Boston the effort of the Americans, and the little force they had in position, may have seemed insignificant indeed. It is possible, even probable that the general feeling—especially among those proud representatives of a haughty breed—was that to make too much of this business would be encouraging to the rebels; that to approach it as a major problem would be too flattering to these unlettered farmers who were only playing at war. It may be that it was believed that a formidable display in front and the threat of cold steel would cause the amateur warriors to melt away like snow in the rays of the summer sun. Clinton expressed some such thought when he wrote: "The general idea was that the redoubt was only a redan, that the hill was open and of easy ascent and in short it would be easily carried. . . ."

The plan finally adopted was for Howe to land with some fifteen hundred regulars at Morton's Point, on the extreme southeast tip of the Charlestown peninsula. Some of these were to make a diversion in front while others marched round the American left flank and rolled it up upon the redoubt. The idea was not without merit and might well have been accomplished exactly as planned, had the American lines remained as they had been when Howe looked upon them early that morning. But if the thing were to be done so, it must be done quickly.

Even dilatory Howe, who was always notable for his procrastination, recognized this and mentioned it in a letter to his brother. But that seems to be all he did. The men were to make an expedition of the movement. They were to sleep on the ground they took, and for this reason they were ordered to take with them their full pack, including blankets, three days' provisions, cartouche box, ammunition, musket and bayonet—in all a weight of some 125 pounds per man, and that on one of the hottest days of the new summer. It took time to prepare all this. Ammunition had to be served out. So did the provisions, which

t turned out, though ordered were not yet ready. The bread had
o be baked, the meat boiled, and the whole lot served out to the
nen. It is impossible now to determine the exact hours at which
he various movements of that day took place, so varied and
conflicting are the reports, but one thing is certain: the morning
vas all but gone before the British troops were paraded, ready
o move; it was well past noon before they landed.

Meantime in the American camp all was confusion. Nothing
apparently had been planned beyond the occupation of the hill.
No orders remain to indicate that any plan of battle had been
drawn up in the event of British resistance. Ward had some six
housand men on whom he could call, but, knowing the British
intention to seize Dorchester Heights, he seems to have been
eluctant to send more troops to Charlestown, lest they be
needed on the other side of the town. Prescott, as soon as he
observed his position, sent for reinforcements, and Putnam,
apparently anxious to make amends for his mistaken judgment,
galloped off to Cambridge to plead with Ward for aid. It was
everal hours before Ward could be persuaded to send Stark
and Reed, with their New Hampshire regiments, to Prescott's
elief. It was not until the fight was well under way that he became convinced that this move was not a feint on the part of the
British to cover a movement against Dorchester, and issued orders for further reinforcements. In the meantime, in the indisci-
pline of the camp, a good many had, fortunately, gone forward
on their own without waiting for orders—or on orders from
other commanders. Some of these arrived in time to be of good
ervice. Others arrived only to turn about and fly. Others gained
he summit of Bunker's Hill and waited, watching but taking
no hand in the fighting below until the last moment, when some
did good service in covering the retreat. Still others reached the
Neck, only to be daunted by the cannon fire from the ships at
he mouth of Willis's Creek Cove, and so never crossed to the

peninsula at all. Putnam did his energetic best. He was here there and everywhere: in Cambridge, at the Neck, behind the rail fence and on Bunker's Hill. His energy was immense, but ineffectual by its very diffusion. As an individual he gave heroic service. But as a commander he appears a failure at this juncture.

While this was going on behind them, Prescott and his men were hastily finishing their defenses, with what feelings may be imagined. They had worked all night, and they were to work all morning and then fight, without rest, without food and without water. The guns of the ships below and of the batteries on Copp's Hill were thundering at them incessantly. Prescott walked the parapet, keeping constantly in sight of the British gunners, to hearten his men and show them how little danger there was. But one man was hit and hastily buried. His death shook the men in the redoubt. The artillery arrived—some six field pieces—and this heartened the men somewhat. But by now Putnam had ordered the entrenching tools back to Bunker's Hill in order to prepare a second line of defense—which was never done—and they had never returned. The cannon had to blast their own embrasures in the parapet. When this was done they fired three or four times, without doing any damage to the enemy, and then ceased firing.

For a few moments the thunder of the guns raised the men's spirits. But when it was seen that they were going to do no more, their doubts rushed back in a flood, bringing fear in their wake and, in some, even rousing suspicions of treachery. Some were convinced that they were to be abandoned to their fate. A few deserted furtively. But to the vast credit of the majority most held their ground with bitterness in their hearts.

The reinforcements had not arrived when the men in the redoubt saw the British barges putting out in a long line from the Boston shore.

Even to the men behind the redoubt, that must have been an impressive and colorful sight. The day was bright. There was no wind. From before their parapet the green pasture swelled and dropped, broken here and there by fences, to dip and disappear from sight. On their right they could just make out the roofs of the village of Charlestown. On the left the bulge of the hill hid the rail fence and the flat meadowland before it from their sight. In that direction the first thing they would have seen would be the Mystic, empty but sparkling blue in the June sunshine. Below them, after disappearing from view for a short space, the ground leveled off and stretched to the low, grassy hillock that stood on Morton's Point, where the British were to land. All around, from the Point, almost to Charlestown they could see the shore line, but there was a piece of it which the swelling flank of the hill hid from view.

On that same side lay the river Charles, with the *Somerset* and the *Lively* and the *Falcon* lying in midstream, the white puffs of their broadsides blossoming along their flanks like flour sacks bursting in the air. Beyond lay the hillsides of Boston, dotted with houses and green trees, and off on one side of them the batteries, which also were spouting smoke and flame. Every window, every rooftop on that side was black with onlookers, and on the river between, the line of boats, each filled with scarlet figures and burnished arms, crept out, longer and ever longer toward the Point below.

As soon as Prescott saw where the British intended to land he detached Knowlton and his Connecticut men, together with the artillery, to oppose the British landing, or, if it was too late for that, to take up such position as might forestall encirclement on the left. Knowlton and the guns filed out at the rear, circled, and disappeared behind the bulge of the hill to the left. Prescott watched for their reappearance below, but he did not see them again. He was a little bitter about that later. He thought they had gone off around Bunker's Hill and deserted him. Actually they had taken post behind the rail-and-stone fence, under the hill, which he could not see.

Meantime the British landed unopposed and formed in three lines upon the little hillock by the Point. Prescott set himself for the attack, but it did not come immediately. Prescott did not understand why, but he was glad enough of the added time it allowed him to make his final dispositions.

What happened was that Knowlton had served better than Prescott knew. Howe, landing, saw that some of the Americans had taken post behind the fence, which ran from the edge of the swamp down to the bluffs overlooking the Mystic, thus opposing his proposed flank march. Knowlton's two hundred, even with the help of the artillery, could not hope adequately to defend the two hundred yards of fence. But they had taken their stand nevertheless. The fence was made half of stone, half of rails, the rails riding on posts embedded in the stone portion of the wall. To this Knowlton's men had added the rails from another fence near by and piled upon these armfuls of fresh-cut hay which was lying in windrows near by. The protection actually afforded by this flimsy barrier was little better than thin air, but from where Howe stood it looked solid enough. Behind it he could see occasional figures moving, and as he had no way of estimating the number of men there, he hesitated and sent back for reinforcements. While he waited for the reinforcements to come over, help began to arrive for the Americans.

These reinforcements were in large part volunteers, parts of companies, portions of regiments, which, having flocked to Bunker's Hill, took in the situation below and filtered down in driblets to take up positions behind whatever cover offered. Some went in behind the breastwork. Some took post behind hastily thrown up barricades between the end of the breastwork and the end of the rail fence, in the marshy ground. Others

slipped into Charlestown, where Prescott had already sent Lieutenant Colonel Robinson and Major Woods, with detachments,
to annoy the enemy on their left flank. These men hid themselves in the houses of the deserted village and began to pepper
the British from that cover.

But the organized portion of the American reinforcement
consisted of Reed's and Stark's New Hampshire regiments.
Stark, who as senior commanded the detachment, marched immediately upon receipt of his orders from Ward. On arrival at
the Neck he found the way blocked by a mob of men who were
unwilling to cross under the raking fire of the ships in the river.
Stark asked for the road and got it easily. Without the least
hesitation then he went forward, taking his own good time and
setting an example to those behind.

Some of his men were nervous and would have him hurry,
according to Dearborn, who marched beside him, and who
apparently shared that feeling. Dearborn wrote some time afterward:

My company being in front, I marched by the side of Colonel Stark;
who moving with a very deliberate pace, I suggested the propriety of
quickening the march of the Regiment, that it might sooner be relieved
of the galling crossfire of the enemy. With a look peculiar to himself,
he fixed his eyes upon me, and observed with great composure, "Dearborn, one fresh man in action is worth ten fatigued ones," and continued to advance in the same calm and collected manner.

At the top of Bunker Hill was Israel Putnam, with whom
Stark had on at least one occasion served in the Old French War.
But if Putnam was a Connecticut general, Stark was a New
Hampshire colonel, and he accepted no orders from the officers
of other provinces—indeed, he accepted none from those of his
own, for in his own eyes he ranked them all. He could see for
himself what was to be done, and without hesitation he marched
his men down and took post behind the rail fence between

Knowlton and the river. There officers and men alike fell to work with rails and hay to make their flimsy barrier more solid in appearance if not in actuality.

But that was not all that Stark did. As has been noted, the rail fence stopped at the low bluff which overlooked the Mystic. At the foot of this bluff, which was perhaps ten feet high, there was a narrow strip of beach which now, because the tide was running out, was growing wider and ever wider. Stark, looking down, at once recognized its danger. If the British should take a route along the beach they might, without being seen, under cover of the bluff, yet flank the American position. Accordingly Stark jumped down with a number of his men and hastily threw up a barrier of stones. Behind this barricade he posted a triple row of defenders.

Now the Americans were as ready as they were ever to be. Because of the steady infiltration of individual volunteers, companies, and detachments which moved on their own, it is impossible to estimate accurately the numbers now on the field. DeBerniere, a young British officer, who sketched the most accurate map of the action, apparently gave up in despair and dotted his plan with little *o*'s, which he marks naïvely as "the rebels behind all the Stone Walls, Trees and brush-wood, &c. their numbers uncertain, having constantly large Columns to reinforce them during the action." The number of those ordered to the field, however, was estimated later at fourteen hundred.

In the meantime Howe also had received his reinforcement and now stood ready to attack. It had been his plan to send the grenadiers and light infantry forward on his right to turn the American left. Behind these were to come the remaining companies of the Fifty-second and Fifth regiments, moving slowly to give the light infantry time to turn the flank, when they, led by the grenadiers, were to attack the line in front. On the left

General Pigot, second-in-command, was to move forward with the left wing, consisting of three companies of light infantry, three companies of grenadiers, the Thirty-eighth, Forty-third, and Forty-seventh regiments, and the First Marines—the two last being the reinforcement for which Howe had sent. This movement of Pigot's was to be an enveloping movement, swinging up the hill between Charlestown and the redoubt, and swinging round to enfold the American position between it and the British right. At the same time Howe's light artillery was to push forward in the center, toward the marshy ground, invisible from below, supported by the Thirty-fifth grenadier company.

To follow this plan in its entirety, however, was now out of the question, owing entirely to Howe's own dilatoriness in starting. The ground before the rail fence was level, an ideal parade except for several fences which ran across it, and which the redcoats would have to scramble over. But the rail fence was now, apparently, heavily manned, and even Howe hesitated to send his light infantry directly against it.

But like John Stark he noticed the narrow strip of beach that ran along the Mystic and determined to take full advantage of it. Accordingly he ordered the light infantry to advance along the beach and get in the rear of the fence, while the grenadiers and right wing, which he himself commanded, moved frontally against that barrier.

While he was coming to this decision an increasing fire from the houses of the village was galling his left. Seeing this, Admiral Graves takes the credit for suggesting that the town be fired by means of carcasses and red-hot cannon balls. Howe acquiesced in this, and presently the *Lively* and the *Somerset* opened fire at point-blank range. Within a short time the town was ablaze.

Now, probably shortly after two o'clock, all was ready for the attack. Howe opened with a brisk cannonade from his heavy guns on the Point and then set his men in motion, "the Line moving slowly, and frequently halting, to give time for the artillery to fire." Even the Americans waiting breathlessly above noticed how slowly that line moved.

But down on the beach the light infantry were not moving slowly. They marched smartly, in column of fours, along the narrow way, not stopping to fire, but bent on taking the flimsy barricade before them with the bayonet. Behind the rock the New Hampshire Yankees waited in silence; waited until the redcoats were almost upon them, before they leveled their motley array of pieces, took aim, and fired.

Every man in the group behind the wall was as much a marksman as it was possible to be with a musket, and the close-order ranks of the British must have been impossible to miss. At the first blast of fire the red ranks split and went down, recoiled on those behind. Those behind pressed forward still. In the narrow confines of the beach, between the bluff and the river, the orderly march fell into confusion.

Behind their barricade of stone the Americans did not all fire at once. True to their tradition, they picked their game and fired at will. Thus while some were firing others were reloading, and so a steady stream of fire and lead spat over the wall and into the dense-packed mass of the British. The companies broke and fell back. And as each one retreated, the one behind tried to come forward in its place, only to face a similar reception. For long minutes the column hung in the narrow way, wavering, while the officers tried to rally their shattered commands and lead them forward. But there was no facing that leaden hail, and in the end the light infantry broke and fled backwards, along the beach.

Up on the level ground above the beach the grenadiers and the regiments forming the right wing advanced still, slowly, for they could not see the beach below the bluff. They must have heard the shooting and the shouts, but it evidently did not occur to them that their comrades could be thrown into disorder by a handful of rebels behind a fence. Doubtless they believed that the light infantry had carried the position and were even now swinging in to catch the defenders of the rail fence in the flank and rear. They went forward in line abreast, keeping beautiful order, according to their commanders, except where they were forced to climb over the fences that stood across their line of march.

Tradition has it that John Stark, even as they came forward, stepped over the fence and paced off fifty yards in front of it. There he jabbed a stick into the ground and returned deliberately to his waiting lines.

"There," he is reported to have said, "don't a man fire till they come up to that stick."

Or words to that effect. Whether he spoke so or not, it is a matter of record that he urged the men to hold their fire. So did old Seth Pomeroy, seventy, and also a veteran of the Old French War, who was behind the fence as a volunteer, having been commissioned a general by Massachusetts but not yet having received his commission. With commendable steadiness the fire was withheld until the British were within close range, when here, too, the devastating fire broke out all along the line.

Here, as on the beach, it was not a single volley that blazed forth, but a sustained blast of sheeting flame that continued until the British line wavered, stood, then broke and fled, leaving their dead and wounded behind them, to use Stark's own picturesque description, "thick as sheep in a fold."

The Americans, seeing British backs turned and flying, were for swarming out after them. Some did break over the fence and into the field, but Stark wisely got them back again into position before the British could rally and attack again.

In the center and on the left the British fared no better. The artillery—the light six-pounders—going forward in the center soon found themselves mired in the marshy ground. And when they were finally brought about to bear upon the American positions it was discovered that the wrong-size ball had been sent with them, so that for the time being they were utterly useless.

On the left Pigot's column advanced, in much the same way that the grenadiers and the right had advanced against the rail fence. Inside the redoubt Prescott and his men waited for them, as Stark waited for the right wing down below. With Prescott by now was Dr. Warren, also lately voted a major general but not yet commissioned. Like Pomeroy he had come up as a volunteer, and when Prescott offered him the command he refused it. Conspicuous in his fine clothes among the homespuns surrounding him, he fought along with the farmers that day, and fell only in the last fierce melee, as his comrades were withdrawing.

But now there was tension and silence in the redoubt. Only the whispered voices of the officers, cautioning the men to be steady—to hold their fire—to aim for the crossbelts—to wait until the knee button on the regulars' gaiters showed above the hill—sounded there. Off in the river the cannon still bellowed, but no one paid heed to them. Down in the village, which by now was burning briskly, a few muskets still crackled. But in the redoubt it was quiet. "Don't fire until you see the whites of their eyes," Prescott is supposed to have said. Perhaps he did say it. The phrase was not unfamiliar to most Americans who were avid students of the memoirs of Frederick's wars.

Up came the British, in their faultless order. The caps of the grenadiers would be first to come in view, followed by the lower hats of the line companies. Next came their heads and then their shoulders, now their bodies and crossbelts, the whole line moving steadily and in perfect parade, pausing only here and there to climb over a fence, firing no more than the Americans fired, waiting to come in close enough to use the bayonet.

But they never came so close—at least in this assault. All along the line of the breastwork and the redoubt the smoke and flame burst suddenly forth, and, as with the right wing below, Pigot's line halted, wavered and broke, and fell back.

Back on the level ground Howe re-formed his columns. There was no change in their order, save that the light infantry came up from the beach—what was left of it—and joined the right wing. Howe also saw that it would be well if the American line behind the fence and behind the breastwork could be en-filaded from the Mystic. Accordingly he sent orders to the two floating batteries in Willis's Creek Cove to come around to that side. The tide in both streams set against the craft, however, and they never arrived in time to be of any assistance.

Howe now flung his attack forward once again, and again his lines met with that same searing fire. They held more steadily this time, trying to face it out, trying by sheer dogged persist-ence to force their way against it. But the slaughter among them was terrific. Again they were forced to retire. Howe said it was the fences that delayed his men in the crossing and made them clear marks for the Yankee fighters. But an unnamed soldier who was present tells a different story:

As we approached, an incessant stream of fire poured from the rebel lines; it seemed a continued sheet of fire for near thirty minutes. Our Light-infantry were served up in Companies against the grass fence, without being able to penetrate—indeed, how could we penetrate? Most of our Grenadiers and Light-infantry, the moment of presenting them-selves lost three-fourths, and many nine-tenths, of their men. Some had only eight and nine men a company left; some only three, four, and five. On the left, Pigot was staggered and actually retreated. Observe, our men were not driven back; they actually retreated by orders.

Once more out of range, Howe now tried to re-form his lines once more. He looked for the floating batteries but saw them still too far away to be any help. He asked why the artillery was silent and was informed that they had twelve-pound shot for six-pound guns. But they had grape. He ordered them forward to flank the breastwork and to open with grape. At the same time he sent to Clinton a request for more reinforcements, but Clinton himself was already on the way. Howe did not know this. But he did know that he could not wait for his message to be delivered and for the help to arrive, for even he could see that the Americans were constantly being reinforced from the top of Bunker's Hill. He must go forward now and take the position, or it might be too late.

It is said that some of his officers tried to persuade him not to make a third attempt. But he was stubborn. His military reputation, he thought, was at stake. He was apparently unaware that that was already lost.

Realizing, at last, the senselessness of sending in men so burdened, he had his remaining troops lay aside their packs and every article of equipment not absolutely essential to the attack. This done, he regrouped his troops, ordered the light infantry to make a feint against the rail fence, and shifted the rest of his force to the left to support Pigot's assault upon the redoubt. Once again the red lines swept forward, and as they went Clinton landed with the Second Marines and the Sixty-third Regiment and moved to the assault on the left.

Within the redoubt on the hill jubilation was tempered with misgiving. The powder was giving out. Some men had no more than a single round left. None, evidently, had more than four. Fortunately some of the artillery cartridges that had been left behind when the cannon went off to the rail fence were found and broken open, their contents meticulously distributed to the men. Thereafter they waited, knowing that if they drove them back this time the hill would probably be theirs, but at the same time painfully aware that, with ammunition short as it was, their chances of throwing the British back a third time were small. Yet not a man of them left the redoubt.

They had some time to wait, but at last the British came on again. This time the grenadiers and the Fifty-second moved against the breastwork, while the artillery, in spite of fire from the trees in the marsh, worked around to a position whence they could rake the barrier, driving the defenders either away or into the redoubt. The rest, except the light infantry, which made a halfhearted gesture against the rail fence, converged on the hilltop. Inside the little fort the defenders again held their fire until the last possible moment, and again they loosed it just as the red ranks seemed within bayonet reach. Again the British reeled and wavered. But this time they kept on, and some got close under the redoubt wall, where the angle prevented the defenders from depressing their pieces sufficiently to dislodge them. These held their ground and rallied others. The line swept forward again, and officers scrambled up the earthen flanks of the redoubt.

As the first heads appeared above the works there was another blast of fire from the defenders. Then, in the words of a survivor, the American fire sputtered and "went out like an old candle."

There was no more powder.

Even if there had been, it is doubtful if it would have made much difference. The redcoats were already flowing around the redoubt on the one hand, while on the other the grenadiers were over the breastwork. It was time to withdraw, and in spite of the carnage and the bayonet work of the enfuriated marines the Americans withdrew in good order, leaving, according to a British source, only thirty dead in the redoubt. One of those dead was Joseph Warren. But Colonel Prescott got off without a scratch, though he refused to run. He "stepped long with his sword up," parrying the thrusts of the bayonets that were made at him, and although some pierced his clothing, and his coat and waistcoat were badly cut, not one of the blades touched him.

The retreat from the redoubt was well covered from the slopes of Bunker's Hill above and from behind the rail fence below. The British, sweeping on to victory, would have pursued, but there were veterans on the other side as well, who held their men in order and held them back until the defenders of the redoubt could make good their escape. Then they, too, withdrew.

Some there were who would have stayed and fought it out on different ground. Putnam was one of these. So, perhaps, was Stark. But as the minutes flew it became clear to all that such an attempt would be futile. The best that could be hoped for was an orderly retreat.

The withdrawal of the Americans was hardly that, but at least it was well done and bitterly fought every step of the way. John Stark, from behind the rail fence, forced the British to fight doggedly for every inch. From fence to wall to tree to bush to rock they fell back, even taking their wounded with them, until they came to the Neck. There for a time they streamed across, under fire still from the guns of the warships. But as the sun set and darkness fell, the last of them slipped over, leaving the British on their dear-bought field, and promptly took up fresh positions on Prospect Hill, on the far side, in case the redcoats should, in the morning, take up the pursuit.

CHAPTER XV

End of an Era

THE Battle of Bunker Hill—or Breed's Hill, if you prefer it so—was, like many another battle, both victory and defeat for both sides. In the purely local sense, the Americans lost their position, but covered themselves with glory. The British took their hill, but at what cost! Casualties on the American side totaled some 431, out of an estimated 3,200 involved, either on the front line or in skirmishing in the rear, at one time or another through the day. Of these the killed numbered 140, the wounded 271, the captured 30. Most of these fell at the rail fence or in the retreat. Oddly enough, as has been noted, the British themselves reported that at the redoubt, where the stand had been most determined and the fighting most desperate, there were only thirty dead left behind. In spite of the raking cross-fire of the ships upon the Neck, and in spite of the hesitancy of the provincials to expose themselves there by crossing, the casualties at that point were very light. Yet one of them, indeed the final casualty of the battle, was a sore blow. Major McClary, of Stark's regiment, had crossed the Neck in safety and was already on the mainland with his men, when he noticed a movement among the British on the Charlestown side. He thought they might be making a move to cross, and returned to the Neck to hold them at that point, should they attempt it. But when it became evident to him that no such move was intended, he turned about to return to his regiment's position on the hills behind him, and at that moment a ball from one of Clinton's cannon, now posted on the heights overlooking the Neck, killed him.

On the British side the casualties were much heavier. All told, killed and wounded, they totaled something over 56 per cent of the entire force engaged. Of between 2,200 and 2,300 men, Howe lost 226 killed and 1,054 wounded—too great a price to pay for any success. But this does not tell all. Of those killed and wounded many were officers. Their numbers killed and wounded, in proportion to the numbers involved, were much higher than those of the ranks. Altogether nineteen officers were killed and seventy wounded. But even worse than this was the fact that among the ranks the casualties were highest among the veterans and picked troops. The grenadiers and light infantry formed the flank companies of British regiments of the day, and each man of them was especially selected for military quality. Since these companies bore the brunt of the slaughter on the hill, the casualties among them were frightful. Of the grenadiers of the Fourth, or King's Own, all except four were killed or wounded; of the Twenty-third, or Royal Welsh Fusiliers, only three remained. In the attack on the beach we have seen that the light infantry suffered quite as severely.

The battle was reported in Europe as a British victory, but it was Vergennes who remarked dryly: "Two more such victories and England will have no army left in America." "What have we conquered?" asked John Wilkes in Commons. "Bunker's Hill with a loss of twelve hundred men. Are we to pay as dearly for the rest of America?"

Thus the triumph of victory was tempered by gloom at its cost for the British. In the American camp, too, the reactions were mixed. Prescott and those who had served with him were bitter. They had not been adequately supported, either with ammunition or reinforcements. Prescott offered heatedly to return, given three fresh regiments, and retake the position, so aroused was he. Fortunately Ward recognized the futility of the move and refused to order the regiments out, thus preventing the situation from taking a still more adverse turn, for the British were by then well entrenched on the peninsula.

As for the men, they had tasted defeat. It is hardly to be expected that they would be anything but downcast.

What was needed was perspective. Just as in Britain the dubiousness of the victory was immediately recognized, so, as the news of the battle traveled southward, did Americans see behind the mere loss of an unimportant position the true significance of what had occurred. Americans could and would fight, not merely from behind trees and stones and walls, Indian fashion, harrying a broken enemy's retreat, but on the field of battle, in prepared positions, and in the face of veteran British troops, and when things became too hot for them they could retire in good order. They could inflict unheard-of losses upon those hitherto seemingly invulnerable redcoats. Another time, given proper support and ammunition, they might do even better. The thought was a tonic to all the colonies, from Maine to Georgia.

But the Battle of Bunker Hill had still another effect which in its own way was even more important than all of these. On the one hand it impressed the British commanders with American fighting ability to such an extent that they abandoned their plan to seize Dorchester Heights and never again sent an expedition out of the town, while, on the other hand, it gave the Americans a sense of confidence in their own ability to stand up against the weight of British attack; a sense that was utterly false because of the disorganization, the lack of training, and the scarcity of weapons and materials of war prevailing in the American camp, but nonetheless effective for that, since it welded them together solidly behind their cause and held the camp intact, strengthened their defenses and their determination to hold the enemy inside Boston.

This reaction to the battle had already begun to take effect when Washington, who had been appointed to command of the Continental Army by Congress on the very eve of the event, arrived in Cambridge. He was quick to view the situation with a realistic eye, and he set to work promptly upon the reorganization of his army and their training. All that long hot summer, and on into the fall and winter, he struggled to whip his unruly forces into shape, and all through that time he scarce dared admit, even to himself, the desperate shortage of powder and weapons that bid fair to hamstring him when the day of battle should come. To remedy the defect he left no stone unturned, and in the meantime he tightened his lines, strengthened his defenses. He bolstered the blockade of Boston on the land side, while to seaward he commissioned privateers to cut off vessels approaching with stores and supplies for the enemy in Boston. Some of these had good luck, and some military equipment intended for the British found its way to Washington's camp. But in spite of his slowly gathering strength Washington lived in constant fear of a British sortie.

While Washington was dreading the possibility of a British attack, the British themselves, inside the town, were quaking lest Washington come in. They could observe his numbers and his strength, but they could not divine his weakness. So they sat down behind their defenses and waited.

Within the town it was a period of hardship. On the night after the battle, and during the days that followed, Bostonians were given ample opportunity to see for themselves the full horror of war. The stream of wounded and dying that poured

across the river seemed endless. The town's facilities for caring
for them were taxed to the utmost, and many, especially those
wounded among the prisoners, were left lying on the wharf
until arrangements could be made for them.

But this was just a beginning. As the blockade grew tighter
and the raids of the Americans in the harbor became more frequent and more effective, the town began to feel desperately the
lack of provisions. At the outset meat was the greatest need.
Boston could still raise a good part of its own vegetables. But
meat had to come in from outside. Before midsummer the harbor
islands were denuded of livestock and hay, and it was necessary
for Gage to insist that the admiral send marauding expeditions
up and down the coast. Even this expedient was not very productive, however. A thousand sheep was the biggest haul, and
that did not go far toward feeding twenty thousand people.

A few individual presents of provisions went in. Putnam sent
his old comrade in arms, Moncrieffe, a note and a present of
fresh meat, which Moncrieffe sent to the hospitals. Toward the
end of July, Daniel Parker sent Andrew Eliot, his pastor, who
had remained in town, two quarters of fresh mutton from
Salem. Eliot used them to make broth for thirty or forty sick
people. By late summer cattle at auction brought fifteen to
thirty-four pounds, while sheep went for thirty shillings and up
—tremendous prices for those days and in that place, where few
men had been granted the privilege of making a living since the
closing of the Port, more than a year before.

Even in July the British began killing off their milk cows.
Efforts were made to send provisions from England, but few of
these succeeded, and at one time it was said that the English
Channel was white with the bodies of sheep that had been
shipped to the garrison of Boston, but, owing to bad weather,
had to be thrown overboard before the ships were much more
than out of sight of land. During the winter the situation became

worse, as is testified, not without humor, by the case of Winifred McOwen, a camp follower, who was sentenced to be
whipped "one hundred lashes on the bare back in the most public places of the town" for having killed the town bull, aged
twenty years, and sold his meat.

With the approach of winter, too, food proved to be only
one of the vital necessities that was lacking. Fuel also became a
problem. As it grew colder, first fences began to disappear, then
trees, then whole buildings. Some soldiers made a good thing of
selling firewood—which they took from houses abandoned by
their owners who had fled to the country. So bad did this situation become that at one time the provost marshal was sent on
his rounds accompanied by an executioner with orders to hang
on the spot anyone caught wrecking a dwelling house. But even
this did not put a stop to it. One of the buildings so torn down
was the old Governor Winthrop House, standing these 145
years.

Among the first victims of the soldiers' axes was the Liberty
Tree, which is said to have yielded fourteen cords. Since it was
elm, one wonders if it did not, in just keeping with its character,
make but a poor fire for the redcoats. John Andrews, in a letter,
complained of having to pay twenty dollars for a cord of wood
—though perhaps this should not be mentioned as a severe hardship. The writer himself can testify that in the winter of 1942-
43, without benefit of siege, the price of wood in Boston went to
thirty-two dollars a cord, and most of it, he is willing to bet, did
not burn half so well as the green old elm of the Liberty Tree!

The shortage of food and fuel produced their inevitable results in pestilence and misery. It is said that after Bunker Hill the
deaths in the town never, during the entire siege, dropped below ten a day, and often exceeded thirty. Smallpox broke out,
together with various fluxes. At the same time a virulent dysen-
tery raged in the American camp.

In the circumstances it was perhaps as well that Boston was not so large as it once was. A good many Whigs had fled, and since the Americans would allow no more Tories to enter the town, the population now declined steadily. Just before his recall to England in October, Gage had a census taken. The return showed a military population of 13,500, a civil of 6,573. Of these last it was estimated that not much more than two thousand were Whigs. Even some of these were allowed to leave later, and as more and more of them slipped out the authorities began to fear for the town. In November, Captain Manly, of Salem, intercepted the *Nancy*, an ordnance ship with large supplies of ammunition for the British. On hearing the news, Howe, who was now in command, wrote home that he expected an attempt would soon be made to burn the town, now that the Americans had the means to do it. Nor were his fears altogether groundless. Patriot correspondence of the time is full of proposals to "smoke out the pirates," and Congress, censuring Washington for his apparent inactivity, more than hinted at it.

When the town was not burned, Howe began to worry lest, when the ice was strong enough to hold troops, Washington would attack across the Charles and the Back Bay. Washington himself seems to have had some such notion, but the winter was mild again, and the ice never formed.

But if these major worries did not materialize, the season was not without its alarums and excursions. Several times there were minor clashes among the islands of the harbor, and once the rebels crossed the mill dam into Charlestown under Captain— by this time Major—Knowlton, who had stood behind the rail fence and pulled down and burned what remained of the village and retired, after throwing a few shells across the river into the town, creating an alarm which interrupted an evening of diversion for some of the officers stationed there.

For, in spite of the hardship of their station, the British officers found ways to amuse themselves. As cold weather came on, making outdoor riding uncomfortable, the Old South Meeting House was selected for a riding school. Undoubtedly this choice was made because of the associations of the building with the cause of the rebels. The pews were cleared out, sawdust scattered on the floor, and the place turned over to the Seventeenth Dragoons, who made the rafters echo with their shouts as they took the jumps erected in the ring. It is said, too, that one of the pews was left to serve as a pigsty, but there seems to be no confirmation of this.

If this were not scandalous enough to the pious people of Boston, the officers' theater must have added the crowning blow. Faneuil Hall for a time following the beginning of the siege was used as a place to store furniture and other property taken from the houses abandoned by the Whigs in their flight. These things were taken from the building and stored elsewhere, many of them in the prison, under the care of the provost, the infamous William Cunningham, of whom more anon, and the old hall that had been the scene of so many town meetings was turned into a theater in which officers took places in the cast for the amusement of their fellows, themselves, and the Tory society which now ruled the town. It is said that some of the feminine parts were taken by young ladies of Boston, whose names have not come down to us. When we stop to consider the light in which the theater was viewed in those days, however, especially in Boston, and when the names of the ladies in question are unknown, and, finally, when a number of accounts tell of various officers dressed for female parts, we may be excused for doubting it.

The first play performed seems to have been Voltaire's tragedy of Zara, with a prologue written by Burgoyne and spoken by Lord Rawdon, who was reputed to be the "ugliest man in

Europe," though his bravery and gallantry were unquestioned. Another play was *The Blockade of Boston*, written entirely by Burgoyne, but not performed until after he had sailed for home in January. This was a lampoon, scurrilous and somewhat bawdy, as the wit of the day was often inclined to be, of the siege—especially of the besiegers. The play was never printed, apparently, and only a few lines of it remain to us, handed down in a broadside, headed "A VAUDEVIL, Sung by the Characters at the Conclusion of a new Farce, called the BOSTON BLOCKADE."

In this curious handbill, says Doodle, a character whose exact status seems a little obscure:

> Ye tarbarrell'd Lawgivers, yankified Prigs,
> Who are Tyrants in Custom, yet call yourselves Whigs;
> In return for the Favours you've lavished on me,
> May I see you all hang'd upon Liberty Tree.
> Mean Time take Example, decease from Attack,
> You're as weak under Arms as I'm weak in my Back.
> In War and in Love we alike are betray'd,
> And alike are the Laughter of BOSTON BLOCKADE.

And Fanfan, evidently intended to be a Negress, drops an unconscious commentary on the manners and society of the day:

> Your Pardon my Massa's one Word to intrude,
> I'm sure in my Heart you won't all tink me rude:
> Tho' in Public you scoff, I see many a Spark,
> Would tink me a sweet pretty Girl in the Dark.
> Thus merily runs the World on with Fanfan,
> I eat good salt Pork and get kiss'd by white Man:
> I do Misses Business, she pleas'd and I paid,
> Egad I no tir'd of BOSTON BLOCKADE.

Beyond these few lines we know only that Washington was caricatured as a man with a great belly, an enormous wig, and a long sword, over which he doubtless tripped, to the delight of the audience.

Evidently the theater took in Boston, however, for on the re-occupation of the town by the Americans revenge was taken by the production of a farce by an anonymous Yankee, entitled *The Blockheads; or the Affrighted Officers*. This production was no nicer than Burgoyne's work had been, evidently, though we know somewhat more about it, for copies of it have survived. In it the British and their friends were characterized under such names as Captain Bashard for the admiral, Puff for the General, L—d Dapper for Lord Percy, Shallow was Gilbert. Dupes was "Who you please," some say Burgoyne. Surly was Ruggles. Brigadier Paunch was Brattle, and so on. The prologue ran:

> By Yankees frighted, too! Oh, dire to say!
> Why, Yankees sure at Red-coats faint away!
> Oh, yes! they thought so too, for lackaday,
> Their general turned the blockade to a play.
> Poor vain poltroons, with justice we'll retort,
> And call them blockheads for their idle sport.

But that came later.

It was the *Boston Blockade* which was playing on the night Knowlton and his men made their raid upon Charlestown. Doubtless the Americans knew exactly at what hour the curtain was to rise, for they had extraordinarily good information of all that went on in the town. It is told that just as the curtain was going up on the new play a sergeant rushed upon the stage, crying, "Turn out! Turn out! They're hard at it hammer and tongs!"

He was applauded by the audience, who thought him a part of the farce until the sound of the cannon and musketry across the river fetched them suddenly to the realization that he was in earnest. Then the show came to a sudden end for that evening, and officers, without stopping to remove costumes or grease paint, rushed to their stations, to the vast amusement of the town Whigs. There were some in the pit, it seemed, who appreciated the action now taking place, on the stage and off, far more than they would have relished the production they had come to see. Wrote one of them:

Much fainting among the women, but the best joke was the Actors who now had another part to perform, than of Women and Negroes, for which they were prepared. One Officer was running to his Corps in his petticoats, and another with his face blacked and in a Negroes dress.

There appears to have been a good deal of complacency among those ladies of the town who had not gone to the performance over the plight of their sisters who had gone and had screamed and fainted and in the end been forced to go home without escorts.

But life in Boston for the British forces, officers and men, was not all beer and skittles and play-acting and dancing. Lord Rawdon was stationed for a time at Charlestown, with the outpost stationed there to hold the peninsula. His picture of conditions there as winter approached is in sharp contrast to the life in Boston:

It is very bleak at present upon these Heights, (October 5) and the duty of the officers is severe. At our lines neither officer or man have the smallest shelter against the inclemency of the weather, but stand to the works all night. Indeed in point of alertness and regularity our officers have great merit. I have not seen either drinking or gaming in this camp. If anything, there is too little society among us. In general every man goes to his own tent very soon after sunset, where those who can amuse themselves in that manner, read; and the others probably sleep. I usually have a red herring, some onions, and some porter about eight o'clock, of which three or four grave sedate people partake; we chat about different topics, and retire to our beds about nine. There is not quite so much entertainment in this way of life as in what . . . the troops in Boston enjoy.

A little later he continues:

For some days past it has not ceased raining; every tent is thoroughly wet, and every countenance thoroughly dull. A keen wind which has accompanied this rain, makes people talk upon the parade of the com-

Boston: Cradle of Liberty

forts of a chimney corner; and we hear with some envy of several little balls and concerts which our brethren have had in Boston. Many officers as well as private men have been very ill with fluxes, agues, and other disorders proceeding from the damp and cold.

And toward mid-December he writes:

On Charlestown Heights indeed the men began to fall sick very fast latterly, from the great severity of the duty. We came into winter quarters two days ago. It was full time, for our tents were so shattered that we might as well almost have lain in the open field.

The Navy also had its troubles. Admiral Graves was severely criticized by all for his inactivity. Doubtless it was because he was so busy writing letters and reports. When he was recalled he wrote an extensive apology for his conduct, and for this we are indebted to him, for he left us many more pictures of conditions during the siege than did anyone else. One, complaining of the hardships suffered by the sailors, is particularly vivid:

The fatigue to men and officers was prodigious. It became unavoidably a perpetual source of Complaint. The Boat duty to the ships at Boston, and the stress of weather and danger of the seas to the Cruizers to the Northward between Capes Ann and Codd, especially in winter when snow storms are usual, rendered the service intolerable to most tempers, even of the most resolute make. This sort of storm is so severe that it cannot even be looked against, and by the snow freezing as fast as it falls, baffles all resistance—for the Blocks become choaked, the Tackle incrusted, the Ropes and Sails quite congealed, and the Whole Ship before long one Cake of Ice. And at times of less inclemency the Sea freezes upon whatever part it falls and soon covers the forepart of a ship with ice. So that whenever there can be occasion to form another route by changing the course, or from the violence of the tempest to hale up a lower sail it is necessary to pour boiling water upon the tacks and sheets and with clubs and bats to beat off the Ice, before the cordage can be rendered flexible. Indeed if the severity of the winters be such in this Climate that the Centinel on shore is frequently found frozen to death upon his post, tho' relieved every half hour, the reader may frame some Idia of what the seamen of a Watch, especially in small vessels, must suffer, exposed to the successive dashings of a freezing wave, during four hours, in handling and working of iccy tackle; and yet the weakness of the complements would not admit of their being divided into more watches.

Boston seamen, of course, were accustomed to such weather as all in the day's work. But the admiral and his British sea dogs appear to have thought it somewhat severe. Notwithstanding his words, it is a matter of record that that winter was unusually mild, and there is no report to be found—other than this one of the admiral's—of any "Centinel . . . frozen to death upon his post."

But while soldiers and seamen were suffering, and while officers played, others were suffering also. Nor were all the officers playing. Some were lining their pockets.

The lot of prisoners was far from easy. A few prisoners had been taken by the British at Bunker Hill, most of them wounded, and a few more had been picked up at intervals. These were all lodged in the jail, without discrimination as to rank. Washington, hearing rumors of this, coupled with tales of their mistreatment, wrote in protest to Gage. Gage's reply was written by Burgoyne:

Britons ever pre-eminent in mercy, have overlooked the criminal in the captive. Your prisoners, whose lives by the law of the land are destined to the cord, have hitherto been treated with care and kindness;—indiscriminately, it is true, for I acknowledge no rank that is not derived from the King.

Washington knew better, with all due respect to Gage and Burgoyne. He was obliged to retaliate by recommending the removal of British prisoners to the interior and the dank mines at Simsbury, Connecticut.

In justice to the British commanders it may be that they were unaware of the abuses practiced by their officers—Cunningham and Loring. The generals had their report from the prisoners' surgeon, and he appears to have been no paragon of humanity.

But it seems strange that Gage should not have been aware of the type of men he was dealing with.

Strictly speaking, neither Cunningham nor Loring was of the Army. Both were civilians appointed to administrative positions, under martial law, by the commander. Cunningham, the provost marshal, in charge of the jail and the prisoners of war, was the son of a trumpeter, born in Dublin in barracks and, by all accounts, a natural bully. He had come to America in 1774 and, for a time, had broken horses and operated a riding school in New York. With the approach of hostilities, however, his loyalist sympathies had made him unpopular there and he had fled to Boston. How he had worked himself into such a responsible post is a mystery.

Joshua Loring, the sheriff and vendue master, in charge of the prisoners' commissary, on the other hand was a bird out of a different nest, although, apparently, of somewhat similar plumage. He came of an old Boston family, owned extensive estates, had been high sheriff of Massachusetts and mayor of Hingham, and was quite socially acceptable—at least to the Tories. That he was mean, avaricious, and contemptible is borne out by a saying which the prisoners in New York, where he later held a similar position, had of him: that he starved the living and fed the dead. By this was meant that he withheld the rations issued for his charges, in order to sell them for his own profit; and failed to report the deaths of some prisoners, that he might continue to draw their rations. Perhaps the most eloquent commentary upon his character, however, is the fact that he was willing, even pleased, that throughout that general's stay in America his wife should serve as mistress to Lord Howe in order that he himself might enjoy favor and so profit by the connection.

Such were the men in whose care the American prisoners were placed. Not all of those prisoners were captives. Some were suspects picked up from time to time inside the town. One of these, John Leach, has left us a vivid picture of conditions in the prison:

The poor sick and wounded prisoners fare very hard; are many days without the comforts of life. Dr. Brown told me that they had no bread all day and the day before. He spoke to the provost, as he had the charge of serving the bread, who replied, "Let them eat the heads of the nails, and knaw the planks and be damned." The comforts that are sent us by our friends, we are obliged to impart to these poor sufferers, and fee the soldiers and others with rum to carry it to them by stealth, when we are close confined and cannot get to them. They have no wood to burn for many days together to warm their drink, and dying men drink theirs cold. Some of the limbs which have been taken off, it is said, were in the state of putrifaction, and not one survived amputation.

Cunningham was evidently already practicing the art in which he was later to become quite perfect. Another excerpt, however, reveals a bolder swindle:

Many goods of the inhabitants have been plundered by the provost and sheriff Loring, and brought to the prison-house. . . . They made a vendue of them in the prison-house, Loring vendue master: the provost, his son and Dyer [he was deputy provost], the bidders—a most curious piece of equity.

Aside from cheating helpless prisoners of their food, giving balls and plays, and standing guard in the cold, the British were quite inactive. Clinton, it is true, led one small sortie against Roxbury, but his plans miscarried owing to misunderstanding between the Army and the Navy, and nothing came of it except to show the Americans where the lines should be strengthened. It was not tried again. Graves, too, sent a party to destroy some whaleboats lying in the Germantown River, at Weymouth. But these never even found the river.

In large matters the Americans were scarcely more lively. But on a small scale they were active as fleas. A great number

of whaleboats were concentrated around the bay, and the operations of parties of Americans in these were constantly giving
alarm to the British. In mid-July they burned Boston Light. The
British promptly set about rebuilding it, for if their supply
ships were ever to find them the Light was necessary. Before it
was completed the Americans in whaleboats swooped down
again upon the island, killed or captured some fifty-three of the
British stationed there to protect the carpenters, burned the
works to the ground again, and escaped over the neck between
Hull and Allerton Point with a loss of one killed and two "just
grazed by balls." The following night one of the transports in
the Charles nervously reported having sighted a great number of
whaleboats softly rowing towards Boston. When the alarm was
given, this flotilla melted away. On another night forty whaleboats were reported lying near Moon Island together with
"three large Boats masted and in appearance Fire Boats."

The British were very much afraid of fireboats, which could
wreak great havoc in the fleet if ever they should get in among
the ships.

The pestiferous activities of these boats emphasized the inactivity of the admiral and led to long recriminations, not the
least of which was Burgoyne's summary in a letter home:

It may be asked in England, "What is the Admiral doing?"
I wish I were able to answer that question satisfactorily; but I can
only say what he is *not* doing.
That he is *not* supplying us with sheep and oxen, the dinners of the
best of us bear meagre testimony; the state of our hospitals a more
melancholy one.
He is *not* defending his own flocks and herds, for the enemy have
repeatedly plundered his own islands.
He is *not* defending the other islands in the harbour, for the enemy
in force landed from a great number of boats, and burned the lighthouse at noonday (having first killed and taken the party of marines
which was posted there) almost under the guns of two or three men of
war.

He is *not* employing his ships to keep up communication and intelligence with the King's servants and friends at the different parts of the continent, for I do not believe General Gage has received a letter from any correspondent out of Boston these six weeks. [The Americans could have told him something about that, for they were intercepting the general's dispatches regularly.]

He is intent upon greater objects, you will think—supporting in the great points the dignity of the British flag, and where a number of boats have been built for the enemy, privateers fitted out, prizes carried in, the King's armed vessels sunk, the crews made prisoners, the officers killed—he is doubtless enforcing instant restitution and reparation by the voice of his cannon and laying the towns in ashes that refuse his terms? Alas! he is *not*. British thunder is diverted or controlled by pitiful attentions and mere Quakerlike scruples; and, under such influences, insult and impunity, like righteousness and peace, have kissed each other.

The general failed to say what the generals were *not* doing.

On the other side of the fence there was similar criticism of the inactivity of leaders. Congress was beginning to wonder openly when Washington would take the initiative, quite overlooking the shortage of supplies of war. John Adams wrote from Philadelphia that he hoped Mrs. Washington's arrival in Cambridge might have the effect of rousing the general to action, and Congress authorized him to burn Boston if it should become necessary, hoping that, thus prodded, he might be induced to move. But Washington was not ready yet. And he was too wise to attack half-armed.

Meantime the months sped by. In December, Burgoyne returned to England—two months behind Gage. Howe, the dilatory, assumed complete command. In January, Clinton departed joyously to make his attempt on Charleston, South Carolina. Washington, uncertain as to his destination, detached Charles Lee, who was still being taken seriously by Americans, to follow him along the coast. February was quiet, but one event of paramount importance occurred that month; Henry Knox, the former bookseller of Boston, arrived at the American lines with the cannon from Ticonderoga and Crown Point—forty-three of them—and sixteen mortars, hauled overland, all the way, upon the snow.

In the meantime powder had been coming in, too. Not great quantities of it, but a cupful here and a cupful there; here a barrel, there a cask, and every now and again a cartload. Despite the British blockade some ships still managed to bring in military stores to ports up and down the coast. Outside of Boston the commanders of practically all the British ships on station in different ports depended upon the shore for fresh provisions, and nearly all of them had agreements with the local folk whereby, so long as they did not interfere with the local trading vessels, they would be so supplied. At some points, as at Portsmouth, the British commanders kept the local vessels under such surveillance that tempers were constantly stirred and it was impossible to bring in much in the way of warlike supplies. But at New York scarcely a ship entered but brought in something. Late in February one ship arrived there with three tons of the precious stuff, and more was expected daily.

By the first of March, then, Washington had the guns and he had the powder. It was time to act.

On the 13th of February the British suffered an alarm. They heard that Washington was quietly planning to seize Dorchester Heights. This was an old bugaboo, and it seems strange that it should have lain so long forgotten. Stranger still is the rumor that alarmed the British, for there is not the least evidence to indicate that, at this time, the Americans intended such a move. Rather everything points to the fact that Washington was considering an attack across the ice of Back Bay—which had now formed thick enough to hold the troops. If Dorchester entered into the scheme no mention is made of it, and the plan was voted down in council.

However, Howe wrote that he heard rumors of an American plan to seize the nearby heights, and his subsequent action shows how seriously he took it. On the night of the 13th he ordered Colonel Leslie, at the Castle, to cross the ice to Dorchester Neck and destroy every house and every kind of cover the troops might find there. They moved in the early morning of the 14th and found the peninsula empty. There were no military stores. There were no troops other than a few pickets, who were seized. There was not the least evidence that any move in that direction was planned. But the soldiers burned a few vacant houses and sheds and withdrew.

They would have been wiser had they remained and occupied the heights themselves. If Washington had not thought of it before—and no doubt he had, but kept his own counsel in the matter—he could have been given no more blatant reminder. Nor could he have been more directly informed of what Howe thought of American ability to seize and hold the position than by the British neglect to remain there once they had landed. Their very withdrawal said in effect that they looked upon the place as untenable by any considerable force, and that they were supremely confident of forestalling any move in that direction. Their very attitude was a challenge.

Washington was too good a commander to put all his eggs in one basket, or to plan an attack anywhere along the lines without first making certain that his entire front was strong enough to withstand a counterstroke. All through the fall and winter he had been quietly strengthening the lines, throwing up forts and batteries at strategic points. The lines at Winter Hill, Ploughed Hill, and Prospect Hill covered Charlestown Neck and were purely defensive, designed to prevent any sortie on the part of the British in Charlestown. But down on Lechmere Point, within easy range of Boston across the Back Bay, and up on the Roxbury lines the men had been busy all winter with pick and shovel, throwing up strong works which needed only artillery to make them threatening.

The artillery had now arrived, and some of it was mounted at Lechmere Point and at Roxbury. The rest was reserved for a still more offensive move.

The proposal which Washington made now, to seize and fortify Dorchester Heights, whence the seaward approaches, the anchorage, the wharves, and even the town of Boston itself could all be commanded, was, as we have seen, his second choice. There is reason to believe that he would have been content with that move alone, trusting to the rest of his lines to play a purely defensive role. But he had not yet the absolute power as commander in chief which necessity was later to confer upon him. Congress was forever making suggestions, even sending him orders, which he felt bound to obey, and his generals had not yet that complete confidence in his judgment that would prevent their overriding his decisions.

So it was now. Over his opposition it was determined that while Dorchester was being fortified and occupied, a force of some four thousand, under Sullivan and Greene, was to be held in readiness to attack Boston across the Back Bay by boat, the ice, by early March, having so far broken up as to make approach upon it impossible. Signals were arranged, to be relayed through Roxbury, and if the British attacked the works on Dorchester the Americans were to counterattack from Cambridge. Thus while they were being attacked on the one hand they were to be attacking on the other; a precarious plan and one which, fortunately, it was not necessary to follow out, for had the Americans attacked from that side, as matters went, the British were quite prepared to lay the town in ashes rather than surrender it peaceably as they did.

With so much planned, one difficulty inherent in the scheme now became apparent. As in the case of the earthworks on

Breed's Hill, it was necessary, at Dorchester, to throw up defenses in the course of a single night. In Charlestown this had been easy, for it was late spring and the ground was soft and workable. At Dorchester, however, the ground was frozen to a depth of eighteen inches, and anyone who has attempted to uncover frozen water pipes at that season of the year can testify that the raising of works there could be neither quick nor silent.

At this juncture a suggestion, said to have been put forward by Colonel Rufus Putnam, was made to make the breastworks of fascines, bundles of sticks, which could be supported by a wooden framework known as a chandelier. The proposal was adopted with enthusiasm, and men were at once set to work to prepare great numbers of the fascines and frames.

On the 4th of March, with great secrecy, that being the eve of the anniversary of the Boston Massacre, when every man could be counted upon to do his best, the militia from the surrounding towns were assembled. At the same time great numbers of carts and teamsters, entrenching tools, and a huge quantity of marsh hay were gathered.

Everything was ready. A blind was to be thrown up on the causeway from Roxbury to Dorchester, "especially on the Dorchester side, as that is nearest the Enemy's guns." Two hundred and fifty axmen were to fell trees for an abatis, and others were to get them in place, set the chandeliers, and fill them with fascines. Seven hundred and fifty men were to be posted on the lower hills, near the shore, and sentries posted between the detachments, to cover the workers. Casks and barrels were to be filled with earth and stones and distributed along the higher hills, to be rolled down upon the enemy in the event of an attack. "The Hoops should be well Naild," wrote Washington, "or else they will soon fly, and the Casks fall to Pieces." Gridley and Knox were to go in on the 4th and lay out the works, and on the morning of the 5th Thomas was to move in with two to three thousand men to occupy the works. In this force were to be five companies of riflemen, who had already proved their deadly marksmanship. "They will, I think," opined Washington, "be able to gald the Enemy sorely in their march from their Boats in landing."

Washington, throughout the operation right to its final carrying out, was never sure that the enemy did not mean to forestall him. Accordingly he made plans to divert them—"amuse" them, he called it. On the night of the 2d, Saturday, the new heavy artillery began to fire all along the line. Sunday night, the 3d, the bombardment was resumed, and under its cover hay and straw were scattered along the Dorchester road to muffle the sounds of the carts' passing. On the night of the 4th came the heaviest fire of all, and to this the British responded more noisily and heavily than the Americans, thereby quite unwittingly helping Washington to carry out the basic portion of his plan. Under cover of the uproar the Americans moved stealthily out upon the peninsula and went to work, and the British, deafened as much by their own fire as by that of the Americans, never heard them until the works were well on the road to completion.

Dorchester peninsula thrust out from the mainland in an L-shaped hook. At the northwest corner, at the heel of the hook, rose Nook's or Foster's Hill, which dominated the wharves and town of Boston at point-blank range, and even commanded the rear of the British lines at Roxbury Neck. At the tip of the L, on the southeast, a high point thrust directly at the Castle, on Castle Island. These points, eventually to be fortified, were on this night merely to be occupied by covering parties, while the main work went forward on the ridge of high hills in between, which overlooked the harbor and the Boston waterfront.

It was a fine night for the work. It was mild, and the hills were lighted by a bright moon, but a mist rose from the water which formed a screen against watchers on the town side, while such wind as there was carried the sounds of labor away from the town, the ships, and the Castle. Apparently some changes were made, for General Thomas oversaw the work, which went on smoothly and steadily. Each man knew his task. The wagons creaked back and forth across the Neck, fetching up fascines and chandeliers and returning for another load. Axmen went to work in the orchards facing the town. Some of the working party hauled the trees into place along the abatis. Others fell to filling the barrels to be rolled down upon the enemy. And still others fell to with pick and shovel to break out a ditch before the breastwork and thicken the outer walls.

Toward ten o'clock there must have been a lull in the firing, for at that hour a sentry reported to Brigadier General Smith —the same who, as colonel, had led the main party on the day of Lexington and Concord—in the British lines that the rebels were at work on Dorchester Heights. If Smith was impressed he gave no sign. The matter was never reported to Howe. If it had been, it might have made little difference. Howe himself was never noted for swiftness of action, and even if he had struck he would have found the Americans not badly pre-pared. At the very time the sentry was making his report to Smith, General Thomas is said to have pulled out his watch and noted that by ten o'clock "they had already got two forts, one upon each hill, sufficient to defend them from small arms and grapes shot."

Work went faster when the shovels bit below the frost line. At three in the morning three thousand fresh men came up, partly as a relief to the workers—note how much more care-fully this operation was planned and executed than that of Bunker Hill—partly to man the works. With them came the artillery which was promptly wheeled into position and placed.

With them, too, came the five companies of riflemen. The relieved men fell back, but only to alarm posts, and the work went on until daylight and beyond, until the guns in the batteries in Boston and on board the ships served notice that they were discovered.

Had any lingering belief in witchcraft still remained in Boston at that late date, the British might well have snatched at it as a straw in explanation of a seemingly impossible phenomenon. When they had gone to bed the night before, the heights of Dorchester had been bare and barren of defenses as an egg. Now, in the space of less than twelve hours, they were bristling with earthworks, raised as if by magic beneath their very eyes. Worse, they mounted heavy artillery in such strength as the British did not suspect the Americans possessed; and these guns were so mounted as to make untenable the harbor, the Castle, and even the town itself. Indeed, if they so wished, the Americans could make the passage out to sea, by the only deep channel, between Castle and Governor's islands, extremely uncomfortable, if not altogether impossible.

The British were taken completely by surprise.

General Howe estimated that the Americans must have had twelve to fifteen thousand men at work all night to have accomplished so much. His engineer Robertson placed the number even higher. Admiral Shuldam—Graves had been relieved in January—is said to have notified Howe promptly that the fleet could no longer remain at its anchorage. Neither, it was obvious, could the troops remain in the town. Bombardment did no good, for the elevation of the works was such that the British guns could not be brought to bear, while the American guns could fire at will and with impunity upon the town, the Castle, and the ships below.

But that was not all. As yet Nook's Hill and Dorchester Point remained unfortified, but since Washington had moved in on

Dorchester, Howe could no longer afford to assume that he would continue to neglect those points. Once Nook's Hill was occupied, the Americans would be in a position to sweep the British lines on Roxbury Neck from behind. From Dorchester Point they could pulverize the Castle at will. Howe had only two alternatives. He must either attack at once and dislodge the Americans before they could consolidate their position, or he must evacuate the town.

Even in the early morning it must have been apparent that attack would be a forlorn hope. Already the Americans were far more strongly posted than they had been on Breed's Hill, and as the day wore on, it became still more evident that this would be a different story, for all through the day the work continued. Nevertheless, for his honor as a general and for the honor of the troops, Howe seemed to think that an attack was necessary. The move was decided upon, and during the day seven regiments were sent down to the Castle, under Brigadier General Jones, to carry out the assignment. In the meantime, at a hasty council of war, it was decided to hold troops in readiness to attack at Roxbury, in case the assault at Dorchester were successful; and at the same time other regiments were told off to guard against American attacks from other quarters. However the generals may have felt about it—it is a curious fact that the troops were ordered to make the assault with unloaded weapons, depending upon the bayonet alone!—the men themselves had little relish for what lay ahead. An American resident of Boston who watched the troops, as they waited to embark for the Castle, said that "they looked in general pale and dejected, and said to one another that it would be another Bunker's Hill affair or worse."

They put it conservatively; it would have been very much worse. Here was no improvised breastwork planned on the spot in the darkness and hastily thrown up, defended by men exhausted by a long night and day of labor, without provisions, short of powder, unsupported by adequate artillery or reinforcements. Here was a carefully planned and executed work, strong in artillery, manned by fresh troops spoiling for battle, adequately supported by strong reinforcements and with plenty of powder. Here, too, were the riflemen, the accuracy of whose fire, the war was to prove, was even more deadly than that withering hail of musketry that had twice hurled back the red-clad ranks at Bunker Hill. Here was a bristling abatis through which the British must force their way; and here was a new engine of war—the rolling casks. No, it would have been very much worse than Bunker Hill, and with odds on it would have had a very different result. As the British troops embarked and dropped down the harbor toward the Castle, the Americans expected an immediate attack. A ripple of anticipation ran through the lines. Washington is said to have remarked to those nearest at hand, "Remember it is the fifth of March, and avenge the death of your brethren." He may have said it. It was a day when commanders were given to such exhortations to their men. "It was immediately asked," the account continues, "what the General said, by those that were not near enough to hear, and was soon answered; and so from one to another thro' all the troops, which added fresh fuel to the martial fire before kindled."

The attack never came off, however. Late in the afternoon it began to rain, the clouds swooped low, and the wind blew. According to Timothy Newell's diary it was "a Hurrycane, or terrible sudden storm." Gordon said it "was such a storm as scarce anyone remembered to have heard." All night it blew, driving some of the transports ashore and piling up such a surf on Dorchester beach that no boat could live in it. In the morning the American works were complete and any attack was hopeless. Howe wrote in his orders: "The General desires the

Troops may know that the intended expedition of last Night was unavoidably put off by the badness of the Weather."

That was Howe's story, and it is the one that has been generally accepted, but recent evidence gives reason to believe that by evening Howe had already made up his mind not to attack and had so given his orders. The storm was an opportune accident which enabled him to save his face. By the morning of the 6th the decision was already taken to evacuate Boston.

It required eleven days to carry the evacuation into effect, and they were eleven long days of disorder and confusion. There were ships enough and in plenty for everybody and everything, but there were not near enough seamen to man them nor time enough to load them all, and in consequence ships and property and military stores in considerable quantities had to be left behind. But who was to go, and in what ships, and what might they take with them? Those were the questions that were uppermost in everyone's mind.

The work began early on the morning of the 6th. The transports were warped in close to the wharves, and the task of loading the heavy stores and equipment began. For the infantry this was no large problem. For the dragoons and the artillery it was something else again. All the horses had to be abandoned. Much of the artillery had to be left behind. Such guns as they could, the British spiked or burst, but there were many which they did not destroy. Similarly there were great mountains of military stores for which they could not find space, and here again they destroyed what they could and left the rest.

While this was being done there was another side of the picture that was distressing. To the Tories, all those who had flocked into the town in order to save their lives and their belongings, the decision to evacuate the city was a sentence of banishment or death. It came upon them suddenly as a clap of thunder and left them stunned with its implications. But as they began to recover from the first shock of it they, too, began to make preparations to leave. By hundreds they besieged Howe with applications for space and the means to convey their belongings aboard. Ships were assigned to them, and they were left largely to their own devices in getting aboard. Those who could took what they were able, but there was much that had to be left, and there were many who took nothing but themselves. The conditions on these refugee ships must have been desperate. Proud Benjamin Hallowell was forced to sleep in a cabin with thirty-six others, "men, women and children; parents, masters and mistresses, obliged to pig together on the floor, there being no berths."

As if this were not enough, the confusion was made worse by Howe's decision to remove everything that might be of use to the Americans. To this end he appointed as agent one Crean Brush, a bird of a feather with Sheriff Loring and Jailer Cunningham. Brush was instructed to save such goods as the rebels might want, and to this end he was given an order to seize whatever might not be turned over to him willingly. A ship was placed at his disposal, and Brush and his men went about their task, translating their orders liberally to cover anything that might take their fancy. They broke into warehouses and stores, plundering and looting at will, under cover of their orders, and it is a matter of record that not only did Brush plunder where he willed, but his men also plundered from him.

Brush and his vessel were later captured on the way to Halifax and brought back to Boston. Joshua Wentworth wrote of his findings on board:

There appeared from the Pillage of this Cargo . . . the Property was in him that cou'd secret the most, for when examining the Chests and Bedg. of the Prisoners, I found great Qty. of Goods, that they had Collected while on board, wh. were taken out of Warehouses without packing, and hove promiscuously on board the vessel, even the Sailors had provided for their disposal at pleasure. In fact the distruction of Property, (under Cover of General Hows Proclimation) is unparrel'd.

The activities of Brush and his men encouraged soldiers and sailors to follow their example and line their pockets while they could, and these, in turn, gave the signal to bands of unprincipled hangers-on to follow suit. To do Howe justice, he issued emphatic orders against looting, but there were not officers enough to enforce them, and the game went on. John Andrews, a Whig who had remained in town, has left us, in a letter, a vivid picture of the general conditions:

By the earnest perswasion of your uncle's friends and with the advice of the select men, I moved into his house, at the time the troops etc., were preparing for embarkation, and under every difficulty you can conceive at such a time, as every day presented us with new scenes of the wantonness and destruction made by the soldiers. I had the care of six houses with their furniture and as many stores filled with effects for eleven months past, and at a time like this I underwent more fatigue and perplexity than I did through the whole siege; for I was obliged to take my rounds all day, without any cessation, and scarce ever failed of finding depredations made upon some one or other of them, that I was finally necessitated to procure men at the extravagant rate of two dollars a day to sleep in the several houses and stores for a fortnight before the military plunderers went off—for sure as they were left alone one night, so sure were they plundered.

In the meantime the selectmen began to fear for the town, should Washington attack. They applied to Howe for assurances, and the general replied that he had no intention of burning the city unless some move was made by "the armed force without" which might interrupt his preparations for departure. The selectmen hastily then sent this word off to Washington, under a flag of truce, begging assurance that he would not thus force matters. The next day Washington's reply was returned, which was to the effect that as the message from the selectmen "was an unauthenticated paper without an address and not obligatory upon Gen. Howe, he would take no notice of it." This was in the hand of Colonel Learned, for Washington himself would not reply, but the implication seemed to be that if the British would proceed with their withdrawal the Americans would not force them to further destruction of property.

It did not, however, mean that the Americans would sit still. On the night of the 8th they raised a small redoubt on Dorchester Point, as a protection against any landing there by the British, and on the 10th the British noticed that preparations were being made to fortify Nook's Hill. A cannonade through the night retarded this somewhat. On the 10th, too, the first ships of the fleet—transports loaded with refugees—fell down the harbor to King Road—now President Roads. The Americans, observing this, feared lest some project of attack might be afoot, and reinforced the lines at Dorchester. But no attack came.

So the days dragged on with the Americans impatient to enter the town, and the British impatient to be off. By the 14th all was ready, but the wind remained foul and the troops were not embarked. On the 15th the regiments were paraded, ready to go on board, but just at the last moment the wind shifted to east, and once more they marched back to their barracks. On the next day there was not sufficient wind to move the ships, so the troops remained on shore.

In the meantime Washington was impatient but alert. At any moment Howe might do an about-face and, gathering his forces swiftly, strike at any point along the American line. It was to prevent any such move that on the night of the 16th Washington served what has been called his notice to quit. That night he fortified Nook's Hill and from there was in a position to sweep the wharves of Boston as the troops embarked. If they did not choose to embark he could sweep the lines at Roxbury from the rear and open the way for his own men to enter Boston.

End of an Era

Saint Patrick's Day of '76. There was no longer any choice for Howe. He must get out or be annihilated. He decided to get out. As the dawn came up, a Lieutenant Adair, of the marines, was sent outside the Roxbury lines to scatter caltrops—a sort of entanglement also known as crow's-feet, four pointed irons which, falling always with one point up, served the same purpose as modern barbed wire. "Being an Irishman, he began scattering the crow-feet about from the gate towards the enemy, and of course, had to walk over them on his return, which detained him so long that he was nearly taken prisoner."

By nine o'clock all the troops were safely embarked save Montresor and Robertson who, with a few men, remained to "shut the Chevaux de fries on the long Wharff and to fire houses if there had appeared any Enemy in our rear, but none appeared." Presently they too took to their boats and rowed out to the waiting ships. With their departure British rule in Boston came to an end.

Index

Acadia (Nova Scotia), 61, 133, 135
Act, Molasses (1733), 81–83
Act of 1660, 56
Act, Quebec, 209–10
Acts, Intolerable, 208–10
Acts of Trade and Navigation, 55–56, 58, 61, 65, 67, 72, 102, 132, 163
Acts, Regulating, 209, 216–17
Acts, Townshend. *See* Townshend Acts
Adair, Lieutenant, 315
Adams, Mrs. Abigail, letter to her husband, on the siege, 254
Adams, John, counsel for British soldiers, 187–88
  criticism of Washington, 301
  letter from his wife, on the siege, 254
  on James Otis, 151
  on the Tea Party, 207
Adams, Mrs. John. *See* Adams, Mrs. Abigail
Adams, Sam, 151, 152, 160, 161, 164, 168, 175–76, 190–92
  at Lexington, 232, 235
  at the Tea Party, 192–98, 201–3
  at the time of the Boston Massacre, 175–76, 180
  chairman of meeting in the Old South Meeting House, 224–26
  escape from the city, 241
  excepted from offer of pardon, 262
  flight to Lexington, 229
  letter to the colonies after the blockade of the city, 213
  on tea from Cape Cod, 208

  share in American action in the Boston Massacre, 186–87
Address by Joseph Warren, in the Old South Meeting House, 225–26
Admiralty Courts, without juries, 147, 149, 163
Adventure Galley, Captain Kidd's ship, 107, 112
Advertisements of Negroes for sale, 85–86
Advice, His Majesty's ship, 110
Agent, colony, in London, 73, 168
Agriculture, 21–22
Aix-la-Chapelle, peace treaty of, 141
Alarm over approach of the French fleet (1746), 137–39
Allerton, Isaac, 1, 24
Allerton Point, 300
American Revolution. *See* Revolution, American
American Weekly Mercury, account of cruelty of the pirates, 101
Amity, pirate ship, 113
Ammunition and arms, 219–34
  attempts by British to seize, 219–34
  ban on importation, 223
  collection and storage, 223–24
  patriots', seizure of, 219–22
Amory, Thomas, 129
Amsterdam, 101
Andrews, John, 290, 313
Andros, Governor Edmund, 66–71, 104, 146
Ann, Cape. *See* Cape Ann

Index

Annapolis, Nova Scotia, 139
Anne, Queen of England, 106
Anti-piracy law, first, 103–4
Anti-Semitism, Hitler's, 126
Antonio, 103–4, 109
Anville, Duc d', 138–39
Apparitions, 48–49
Apthorp, Charles, 129
Apthorp's Wharf, 121
"Aristocracy, codfish," 117–30
Arlington (Menotomy), Massachusetts, 237, 243, 244
Armada, Spanish, defeat of, 8
Armies, English and colonial, 141–42
Arms and ammunition, attempts by British to seize, 219–34
   ban on importation, 223
   collection and storage, 223–24
   patriots', seizure of, 219–22
Army, British, in the city, 260
   on American soil, in the Townshend Acts, 167, 169, 171–72
Army, Continental, 141–42, 247
   headquarters at Cambridge, 261
Articles, or laws, of the pirates, 96–97
Assembly, General Massachusetts, 164, 168, 173, 223
   meeting at Salem, 214
Assistance, Writs of, 82–83, 147, 149, 150, 166
   legalization in the Townshend Acts, 167
   upholding of, by the Court, 151
Atkins, Captain Henry, voyage of, 76
Atlantic Avenue, 121
Attempts by the British to seize arms and ammunition, 219–34
Attucks, Crispus, killed in the Boston Massacre, 183–84
Atwood, Samuel, 177–78
Austrian Succession, War of, 141
Azores, 36

Back Bay, 20, 230, 248, 253, 260, 291, 302, 303
Baker's Isle, 1
Balfour, Captain, 226
Ball, Captain, 125
"Ballad of Chevy Chase," 240
Barker, Thomas, 28
Barnard, Captain Nathaniel, 170
Barrels, rolling, new weapon, 307, 310
Basques, early fishermen, 4, 5
Batteries, North and South, 121

Beacon Hill, 16, 19, 69, 248
Beacon Island, 124
Beaver, tea ship, 199
Belknap, Jeremy, on the Plymouth Company, 9
Bellamy, Captain Samuel, pirate, 106, 124
Bellomont, Governor the Earl of, 107–11
Bendall, Edward, 37
Bentley, Joshua, 232–33
Bermuda, trade with, 32, 33
Bernard, Governor Sir Francis, 156, 159, 160, 165, 168–69, 172
Bethel, privateer, 115
Beverly, Massachusetts, minute men, 228
Birchall, George, 90
Bird Island, 20, 106
Blanchards, 127
Blaxton, William, 10, 16
Blessing of the Bay, The, 27–28, 30
Block, Adrian, 27
Block Island, 97–98
Blockade, port. *See* Port—Blockade
Blockade of Boston, The, play by Burgoyne, 293
Blockheads, The; or, The Affrighted Officers, play, 294
Bloodshed, first, of the Revolution, 161–64
   claim by Salem, 227
Blossome, 39
Blowing up of ships, 48–49
Blue Hills, 8
Board of Commissioners, 168
Board of Trade and Plantations, The. *See* Lords of Trade and Plantations
Boatbuilding. *See* Shipbuilding
Bonner, John, plan of the city (1722 and 1769), 119
Boston Blockade, play, 294
Boston Light, 123–25
   burning by Americans, 300
Boston Massacre (1770), 161–84
   effect, 185–88
   victims, 184
Boston Tea Party, 193–204
Bourne, Nehemiah, 29
Bowdoins, 127
Boycotts (non-importation and non-consumption agreements), 152–53, 168, 214–15

Index

Boylston, Thomas, 129
Boylston's Alley, 176–78
Bradford, William, *History of Plymouth Plantation*, 113
Bradish, Joseph, pirate, 107
Bradstreet, Governor William, 64, 69, 70
Braintree, Massachusetts, 254
Brandy, 78
Brant Rock, 123
Brattle, General William, 220
  caricatured in a play, 294
Brattle Street (Corn Hill), 176–78
Bredcake, Captain Thomas, 45, 115
Breed's Hill, 252, 253
  and Bunker (Bunker's) Hill, 252, 253, 264–65
  Battle of. *See* Bunker Hill, Battle of
Breed's (Hog) Island, 255
  raid on, 255–58
Bretons, early fishermen, 4
Bridge, Cambridge-Brighton, 242–43, 245
Bridge, Colonel, 264
Bridgewater, Massachusetts, 218, 254
Brighton-Cambridge bridge, 242–43, 245
Britain and the British. *See* England
Britannia, 256
Brush, Crean, 312–13
Buccaneers, 92–116
Buildings, wooden and brick, 118, 119
Bull, Dixey, pirate, 44, 102, 133
Bull Inn, 128
Bullivant, Justice, 68, 69
Bunch of Grapes Inn, 128
Bunker (or Bunker's) Hill, and Breed's Hill, 252, 253, 264–65
  attack, British, and repulse, 278–84
  Battle of, 225, 245, 259–84
  blunders and heroism on both sides, 263–64
  British plan of attack, 260–61, 270, 276–77
  British soldier's story of attack, 281
  casualties on both sides, 285–86
  defense, Continental Army, confusion in, 271
  effects, 286–88
  number of Continentals engaged, 276
  withdrawal of the Continentals, 283–84
Bunker Hill Monument, 20
Burgoyne, General John, 259–61, 267, 292, 297, 300, 301
  caricatured in a play, 294

play, *The Blockade of Boston*, 293
playwright, 294
Burning of the city, authorized by Congress, 301
  expected by the British, 291
  fear of, during the evacuation by the British, 313–14
Business. *See* Trade
Bute, Lord, 154

Cabot, John and Sebastian, 3–4
Cahoon, Captain James, 97–98
Caldwell, James, killed in the Boston Massacre, 184
Cambridge (old name, Newtowne), Massachusetts, 22, 220, 230, 237, 240, 243, 244, 252, 261, 264, 268, 288, 304
  headquarters of the Continental Army, 261
Cambridge-Brighton bridge, 242–43, 245
Canada, Quebec Act, 209–10
  recognition of the Roman Catholic religion, 209–10
Canary Islands, trade with, 38
Cape Ann, 1, 5, 24, 123
  naming of, 7
  settlement on, 10, 13
Cape Breton Island, 136, 139
Cape Cod, 27, 124, 208
Capital of New England, 35
Carr, Patrick, killed in the Boston Massacre, 184
Carrying trade, 40–41, 53–54
Cartier, Jacques, 4
Casks, rolling, new weapon, 307, 310
Castle, The. *See* Castle William
Castle Island, 20, 49, 260
Castle William, 135, 138, 140, 159, 165, 172, 185, 197, 199, 200, 208, 215, 227, 240, 259, 303, 306–9
Catholics, prejudice against, 125, 126
  recognition of religion, in Canada, 209–10
Cayman Islands, pirates' rendezvous, 95
Cerberus, 260
Chaddock, Captain, 49
Champlain, Sieur de, explorations, 6
Charles I, King of England, 15
Charles II, King of England, 56, 66
Charles, privateer, 104–6, 112, 115
Charles River, 16, 18–20, 230, 240, 253, 260, 264–66, 291
  naming of, 8

[319]

Index

Charlestown, Massachusetts, 2, 10, 16, 19–21, 120, 220, 233, 240, 244, 245, 252, 255, 260, 262, 264, 268, 271, 291, 303
  fire set by British cannon balls, 277
  landing at, 2
  life in, during the winter of 1775, as seen by Lord Rawdon, 295–96
  occupation of Breed's Hill by the Continentals, 263
  raid upon; interruption of a play, 294–95
Charlestown Ferry, 120, 211
Charlestown Navy Yard, 18
Charlestown Neck, 245, 252, 264, 268, 269, 271, 275, 285, 303
Charter, Massachusetts Bay Company (old charter), 15
  revocation of, 65, 67
Charter, new, 73
  Lord George Germain on abrogation, 206–7
"Chebacco" boat, 23
Chelsea (old name, Winnesimmet), Massachusetts, 10, 255
Chelsea Creek, 255, 256
Cheuyot Hills, 8
"Chevy Chase, Ballad of," 240
Child, first white born in the New World, 2–3
"Christopher Island" (Saint Kitts), trade with, 32, 36, 37
Church, Dr. Benjamin, 229, 241
Church, rule by the (theocracy), 73
Churches, number of (1680 and 1699), 118; (1721), 119
  pre-Revolution, 121
Cilley (New Hampshire soldier), 247
Civil Wars, English, 54
  in New England, 45–48
Claim of the city to title, "Cradle of American Liberty," 205–7
Clark, Richard, 194
Clark Parsonage at Lexington, 229
Clark's shipyard, 122
Clark's Warehouse and Wharf, 121, 194
Climate, 18
Clinton, General Sir Henry, 259, 266, 267, 269, 270, 282, 299, 301
Club, early, 128
"Coasters, Lord North's," 212
Cod, Cape. See Cape Cod
Codfish, 52–54
  base of the city's prosperity, 129–30

"Codfish aristocracy," 117–30
Coffeehouses (1760), 146
Coffin, Captain Shubael, 164
Cohasset, Massachusetts, 123
Collector of the customs, 59
Colonies, Congress, general, proposed, 213–14
  Continental Congress, 214
  other, appeal to, against the Townshend Acts, 168
  rally behind Massachusetts after blockade of Boston, 213–14
  remote control of, 15
  right of England to rule, by Declaratory Act, 165
  right to rule, assertion by George III, 207
  settlements, early, scattered, 10
  white, early, 22
Colonization of Massachusetts, 1–16
Columbus, Christopher, 3
Commerce. See Trade
Commercial Street, 121
Commissioners, Board of. See Lords of Trade and Plantations
Committee of Correspondence, 197, 219, 220
Committee of Thirty, 236
Committee of Trade and Plantations, English. See Lords of Trade and Plantations
Committee of Safety, 197, 207, 213, 214, 232, 236, 261, 262, 265, 267
Committees of Correspondence, 197, 219, 220
Common, the, 128, 165, 215, 216, 230, 236–38
Commonwealth, English, 61–62
Commonwealth History of Massachusetts, by Albert Bushnell Hart, on the slave trade, 86
Companies, trading, 9
Conant, Colonel, 233
Conant, Roger, 13, 14, 16
Concord, Massachusetts, 223
  Battle of, 235–46
  legends about British move, 230
  move on, to seize arms, 229
Congress, Continental, 214, 219, 288, 291
  burning of the city authorized by the Congress, 301
  criticism of Washington, 301
Congress, Provincial, 219, 223
  counterproclamation, 262

Index

Connecticut, 138
Connell, Captain, 169
Continental Army, 247–48
  headquarters at Cambridge, 261
Continental Congress, 214, 219, 288, 291
  burning of the city authorized by the Congress, 301
  criticism of Washington, 301
Copley, John Singleton, 146, 199
Copp's Hill, 19, 60, 106, 253, 266, 267, 272
Corn Hill (Brattle Street), 176–78
Correspondence, Committees of, 197, 219, 220
Cortereal (explorer), 4
Council, temporary, 65–66
Council for New England, 10, 12, 14
Counterproclamation by the Provincial Congress, 262
County meetings after the Boston Massacre, 218–19
Courier system, 219, 220
Court, Great and General, of Massachusetts, 45, 49
Court Street, 239
Courts of Admiralty without juries, 147, 149
Coytmore, Captain Thomas, 36–38
"Cradle of American Liberty," claim of the city to the title, 205–7
Cradock, Matthew, 15, 23, 27, 28
Cromwell, Oliver, Navigation Act (1650), 55
Cromwell, Captain Thomas, 113–14
Crown, the. See England; names of Kings
Crown Point, 302
Cunningham, William, prison provost under the British, 292, 297–99, 312
Currency, need for, 67
Cushing, Thomas, 151
Custom House, 181, 182
Customs, revenue, 57–59, 132, 147, 148
  collectors, 59
  duties imposed by the Townshend Acts, 167
  enforcement, rigid, 189
  evasion, 148–49
  free trade, 56; assertion of right, 82; death of, 73
  locally imposed, 57
  smugglers. See Smugglers
  tonnage, 57

Customs and manners, early, 128–29
Cutler, Captain John, slaver, 89, 90

Dana, Justice, 160
Dangers of the sea, 123
Dankers, Jasper, description of the city (1680), 118
Danvers, Massachusetts, 215, 227
  minute men, 228
Dartmouth, tea ship (Boston Tea Party), 197, 199, 200
D'Aulnay (Frenchman in Acadia), 41–44
Dawes, William, capture and release, 241
  ride, 230–32
Dearborn, General Henry, 275
DeBerniere, sketch of the Bunker Hill Battle, 276
Declaratory Act, 165
Dedham, Massachusetts, 219
Deer Island, 20
Depression, trade, 67, 152
Description of New England, by Captain John Smith, 8
Descriptions of the city:
  in 1650, by Johnson, in Wonder Working Providence, 59
  in 1671, by Josselyn, 60
  in 1680, by Jasper Dankers, 118
  in 1686, by John Dunton, 118
  in 1699, by Edward Ward, 118
  in 1721, by Captain Nathaniel Uring, 119
Desire, 28, 38
Diana, 256–57
Discoverers, early, 3–10
Discoveries, by Richard Hakluyt, 8
Distilleries, rum, 54, 80–81
Diving bell, first, 37
Dock, Town, 68, 177
Dock Square, 178, 181–83
Dominion of New England, planned, 65, 66, 72–73
Dorchester, Massachusetts, 14, 22, 29, 38, 120, 248, 252, 260, 262, 267, 271
Dorchester Company of Adventurers, 13
Dorchester Flats, 20, 211, 253, 260
Dorchester Heights, 271, 287
  attack planned by the British, 309–11
  fortification by Washington, and plans for action, 302–10
Dorchester Neck, 20, 303
Dorchester Point, 260, 308–9, 314

Index

Dove, 32
Downing, Emmanuel, 40, 84
Dragon, 115
Drinks, favorite, 129
Dudley, Governor Joseph, 65, 71, 106
Dudley, Paul, 106
Dunton, John, description of the city (1686), 118–19
Dutch at New York, 22
  competition with, 55, 56
  in the city, 125, 126
  trade with, 30, 32
Duties. *See* Customs, revenue

East Boston, 20, 255
East Cambridge, Massachusetts, 237
East India Company, 9, 108–9, 111, 196, 208
  tea agents, 192
  tea policy, 191–93
Economists, 79
Edict of Nantes, and repeal of, 126–27
Edwards, Captain Benjamin, 95
Effect, social, of immigration, 128
Eleanor, tea ship, 199
Eliot, Reverend Andrew, 289
Elizabeth, Queen of England, 4, 43
Elm Tree, Great, 154
Emerson, Ralph Waldo, poem of Battle of Concord, 235
Emmot, Joseph, 109, 110
Endecott, Governor John, 1, 14, 16, 23
England, army, occupation of city after the Tea Party, 215
  Army on American soil, in the Townshend Acts, 167, 169, 171–72
  Army, quartering of troops on the City, 172–73, 209; end of, 185–86
  Civil Wars, 54
  Civil Wars, in New England, 45–48
  colonial policy, blunders in, 191
  coming into her own, 8
  Commonwealth, 61–62
  Crown, dispute with, 62
  Crown, prerogatives of, 144–46
  Crown, resentment against, 55
  domination by, in the eighteenth century, 145–46
  finances, demand for American support, 166–69
  in the seventeenth century, 11
  jealousy, English, of the city, 128, 131
  Navy, 43, 112
    arrogance toward merchantmen, 189

    clash with, over impressment, 139–41
    early, 43, 112
    fleet arrival at the city, 259–60
    impressment for, 139–41, 169
    life in, at the city (winter of 1775), 296–97
  Parliament, blamed for ills in the city, 147
  Parliament, representation in, 146, 147, 163
  parties, political, 145
  Rebellion, 61–62
  Restoration, 62
  right to rule colonies, by Declaratory Act, 165
  Tories and Whigs, 145
  trade jealousy, and rivalry, 128, 131
  trade with, 56
English stock in the city, 125–26
Epidemics, 120, 152, 290
Ericson, Leif, visit to Massachusetts, 2
Ericson, Thorwald, visit to Massachusetts, 2
Eskimos, trade with, 76
Essex, Massachusetts, 23
Essex Street, 154
Estournel, Admiral d', 139
Evacuation of the city by the British, 311–15
Evacuation Day, March 17, 315
Evening Post, Boston, on slaving voyage, 90
Exchange alley, 181
Expansion of the city (to 1721), 119; (in the 1740s), 146
Expectation, 63–64
Explorers, early, 3–10
Explosions, ship, 48–49
Exports. *See* Trade

Falcon, 273
Families, leading, 129–30
Fancy, 99
Faneuil, Andrew, 120
Faneuil, Benjamin, Jr., 194
Faneuil, Peter, 89–91
Faneuil Hall, 128, 143, 159, 177, 180, 197, 213
  use as warehouse and theater, 292
Faneuils, 127
Farming, 21–22
Farnsworth, Amos, on Hog and Noodle's Island fight, 256

Index

"Father of the Revolution" (James Otis), 150–51

Fees, port, 57

Fighting during the siege, 251–58

Fireboats, British fear of, 300–1

Fires, great (1631–1760), 117, 119–20

First city in the colonies, 117

Fish, dried, three grades, 74

Fisheries, 22
   barring of patriots from, 223
   base of the city's prosperity, 129–30
   cod, 52–54
   early, 4–5
   importance of, 74–75
   piratical attack on, by Low, 98–99

Fleet, British. See England—Navy

Flucker, Captain James, 96, 98, 99

Fly, William, pirate, 106–7

Folsom (New Hampshire soldier), 248

Forests, New World, 22

Fort, the, 69, 165, 172, 259

Fort Hill, 19, 155, 157, 215

Fort Hill Square, 121

Fort William and Mary, 224

Fortune, 40

Foster, William, 45

Foster's (Nook's) Hill, 260, 306, 308–9, 314

Founding of the city, 20, 21

France, clashes with, 30, 41–44
   rivalry with, 131–43
   trade with, 61
   wars with, 79, 81–82, 104, 105, 108, 115, 131–43
   wars with, Peace of Utrecht, 74, 80

Frankland, Sir Harry, 148

Franklin, Benjamin, first literary work, "The Lighthouse Tragedy," 124

Free trade, 56
   assertion of right, 82
   death of, 73

Freedom, religious, 62

Freeman, Captain Isaac, 115

French (Huguenots) in the city, 125–27

French and Indian War (Old French War) (Seven Years' War), 41–42

French East India Company, 110

French West Indies, trade with, 74, 76, 79

Frye, Colonel, 264

Fur trade, 56, 76

Gadsden, Christopher, 213

Gage, General Thomas, 171–72, 214–16, 218–23, 225, 235–91, 293, 297, 301
   attempts to seize arms and ammunition, 219–34
   on repression, 210
   return to England, 301
   wife an American, 230, 231

Gallows (1722), 120

Gardiner, John, and Gardiner's Island, 109

Garrett, Richard, adventures of, 24–26

General Assembly of Massachusetts, 164, 168, 172, 223
   meeting at Salem, 214

General Court (Great and General Court of Massachusetts), 45, 49

Generals, American, experience in Seven Years' War, 142

George I, King of England, 144

George II, King of England, 144, 147
   death, 142–43
   friend of the city, 143–45

George III, King of England, 165
   accession, 143
   character, 144–46
   enemy of the city, 143–45, 147
   on right to rule the colonies, 207

George's Island, 123

Germain, Lord George, on the abrogation of the charter, 206–7

Germans, in the city, 126

Germantown River, 299

Ghosts, 48–49

"Gibraltar of America" (Louisbourg), taking of, and effect of capture, 137–38

Gift of God, 40

Gillam, James, pirate, 107

Gillan, Benjamin, and Company, 29

Glasgow, 269

Gloucester, Massachusetts, 23, 29
   fisheries, 74–75

Glover, Captain Robert, 115

Goldfinch, Captain, 179–80

Gómez, Estevan, 4

Gorges, Sir Fernando, attempt to form colony, 7
   land grants to, 9–10

Gosnold, Bartholomew, 5, 6

Governor, new method of selection, 73

Governor Winthrop House, demolition for fuel, 290

Governors, colonial, 58, 59
   See also personal names

Index

Governor's Island, 308
Grants, land, 9–10, 14
  confusion in, 9
Grape Island, 253
Graves, Admiral Lord, 253, 255–56, 258, 260, 262, 277, 299, 308
  on life in the British Navy (winter of 1775), 296–97
Gray, Harrison, 201
Gray, Sam, 174–84
  insult to British soldier, 174
  shooting in the Boston Massacre, 184
Great and General Court of Massachusetts, 45, 49
Great Barrington, Massachusetts, 217
Great Brewster Island, 124
Great Britain. *See* England
"Great Tree, The," 154
Green Dragon Inn, 128, 241
Greene, General Nathanael, 248, 304
Grenville, Chancellor of the Exchequer George, 166–67
Greyhound, 95
Gridley, Colonel Richard, 264–66, 305
Griffin's Wharf, 198, 203, 204
Growth of the city (to 1721), 119; in the 1740s, 146
Guinea Coast, slave trade, 39
Gurnett's Nose, 25
Guy Fawkes Day, 151, 160

Hakluyt, Richard, *Principall Navigations, Voiages, Traffiques and Discoueries*, 8
Hall, Captain, master of the tea ship *Dartmouth*, 197–99
Hallowell, Comptroller Benjamin, 158, 170, 171, 262, 312
Hancock, John, 56, 151, 152, 170, 195, 196
  at Lexington, 232, 235
  at the Tea Party, 203
  escape from the city, 241
  excepted from offer of pardon, 262
  flight to Lexington, 229
  Liberty incident, 169–71
Hancocks, accused of being smugglers, 129–30
Hanover Square, 154, 193
Happy Delivery, pirate ship, 95
Harbor, the, 17–18
  first English and French visits, 8
  fortifications, 57
  perils of, 123

Harbors of the world, 17
Hardwick, Massachusetts, 217
Harrison, Collector Joseph, 170, 171
Harrison, brigantine, 164
Hart, Albert Bushnell, *Commonwealth History of Massachusetts*, on the slave trade, 86
Harvard College fire, 152
  President, Reverend Samuel Langdon, 264
Hatfield, Connecticut, 217
Havannah Expedition, 142
Hawkins, Captain Thomas, 29, 36
Hawkins, Thomas (pirate), 104, 114
Hayes, Captain John, 125
Haying expedition, British, 253–55
Hazard, His Majesty's ship, shipwreck, 123
Henry IV, King of France, 126
Herjulfson, Bjarne, Norseman, visit to Massachusetts, 2–3
Higginson, John, 84
Hill, Henry, distiller, 80
Hills, three, of Tremont, 19
Hingham, Massachusetts, 28, 29, 253
Hispaniola, 33
History of Plymouth Plantation, by William Bradford, 113
Hitler, Adolf, 126
Hog (Breed's) Island, 255
  raid on, 255–58
Hollingsworth, Richard, 28–29
Holyoke, Massachusetts, 221
Honduras, logwood trade with, 94
Hopewell, trading ship, 38
Hore, Master, 4
Hotels, early, 128
Houses, number of in 1690, 117; in 1722, 119
Howe, Admiral Earl, 270
  caricature of, in a play, 294
Howe, General Viscount, 251, 259, 260, 266, 267, 269, 270, 274, 276, 277, 281, 282, 291, 303, 307–13, 315
  caricature of, in a play, 284
Huguenots, in the city, 126–27
  persecution of, by Louis XIV, 126–27
Hull, Edward, 114
Hull, John, 45, 114
Hull, Massachusetts, 300
Hutchinson, Oliver, 194
Hutchinson, Governor Thomas, 150, 154, 156, 157, 162, 165, 168–69, 172, 185–96, 200, 202, 261

Index

attack on his house, by mob, 159
 on repression, 210

Immigrants, early, 34, 125–28
 social effect on the city, 128
Import duties. *See* Customs, Revenue
Impressment, 169
 clash over, 139–41
India, trade with, 108
Indians, friendliness to Garrett's men, 26
 kidnaping of, 6–7
 King Philip's War, 62
 Narragansetts, 40
 Pequot War, 33
 trading with, 5–6, 61
 wars with, 33, 61, 62, 66, 133
"Indians" at the Tea Party, 203
Industries related to shipbuilding, 29–30
Ingersoll, Jared, 156
Inns, early, 128, 146
Intolerable Acts, 208–10
Intolerance, 62
Ireland, John, pirate, 108
Irish in the city, 126
Isle of Shoals, 24

Jamaica Plain, Massachusetts, 226
James I, King of England, 11, 43, 55
James II, King of England, 66, 111
 deposition of, 67–68
Jamestown, Virginia, founding of, 9
Jealousy, British, 128, 131
Jenkins' Ear, War of, with Spain, 122
Jews, 126
John Gallop's Point, 49
John of Oxon, shipwreck, 123
Johnson, description of the city, 118
Johnson, Isaac, 21
Johnson, Lady Arabella, 21
Johnson, Thomas, hanging of, 104
Johnson, *Wonder Working Providence*, 59
Jolly Batchellor, slaver, 89–91
Jones, Brigadier General, 309
Jones, John, 89
Jones, Margaret, 49–51
Jonquiere, Admiral la, 139
Josselyn, description of the city (1670), 60
Jury trials, denial of, 147, 149, 163

Karlsefne, Thorfinn, visit to Massachusetts, 2
Kennebec River, 27

Keyser, Thomas, 39
Kidd, Captain William, 107–12, 115
Kilby Street, 155
King George's War, 141
King Philip's War, 62
King Road (President Roads), 314
King Street, 120, 155, 158, 179, 181, 188
King's Chapel, 128
Kirk, Sir David, 42
Kirk, Thomas, tidewaiter, 170
Kirke, Governor Percy, 66
Knowles, Commodore, 139–41
Knowlton, Colonel, 264, 273, 274, 276, 291, 294
Knox, General Henry, 182, 183, 301–2, 305

La Jonquiere, Admiral, 139
Lamb, ban on eating, 153
Land grants, 9–10, 14
 confusion in, 9
Langdon, Reverend Samuel, President of Harvard College, 264
Larkin, John, 233
Larz Anderson Bridge, 240
La Tour (Frenchman in Acadia), 41–43
Law, anti-piracy, first, 103–4
Lawrence, Captain Peter, 115
Laws, or articles, of the pirates, 96–97
Leach, John, on prisoners in British hands, 299
Leaders of the Revolution, 151
Leading families, 129–30
Learned, Colonel, 314
Lechmere Point, 303–4
Lee, General Charles, 301
Leif Ericson, visit to Massachusetts, 2
Leifsbudir, home of Leif Ericson, 2
Leslie, Colonel, 227–28, 303
Letters of marque, 112
"Leveling," 162
Levett (early settler), 1
Lexington, Massachusetts, 229
 Battle of, 235
Liberalization of religion, 73
Liberty incident, 169–71
Liberty Boys and party, 157, 160, 186–88, 190, 192–94, 196–97
Liberty Poles, 163
Liberty Tree, 160, 165, 193, 195, 293
 destruction by the British, 290
 first, 157
Lighthouse, first, 123–25

Index

"Lighthouse Tragedy, The," by Benjamin Franklin, 124
Lights, mysterious, 48–49
Little Isle, 1
Lively, 267, 273, 277
Livingston, Robert, 107
Logwood trade with Honduras, 94
London, province agent in, 73, 168
London, or Virginia, Company, 9, 12
London Packet, 170
Londonderry (Manchester), New Hampshire, 126
Long Wharf, 119–21, 128, 172, 220, 260
Longfellow, Henry Wadsworth, "Paul Revere's Ride," 232, 235–36
"Lord North's Coasters," 212
Lords of Trade and Plantations (later, Board of Trade and Plantations), 58, 122, 131, 132, 168
Loring, Joshua, in charge of American prisoners in the city, 297–99, 312
Louis XIV, King of France, 126–27
Louisbourg, attack on, 82
    capture of, and effect of capture, 136–37
Low, Ned, pirate, 92–102
Lowther, George, pirate, 95–96
Loyal American Associates, 250
Loyal Irish Volunteers, 251
Loyalists in the city during the siege, 250–51
Lumbering, 22
Lynn, Massachusetts, 22

Machias, Maine, 41
Mackintosh, Captain, 158, 160
Madagascar, rendezvous of the pirates, 108
Maine, 133, 136
    Popham Colony, 27
Malcolm, Captain Daniel, smuggling case, 166
Mall, Ensign, 179
Manchester (Londonderry), New Hampshire, 126
Manhattan. *See* New Amsterdam
Manly, Captain, 291
Manners and customs, 128–29
Manufacturing, move to encourage, 153
Map, early, of the city, 17–20
    Bonner's (1722 and 1769), 119
Maps, 8
Marblehead, Massachusetts, 28, 32, 38, 123

aid to Boston in the blockade, 212–13
chosen by England to supersede Boston, after the Tea Party, 209
minute men, 228
slave trade, 84
"Mare-Mount" (Wollaston, Massachusetts), 10
Marshall, Captain John, 170
Marshfield, Massachusetts, 223
    Tories in, 226
Martinique, expedition against, 134–35
Mary, 99
    shipwreck, 123
Mary Rose, shipwreck, 36–37
Maryland, trade with, 32
Mason, Captain John, 14
    death of, 35
    land grants to, 9–10
Massachusetts Assembly, 164, 168, 173
Massachusetts Bay, 3, 6
    visits to, 2–3
Massachusetts Bay Colony, 21
    dispute with the Pilgrims over boundary, 14
Massachusetts Bay Company, 15, 23
Massachusetts Gazette and News Letter, 153
Massacre, Boston, 161–84
    effect, 185–88
    victims, 184
Maverick, Samuel, 10, 26, 27, 30
    shot in the Boston Massacre, 184
Mayflower, 12
Mayhew, Jonathan, 151
Maypole at "Mare-Mount," 10
Maze, William, pirate, 108
McClary, Major, death at Bunker Hill, 285–86
McOwen, Winifred, 290
Medford (Mystic), Massachusetts, 22, 28, 29
Menotomy (Arlington), Massachusetts, 237, 243, 244
Mercantile class, rule by, 76
Mercantilism, 54
Merchant vessels with letters of marque, 112
Merchants. *See* Trade
Mermaid, slaver, 88
Merrimack River boundary, dispute over, 14
Metropolis of the colonies, 131
Middle Passage, slave trade, 86, 87

Index

Military occupation after the Tea Party, 215

Mill Pond, 120

Milton, Massachusetts, 200, 219

Minute men, 228

Mitchell, Mayor, 237

M'Neil, Archibald, 174–75

Molasses, trade in, 76–83, 165

Molasses Act (1733), 81–83, 132

Molineaux, William, at the Tea Party, 203

Moncrieffe (friend of Putnam), 289

Money. See Currency

Monnahiggan, Isle of, 7

Monopolies, trade, English, 9

Monopoly, tea, and implications of policy, 191–92

Montagu, Admiral, 200, 204

Montgomery, Private, at the Boston Massacre, 179, 181–82

Montresor, John, 315

Moon Island, 300

Moore, Captain, slaver, 88

Morton's Point, 267, 270, 273, 274, 278

Moulton, Robert, 23

Murray, Councilor, of Rutland, Massachusetts, 217

Murray Barracks, 176–81

Mystic (Medford), Massachusetts, 22, 28

Mystic River, 18–20, 24, 27, 211, 255, 265, 267–69, 276–78

Nahant, Massachusetts, 24

Nahumkeck (Naumkeck; later Salem), 1, 13, 14, 16, 24

Naming of Boston, 16

Nancy, ordnance ship, 291

Nantasket, Massachusetts, 2, 8, 18, 134, 137, 172, 211

landing at, 2

Nantes, Edict of, and repeal, 126–27

Narragansett Indians, 40

Nationalities in the city, 125–28

Naumkeag (Nahumkeck; later Salem), 1, 13, 14, 16, 24

Naval stores, 22

Navigation and Trade, Acts of, 55–56, 58, 61, 65, 67, 72, 102, 132, 163

Navy, English. See England

Navy Yard, Charlestown, 18

Neck, the. See Charlestown Neck

Negroes. See Slave Trading

Netherlands, the. See Dutch

New Amsterdam (New York), 27, 28, 66, 71, 126

Dutch in, 22

rival, commercial, 147

New Brunswick, 133

New England, capital, 35

news of Lexington and Concord, spread of, 245–46

"New England Company for a Plantation in Massachusetts Bay," 13–14

New Hampshire, 14, 35, 121, 126, 136, 224

New Hampshire Committee of Safety, 261

New York (New Amsterdam), 27, 28, 66, 71, 126

Dutch in, 22

rival, commercial, 147

Newbury (Washington) Street, 154

Newburyport, Massachusetts, slave trade, 84

Newell, Timothy, 310

Newfoundland, 4, 136

Newman, sexton of the Old North Church, 241

Newport, Rhode Island, 223

slave trade, 83

News of Lexington and Concord, rapid spread of, 246

News Letter, 154

article on the slave trade, 86

letter in, on the slave trade, 88

pirates' laws published in, 97

slavery advertisements, 85–86

Newspapers (1760), 146

American Weekly Mercury, 101

Evening Post, on a slaving voyage, 90

Massachusetts Gazette and News Letter, 153

News Letter. See News Letter

Tory plea against, 168

Newtowne (Cambridge), Massachusetts, 22

Nixon, Colonel John, 255

Nix's Mate, 106–7

pirate's curse on, 20

"No taxation without representation," 146, 147, 163

Noddle's (Nottle's) Island, 19, 20, 24, 49, 124, 135, 233

raid on, 255–58

Non-importation and non-consumption agreements (boycotts), 152–53, 168, 214–15

Index

Nook's (Foster's) Hill, 260, 306, 308–9, 314

Normans, early fishermen, 4

Norsemen, visits to Massachusetts, 2–3

North, Lord, 212

North Battery, 121

North Boston, 232

North Cambridge, Massachusetts, 245

North End, 160
shipbuilding, 29

North Station, 120

North Virginia, or Plymouth, Company, 9

Nostra Senhora da Victoria, 100

Nottle's Island. *See* Noddle's Island

Nova Scotia (Acadia), 61, 133

Noyes, Oliver, 120

Nutting, Captain, 264

O. Cromwell's head Inn, 128

Occupation, military, after the Tea Party, 215

Old Brick Meeting House, 180

Old French War (Seven Years' War; French and Indian War), 141–42

Old North Church, 232, 241

Old South Meeting House, 198
use as a riding school, 292

Old State House (Town Hall), 128, 140, 143, 155

Oldham, John, murder by Indians, 33

Oldmixon, John, 121

Oliver, Andrew, 154–56, 160

Olivers, 127

Onrust, ship, 27

Orange Street, 239

Orford, Earl of, 107

Otis, Harrison Gray, on the city on Lexington-Concord day, 239

Otis, James, 150–51

Paine, Timothy, 217

Papillion, Captain Peter, 98

Papists, prejudice against, 125, 126

Parker, Daniel, 289

Parliament, blamed for ills, 147
representation in, 146, 147, 163

"Paul Revere's Ride," by Henry Wadsworth Longfellow, 232, 235–36

Paxton, Collector Charles, 148–49, 166, 262

Peace treaty of Aix-la-Chapelle, 141

Peace of Utrecht, 74, 80

Peirce (early settler), 1

Pemaquid, 1, 24, 44, 133

Penn, William, 84

Penobscot Bay, Maine, 44

Penobscot River, 41

Pepperell, Massachusetts, 264

Pequot War, 33

Percy, Earl, 216–18, 230, 236–40, 242–45
caricature in a play, 294
legend of move on Concord, 230

Perils of the sea, 123

Peter, Reverend Hugh, 28

Philadelphia, rival in culture, 147
rival of the city, 128

Philadelphia Resolves, 196

Phipp's Farm, 237

Phips, Sir William, attacks on Port Royal and Quebec, 134

Pickering, Colonel, 245

Pierce, Captain William, 38

Pigot, General, 277, 280–82

Pilgrims, 11–12
at Plymouth, 10
dispute with Massachusetts Bay colony over boundary, 14

Pinnaces, 26

Pirates, 43–48, 92–112
act of grace for, 108–9
and privateers, 92–116
articles, or laws, 96–97
cruelties of Low, 99–101
curse on Nix's Mate, 20
description of, 92
law against, first, 103–4
laws, or articles, of, 96–97
Nix's Mate, curse on, 20
rendezvous, Cayman Islands, 95
rendezvous, Madagascar, 108

Piscataqua River, 44
settlement at, 6, 10

Pitcairn, Major, 230, 238, 239

Pitt, William, 145

Plague from the West Indies, 48

Plan of the city, engraved, Bonner's (1722 and 1769), 119

Plantations and Trade, Committee of, 58

Play, *The Blockade of Boston*, by John Burgoyne, 293

Ploughed Hill, 303

Plowman, Captain Daniel, privateer, 104–6

Plymouth, Massachusetts, 22, 25, 31, 217
early English visits to site, 6, 8
landing at, 12

Index

Pilgrims at, 10
self-government, 15
Plymouth, or North Virginia, Company, 9
Point Shirley, 20
Political tolerance, 62
Pollard, Anne, 20
Pomeroy, General Seth, at Bunker Hill, 279, 280
Popham, Captain George, attempt to form a colony, 7
Popham, Sir John, attempt to form a colony, 7
Popham Colony, Maine, 27
Population of the city in 1690, 117; in 1722, 119; in 1740s, 146
decline (1775), 291
racial stocks, 125–28
Port. See Trade
Port, blockade (closure) of, 249
aid from other cities, 212–13
bill for closure of the port, after the Tea Party, 208–12
by Washington, 57
Port fees, 57
Port Royal, Nova Scotia, attack on, 133, 134
reduction of, 135
Portsmouth, New Hampshire, 302
cache of arms and ammunition, and Paul Revere's warning ride, 224
Portuguese, early fishermen, 4
in the city, 125
Pound, Thomas, pirate, 104
Powder and arms, attempts by the British to seize, 219–34
ban on importation, 223
collection and storage, 223–24
for the Continentals, 302
Pratt, Benjamin, 151
Prescott, Colonel William, 265–67, 271–75, 280, 283–84, 287
at the Battle of Bunker Hill, 264
"Don't fire until you see the whites of their eyes," order at Bunker Hill, 280
President Roads (King Road), 314
Press, the. See Newspapers
Preston, Captain Thomas, 182–83, 186
acquittal, 187–88
Principall Navigations, Voiages, Traffiques and Discoueries, by Richard Hakluyt, 8

Pring, Martin, 6
Prisoners of the Americans, after Bunker Hill, 297
Prisoners of the British, ill treatment after Bunker Hill, 297–99
Privateers, 112–16
and pirates, 92–116
Privy Council, 58
Proclamation of reconciliation, and counterproclamation, 262
Prospect Hill, 284, 303
Prosperity (1760), 147
based on the fisheries, 129–30
Protestants, persecution by Louis XIV, 126–27
Providence, Rhode Island, 223
Province agent in London, 73, 168
Province House, 155, 165
Provincial Congress, 219, 223
counterproclamation, 262
Pullen Point, 20
Puritans, 2, 11, 15, 20–21, 61, 125
composition, in the city, 22
Putnam, General Israel, 213, 221, 247, 256–58, 264, 271, 272, 275, 284, 289
activity during the siege, 252
responsible for fortification of Breed's Hill, 265–66
Putnam, Colonel Rufus, 304

Quakers, enslavement proposed by Cotton Mather, 84
persecution of, 62
Quarantine, early, 48
Quartering of troops in the city, 172–73, 209
end of, 185–86
Quebec, abortive expedition against (1693), 134–35
attack on (1690), 134
capture of (1759), 143
expedition against (1711), 135–36
Quebec Act, 209–10
Quedah Merchant, 108–10
Quelch, Captain John, 105–6, 112, 113
Quincy, John, counsel for British soldiers, 187–88
Quincy, Josiah, 201
Quincy family, 115

Race track, Suffolk Downs, 255
Races (peoples) in the city, 125–28
Rainbowe, 39

Index

Randolph, Collector and Surveyor of the Customs Edward, 40, 57–59, 61–66, 69, 71, 75, 104, 132

Rasilli, Chevalier de, 41

Rawdon, Lord, 292–93
on life at Charlestown (winter of 1775), 295–96

Rebecca, 28, 32, 96, 98

Rebellion, English, 61–62

Reconciliation, proclamation of, by General Gage, and counterproclamation, 262

Recriminations between British army and navy men, 300–1

Reed, Colonel, 271, 275

Reformation, the, 11

Refugees in the city, 125–28

Regulating Acts, 209, 216–17

Regulation, foreign, resistance to, 57

Regulation of trade, 67

Religion, liberalization of, 73

Religions in the city, 125

Religious freedom, 61

Representation in Parliament, 146, 163

Resistance to regulation from abroad, 57

Restoration, English, 62

Revenue, raising, Law for, 165

Revere, Paul, 146
at the Tea Party, 203
capture before reaching Concord, and release, 235, 241
messenger, on the Tea Party, to New York and Philadelphia, 207
ride, 232–35
warning ride to Portsmouth, New Hampshire, 224

Reveres, 127

Revocation of colony's charter, 65, 67

Revocation of the Edict of Nantes, 126–27

Revolution, American, bloodshed, first, in the Boston Massacre, 161–83
bloodshed, first, claim of Salem, Massachusetts, 227
causes of, 55, 57, 76–77, 131, 132, 147–48
causes of, one-sided accounts of, 161–63
"Father of the Revolution" (James Otis), 150–51
Generals, American, experience in the Seven Years' War, 142
leaders, 151
martyrs, in the Boston Massacre, 186

unification of the colonies by the Stamp Act, 163
Whig and Tory accounts of, 161–63

Rhode Island, 223

Richardson, Captain, 47–48

Richardson, Thomas, 233

Right to rule the colonies, view of King George III, 207

Riots, against the Stamp Tax, 155–60

Risings, general, after seizure of arms, 221–22

Roberval (explorer), 4

Robinson, Captain John, slaver, 88–89

Robison, Colonel, 275

Rogers, Robert, 126

Roman Catholic religion, recognition, in Canada, 209–10
prejudice against, 125, 126

Romney, Earl of, 107

Romney, His Majesty's Ship, 169–71

Ropemakers, fight with troops, 174–75

Rose, His Majesty's Ship, 67, 69, 104

Rotch, Francis, 197–201

Rowe, John, 250

Rowe's Wharf, 121

Roxbury, Massachusetts, 19, 22, 239, 244, 248, 252, 260, 262, 299, 303–4, 306, 309, 314, 315

Roxbury Flats, 19, 20

Roxbury Neck, 120, 230, 231, 239, 260, 309
fortification of, 222

Royal Exchange Lane, 181

Royal Fencible Americans, 251

Royal North British Volunteers, 251

Ruggles, Timothy, 217, 250
caricature in a play, 294

Rule by the church (theocracy), 73

Rum, trade in, 54, 75–83

"Rum," origin of the word, 77

"Rum, niggers and molasses trade," 40, 54, 76

Rut, John, 4

Rutland, Massachusetts, 217

Sabbath observance, 197

Sabotage of the British, by the patriots, 222

"Sacred Cod, the," 53

Saffin, John, defense of the slave trade, 84

"Saint Botolph's Town," 147

Saint Joseph, 115

Index

Saint Kitts (Christopher Island), trade
with, 32, 36, 37
Saint Lawrence Valley, furs from, 6
Saint Patrick's Day, 1776 (Evacuation
Day), 315
Salem, Massachusetts, 27–29, 38, 291
aid to Boston in the blockade, 212–13
attempt by the British to seize arms
and powder, 226–28
chosen by England to be the seat of
government, after the Tea Party,
209
claim to first bloodshed of the Revo-
lution, 227
landing at, 2
military occupation, after the Tea
Party, 215
minute men, 228
settlement at, 10
slave trade, 84
See also Naumkeag
Salons (1760), 146–47
Saltonstall, Sir Richard, 15, 24
Salvaging operations, 36–38
Sassafras, trading for, 5, 6
Saunders, Captain, 125
Savalet, Captain, 4
Scarlett's Wharf, 121
School Street, 239
Scituate, Massachusetts, 223
Scollay, John, at the Tea Party, 203, 207
Scotsmen in the city, 126
Sea, perils of the, 123
Seaflower, ship, 39
Seafort, ship, 29, 36, 45, 112, 114
Search without warrant, 147, 149, 150
case of Malcolm, 166
Sebada, Captain, 114
Seizure of patriots' arms and powder,
219–22
Separation, privateer, 113–14
Separatists (church), 11–12
Settlements. See Colonies
Seven Years' War (Old French War;
French and Indian War), 141–42
Sewall, Jonathan, 262
Sewall, Judge Samuel, 85, 135
attack on the slave trade, 84
Sewall, Chief Justice Stephen, 150
Shallops, early, 23–26
Shapleigh, Major Nicholas, 103–4
Shawmut, 10, 16, 19, 21, 22
Ship explosions, 48–49
Shipbuilding, 23, 27–29, 38, 120–22

and trade, 30
decline in 1760, 146; in 1764, 152
industries, related, 29–30
rivalry with England, 81, 122
timber for, 22
Ships, merchant vessels, with letters of
marque, 112
Shipwrecks, 123
Shirley, Governor William, 136
Shirley Point, 20
Shrewsbury, Duke of, 107
Shuldam, Admiral, 308
Siege of the city, by the Continentals,
247–58
fighting, 251–58
Sigourneys, 127
Silversmiths (1760), 146
Simsbury, Connecticut, mines, 297
Skelton (early settler), 1
Slave trading, 38–40, 54, 83–91
advertisements of Negroes for sale,
85–86
Middle Passage, the, 86, 87
protest against, and defense of, 84
risks in, 87–91
share of the city in, 83–91
Smallpox, 120, 152, 290
Smith, Brigadier (Britisher at Concord),
230, 237, 243–44, 307
Smith, Isaac, 243
Smith, Captain John, 15, 18, 22
Description of New England, A, 8
explorations, 7–9
Smugglers, 56, 82, 130, 148–50, 165, 189
tea, 190
wine, case of Malcolm, 166
Smyth, James, 39
Snorre, first white child born in the
New World, 2–3
Social effect of immigration, 128
Social manners and customs, 128–29
Soldiers, English and Colonial, 141–42
Solebay, 100
Somers, Lord, 107
Somerset, His Majesty's Ship, 230, 233,
241, 252, 253, 273, 277
Somerville, Massachusetts, 245
Sons of Liberty, 160, 173, 175, 185–204,
208
South Battery, 121
South Boston, 20
South Cove, 19, 20
South End, 160
Southack, Captain Cyprian, 115

Index

Spain, war with (The War of Jenkins' Ear), 122
Spaniards in the city, 126
Sparks, Jared, 161
Speech by Joseph Warren, in the Old South, on the blockade, 225–26
Spenser (Connecticut soldier), 248
Spies, British, 229
Springfield, Massachusetts, 217, 221
Stagg, Captain, 46–48
Stamp Act, the, 147
  as unifier of the Colonies, 163
  Grenville, George, Chancellor of the Exchequer, "father" of the Act, 166
  passage of (1765), and agitation against, 152–60
  repeal of (1766), 164–65
  riots against, 155–60
  support by Townshend, 166–67
  Virginia resolutions against, 156
"Stamp Act Congress," 163
Standish, Captain Miles, 31
Staples Act (1663), 132
Stark, General John, 126, 248, 271, 275–77, 284, 285
  order to his men to hold their fire, at the Battle of Bunker Hill, 279
State House, new, dome of, 18
State House, Old (Town House), 128, 140, 143, 155
Stevenson, Robert Louis, Treasure Island, 111
Stillhouses (1722), 120
Stocks, racial, in the city, 125–28
Stone, Captain John, offenses, and his fate, 31–32
Story, William, 158
Streets, number of (1722), 119
Suffolk County Convention, after the Massacre, 218–19
Suffolk Downs race track, 255
"Suffolk Resolves," 219
Sugar, trade in, 79, 80
Sugarhouse (1722), 120
Sullivan, General John, 304
Sunday, observance of, 197
Swallow Frigott, privateer, 114
Symmetry, His Majesty's Ship, 268, 269

Tariff. See Customs, Revenue; Smuggling
Taussig, Charles, 77

Taxation, British right to impose on colonies, 187
  customs. See Customs; Revenue
  implications of the imposition on tea, 192
  meeting of protest before the Tea Party, 196
  tonnage duties, 57
  without representation, 146, 147, 163
Tea, banning from colonial tables, 192–93
  commissioners for cargoes, 194–96
  Dartmouth, Tea Party ship, 197, 199, 200
  East India Company policy, 191–93
  "Indians" at the Party, 203
  meetings of protest before the Party, 196
  Party, 193–204
  Party, reaction to, in the colonies and in England, 207–10
  salvage from the Cape Cod wreck, 208
  ship bringing tea, before the Party, 196, 197, 199
  smuggling, 190
  tax on, 187
  wreck of the fourth ship, 208
Tew, Thomas, pirate, 107, 113
Thacher, Oxenbridge, 151
Thanksgiving, first in New England, 21
Theater in the city (winter of 1775), 292–95
Theocracy (rule by the church), 73
Thevet (explorer), 4
Thomas, General John, 248, 252–54, 305–7
Thompson, David, 10
Thorvald, Ericson, visit to Massachusetts, 2
Thunder, ship, 32
Ticonderoga, 302
Tidewaiter, the, 170
Timber for ships, 22
Tolerance, religious and political, 62
Tonnage duties, 57
Topography, early, of the city, 17–20
Tories, after the Boston Massacre, 216–18
  evacuation from the city, 310–11
  leading, before the Revolution, 194–95
  writers, 145
Tories and Whigs, 145
Town Cove, 48

Index

Town Dock, 68, 177

Town House (Old State House), 128, 140, 143, 155

Town meetings, after the Massacre, 218–19

Townshend, Chancellor of the Exchequer Charles, 166–69

Townshend Acts (1767), 166–69
repeal, 187

Trade, and shipbuilding, 30
boycott of English goods, 152–53, 168, 214–15
carrying, 40–41, 53–54
closure of the port, after the Tea Party, 208–12
aid from the outside, 212–13
companies, 9
competition with the Dutch, 56
concessions by England, 73
depression, 67, 152
early, 26–27, 34–51
expansion, 64, 129, 146
expansion after the Boston Massacre, 188–89
expansion into far regions of the earth, 75–76
exports, early, 75
free, 56
free, assertion of right, 82
free, death of, 73
fur, 76
imports, early, 74
indifference to political issues, 190–91
jealousy, English, 131
laws, change in, 165
laws, English, for regulation of trade, 58–59, 66, 147–60, 188
laws of, in the Townshend Acts, 166–69, 187
logwood, with Honduras, 94
manufacturing, move to encourage, 153
Molasses Act (1733), 81–83
monopolies, English, 9
monopoly in tea, and implications of policy, 191–92
navy's arrogance toward merchantmen, 189
non-importation and non-consumption agreements (boycotts), 152–53, 168
regulation by English laws, 58–59, 66, 67, 147–60, 188

revival after repeal of the Stamp Act, 165
revival after suppression, 73–74
rivalry, English, 58, 131
rum, 54
"rum, niggers and molasses," 40, 54, 76
slave, 38–40, 54, 83–91
sugar, 79, 80
suppression of, 67
tea monopoly, and implications of policy, 191–92
three-cornered, 54–55
Townshend Acts, and repeal of, 166–69, 187
vessels arriving in a week, 61
with various countries:
Bermuda, 32, 33
the Canary Islands, 38
the Dutch, 30, 32
England, 56
the Eskimos, 76
the French, 61
the French West Indies, 74, 76, 79
Honduras, 94
India, 108
the Indians, 5–6, 61
Maryland, 32
Virginia, 27, 30, 53
the West Indies, 40–41, 53, 56, 61, 74, 76, 80

Trade and Navigation, Acts of, 55–56, 58, 61, 65, 67, 72, 102, 132, 163

Trade and Plantations, Board (and Lords) of. See Lords of Trade and Plantations

Tragabigzanda, Princess, 7–9

Treasure Island, by Robert Louis Stevenson, 111

"Tree, Great, The," 154

Tremont, origin of name, 16
three hills of, 19

Tremont Street, 239

Trial, 29, 36, 38

Trial by jury, right to, 147, 149, 163

Trimountaine, 16

Turner, John, 37–38

Union Club, 155

Uring, Captain Nathaniel, description of the city (1721), 119

Utrecht, Peace of, 74, 80

Vergennes, Comte de, on Bunker Hill Battle, 286

Index

Verrazano, Giovanni da, 4
View from the harbor, 18
Vikings. *See* Norsemen
Vinland, 2
Virginia, 22
  resolutions against the Stamp Tax, 156
  trade with, 27, 30, 53
Virginia, 27
Virginia, or London, Company, 9, 12
Visits by Norsemen, 2–3

Wake, Thomas, pirate, 108
Walford, Thomas, 10
Walker, Admiral Sir Hovenden, 135
Walkington, Captain Leonard, 115
War, cost, payment protested, 148
  King George's, 141
  Pequot, 33
  Seven Years' (Old French War;
    French and Indian War), 141–42
  with the Indians, 33, 61, 62, 66, 133
Ward, General Artemas, 248, 262, 263,
  265, 271, 275, 287
Ward, Edward, description of the city
  (1699), 118
Warrant, search without, 147, 149, 150
  case of Malcolm, 166
Warren, Admiral, 137
Warren, Doctor John, 236, 240, 241, 261
  at the Tea Party, 203
Warren, General Joseph, 231–32
  address in Old South Meeting House,
    224–26
  death at Bunker Hill, 283
Wars, of the Austrian Succession, 141;
  peace treaty of Aix-la-Chapelle,
    141
Wars, with France, 131–43
  Peace of Utrecht, 74
Wars with the Indians, 61, 133
Warwick, Earl of, 51, 113
Warwick, 30
Washington, George, 301, 305, 306, 313
  caricatured in a British play, 293
  criticized for inactivity, 301
  exhortation to his troops, 310
  in command of the Continental
    Army, 288, 291
  limit on his power, 304
  plans for action and fortification of
    Dorchester Heights, 302–10
  protest against British ill-treatment of
    prisoners, 297

Washington, Martha, 301
Washington (Newbury) Street, 154
Watertown, Massachusetts, 22
Watson, George, 217–18
Waymouth, Captain George, explora-
  tions, 6–7
Webster, Daniel, 126
Weeden, William, on the slave trade,
  86–87
Weems, Mason L. (Parson), 161
Welcome, ship, 29, 50
Welshmen in the city, 126
Wentworth, Governor Benning, 122
Wentworth, Governor John, of New
  Hampshire, 121–22, 222
Wentworth, Lieutenant Governor John,
  of New Hampshire, 121–22
Wentworth, Joshua, 312–13
Wessaguscus (Weymouth), 10
West Indies, plague from, 48
  trade with, 40–41, 53, 56, 61, 80
Weston, Captain, 10
Wetherley, Tee, pirate, 106
Weymouth (Wessaguscus), Massachu-
  setts, 10, 29, 253–54, 299
Weymouth Back River, 253
Wharves, 120, 121
Wheeler, Sir Francis, 134–35
Whidaw, pirate vessel, 106
  shipwreck, 124
Whigs and Tories, 145
White, John, 13, 15
Wickham, Captain Charles, slaver, 90
Wilkes, John, on Bunker Hill Battle,
  286
William III, King of England, 73
  accession, 68
William and Mary, King and Queen of
  England, 70
Williams, Councilor, of Hatfield, Mas-
  sachusetts, 217
Williams, Inspector General, 171
Willis's Creek and Cove, 265, 268, 269,
  271, 281
Windmill Hill, 46
Wine-smuggling case, 166
Winnesimmet (Chelsea), Massachusetts,
  10, 26
Winnesimmet Ferry, 257
Winslow, John, 68
Winslow, Josiah, 194
Winsor, Justin, 80

Index

Winter, first white men's in the city, 21

Winter Hill, 219–22, 245, 248, 303

Winter of 1775–76 in the city, 289–90, 292

Winthrop, Governor John, 1–2, 15, 16, 18–21, 23, 26–28, 31, 34, 35, 40, 84
  Journals, 2, 46, 48–49; extracts from, 45

Winthrop, Massachusetts, 18, 255

Witchcraft, 48–51, 73

Wollaston, Massachusetts ("Mare-Mount"), 10

Wonder Working Providence, by Johnson, 59

Wood, description of the city, 118

Woods, Major, 275

Woolen goods, manufacture of, 153

Worcester, Massachusetts, 217, 220
  raid on, proposed, 228–29

Worthington, Councilor, of Springfield, Massachusetts, 217

Worthylake, Captain George, 124–25

Writers, Tory, 162

Writs of Assistance, and resistance to, 82–83, 147, 149–51, 166
  legalization by the Townshend Acts, 167
  upholding of, by court, 151

Wyeth, John, at the Tea Party, 203

"Yankee Doodle," 239, 240

Yankees, origin of, 131

Young, Dr., 201, 203
  proposer of the Tea Party, 198